MONSTER KIDS

MONSTER KIDS

How Pokémon
Taught a Generation
to Catch Them All

DANIEL DOCKERY

RUNNING PRESS

PHILADELPHIA

Running Press
Hachette Book Group
1290 Avenue of the Americas, New York, NY 10104
www.runningpress.com
@Running_Press

Printed in the United States of America

First Edition: October 2022

Published by Running Press, an imprint of Perseus Books, LLC, a subsidiary of Hachette Book
Group, Inc. The Running Press name and logo are trademarks of the Hachette Book Group.

The Hachette Speakers Bureau provides a wide range of authors for speaking events.
To find out more, go to www.hachettespeakersbureau.com or call (866) 376-6591.

The publisher is not responsible for websites (or their content) that are not owned
by the publisher.

Print book cover and interior design by Rachel Peckman

Library of Congress Cataloging-in-Publication Data
Names: Dockery, Daniel, author. Title: Monster kids : how Pokémon taught a generation
to catch them all / Daniel Dockery. Description: First edition. | New York, NY: Running
Press, [2022] | Summary: "The first book to explore the evolution of the cultural touchstone
Pokémon, which continues to capture the attention of fans for more than 25 years with video
games, products, and films, Monster Kids is the perfect read for fans of Jason Schreier's Blood,
Sweat & Pixels and Pokémon fans who still want to catch them all."—Provided by publisher.
Identifiers: LCCN 2021058226 (print) | LCCN 2021058227 (ebook) | ISBN 9780762479504
(trade paperback) | ISBN 9780762479511 (ebook) Subjects: LCSH: Pokémon (Game)—
Social aspects. | Video games—Social aspects. | Video games and children. Classification:
LCC GV1469.35.P63 D63 2022 (print) | LCC GV1469.35.P63 (ebook) | DDC 794.8—dc23/
eng/20211215 LC record available at https://lccn.loc.gov/2021058226 LC ebook record
available at https://lccn.loc.gov/2021058227

ISBNs: 978-0-7624-7950-4 (paperback), 978-0-7624-7951-1 (ebook)

LSC-C

Printing 1, 2022

For Mom

CONTENTS

Pallet Town

I was nine years old when I first saw Pokémon—not as video game creatures or anime characters, not even as manga page drawings or trading card art, but as a sticker. And that's all it took.

This fateful meeting occurred as I shopped in a Super Kmart in small-town North Carolina, a department store that, in fall 1998, already seemed on the verge of decrepitude. Its aisles were too close together, its stock seemed to have been so haphazardly placed on the shelves that it risked fall-ing on you, and the whole thing smelled like the automotive section. The entire store rested in a fog of tire and seat cleaner aroma.

The video game area happened to be nestled next to the aisle with the motor oil and air fresheners, meaning that every trip to see the Nintendo 64 and PlayStation mandated plunging into the deep end. But on that day I was far too invested in my discovery to pay attention to the odor. I'd snuck away from my parents to stare at the quiltlike array of titles. Not that I'd be able to afford many of them—my family was firmly middle class and blue collar. It was nice to look, though, and to imagine the fantasies that lay behind labels like *The Legend of Zelda: Ocarina of Time* and *Resident Evil*.

At the far end of the aisle was the Game Boy section, where the handheld console and its wares reigned. These titles often went unnoticed by me at that age, as I figured that its selection of 8-bit adventures was simply a step down from those offered on the bigger (and more expensive) systems. That day, though, I lingered. In the bottom right corner of the glass, emblazoned on a sticker that almost seemed random in its placement, were the words: "POKÉMON! GOTTA CATCH 'EM ALL! COMING FALL 1998."

Below this declaration were three monsters: a friendly yellow mouse with a tail shaped like a lightning bolt, a bipedal turtle with cannons extending from its shoulders, and a large wasp with drills on its forelimbs. Later, I'd come to know them as Pikachu, Blastoise, and Beedrill—just three of the advertised 150 monsters available to capture and train in the first set of Pokémon games—but for now they remained "nice rat," "turtle man," and "nightmare." Nonetheless, I was intrigued. I had to meet these things and, when I did, I had to catch them all.

I would receive *Pokémon Red Version* and a purple Game Boy Color on my birthday in the spring of the following year, after spending months cajoling my parents about its wonder and social benefits and evangelizing the animated series whenever it came on TV. It wasn't the first time I had played it (on a school field trip to the zoo, I borrowed my friend's Game Boy and actively considered robbing him, such was my desire to keep playing *Pokémon*) and as soon as I got the console in my hands, some form of *Pokémon* game would stay there for the next four or so years.

This book is about those four or so years.

Not about me. No one on earth deserves 70,000 words about me trying to sneak *Pokémon Red* into Scout camp multiple times. Or an entire chapter about how I brought my Game Boy to a middle school dance and during Outkast's "Ms. Jackson," it fell out of my pocket, forcing me to scramble around on the floor for it, ruining the awkward gyration of at least four preteens.

Instead, this is about the four or so years that nearly everyone I know experienced, the years when Pokémon came to North America, and the media, along with various school groups, religious organizations, and countless parents, had no idea of how to handle it and its rampant popularity. Many people have referred to these years as "Pokémania," a moniker that treats it less like a capable franchise that happened to be packaged in an extremely effective manner and more like an affliction. Once your kid had the Pokémania, it was over. There was no cure. You were simply stuck buying trading cards and figurines for your ill child until the fever passed, not that anyone at the time had any idea of when it would.

What were some of the symptoms? At first, one could expect their child to wake up early (usually around six-thirty to seven in the morning) to catch *Pokémon* on TV. And, if the disease didn't clear up, then eventually you might find them huddled intensely over Game Boys with friends, connected with a link cable and spreading the virus among one another. They would be sprinting into their local malls to participate in trading card game events. The sick could often be witnessed asking movie theater employees if they had any more special edition cards before dragging their parents along as they crowded into a dark room to watch both a nearly dialogue-free short film about Pokémon playing with one another . . . and then stay for a Pokémon feature film that followed. The truly ailing might even one day ask you to take them to a nearby theater to see the characters perform *live*.

Pokémania came swiftly and without much warning. At first there was the anime on TV screens and then, within weeks, a game on shelves. The 1998 Christmas season saw a solid number of Pokémon offerings, and by the next year's holidays, those offerings had increased exponentially. There was seemingly no stopping *Pokémon*, forcing those out of the loop to wonder just how so much had come so fast out of nowhere.

Of course, despite what the media or critics said, it didn't come out of nowhere. Far, far from it, in fact. *Pokémon* had spent nearly ten years gestating in Japan, first during its exhausting development by the nascent game studio Game Freak and then as Nintendo's new breakout hit that defied all expectations with its consistent success and ability to birth numerous spinoffs. It's important to remember that *Pokémon* was created from a dream about Japan, about its wildlife and about a sense of discovery, which is something that is often paved over, and this book will tell some of those stories, too.

It's also impossible to talk about Pokémania and all that grew from it without talking about the budding games and shows that weren't *Pokémon*. For in its wake as the hype reached fever pitch, other franchises emerged and became entangled with or engulfed by it. In North America, *Pokémon*'s blockbuster status kicked off a pop culture arms race of sorts, one that saw various publishers and licensing outlets attempt to catch 'em all themselves, with "'em" being series based around monster collecting. Some of these companies produced little more than a *Pokémon* copycat to spawn merchandise and then be thrown at any child that would pay attention. Others were treated with more care, as those in charge realized that one size didn't fit all and that what worked for *Pokémon* would perhaps betray the qualities of the product they currently had in their hands. They also have their own stories, some of which we will explore in this book, despite all the finger pointing from pundits that *everything* was simply ripping off Pikachu and its many brethren.

Among these "rip-offs" are *Digimon*, the sibling project to the virtual pet Tamagotchi, whose focus on fighting monsters led to a splurge of tie-in products and an extremely poignant animated adaptation, as well as *Yu-Gi-Oh!*, which began as a manga author's eureka moment and evolved into a trading card game of gargantuan proportions. There's also *Medabots*, a series about collectible fighting robots that is eternally underrated; and

Monster Rancher, which provided an intriguing system of creating monsters, but would unfortunately fossilize itself; and many more, including *Cardcaptors*, an anime that wasn't supposed to be like *Pokémon* in the first place.

What unites all these franchises, or at least the best of them, isn't just the focus on finding and training monsters, nor is it the varying levels of outrage, confusion, and critique that each received. Rather, it's the focus on connection, on the idea that each of these series was deeply interested in how we play and, more importantly, how we play with others, whether it's done in the spirit of calm collaboration or heated competition. Each of these was created with that in mind, and it's in these intentions that the franchises have their beating hearts. What *Monster Kids* is truly about is how the hearts of Pokémon and its rival franchises were revealed to the world, how they were presented, and sold, and altered in ways that garnered millions and millions of fans. I believe that everyone has the capacity to be a Monster Kid, able to relay their thoughts and desires through outlandish worlds and surprisingly thoughtful creatures. We are meant to dream as youths, and some of us are meant to dream of monsters. What these series did, all popping up over the course of a few years, was provide an outlet for kids like me and our dreams.

In the process of writing *Monster Kids*, I interviewed dozens of people who helped make these franchises happen. Some worked on acquiring *Pokémon* and these other properties from Japan, seeing the promise in them and deciding that they deserved to be shared. Some worked on localizing them, translating the games and anime and, in many cases, retooling them to reach the widest audiences possible. Some worked on providing voices, bringing our favorite characters and monsters to life in ways that are often equal parts nostalgic and ridiculous. In talking with these people, I've learned that some continue to love the series that they worked on, while others haven't thought about it for years. There are a few who would do things differently now and those who thought that the fictional characters and worlds they'd become attached to weren't destined for success at all, but rather doomed to be cautionary tales of the dangers of imported media.

Regardless of intentions or outlook, their stories are important. Things are very different now. Pokémon is no longer an untested concept, and franchises like Digimon and Yu-Gi-Oh! are far past being monster-collecting underdogs. Each has produced some of the most recognizable and financially successful series that the world has ever seen and revolutionized their mediums of choice. In fact, fans of Pokémon (or Digimon, or Monster Rancher, or, hopefully, Medabots) became fans of not only their favorite franchise, but of mediums that continue to change the tides of whole industries. Before Pokémon, the Game Boy line was thought to be on its last legs, a relic better left in a museum than a bedroom. Pokémon would breathe new life into it and completely overhaul what we consider to be the capabilities of handheld systems. Because of Pokémon, some fans were introduced to Japanese animation, or anime, on a grand scale, which was localized and placed alongside some of the heaviest hitters that Western cartoons had to offer at the time. This created lifelong devotees and often influenced other companies to give anime a chance, whereas before they'd seen it as the exclusive interest of niche enthusiasts.

Admittedly, in writing this book, it is easy to see that Pokémon occupies an undeniably weird spot in pop culture. The fact that it's a fairly benign story about befriending others and caring for the world that was turned into a cross-market goliath of rampant branding is not lost on me. As with all art, we often must wrestle with and reconcile how it is created and how it is sold. Monster Kids also looks at how children are seen as potential consumers waiting for advertising's pied piper and clever identifiers of their own distinct personal tastes, something that wasn't lost on the gaming and animation industries.

My discovery of Pokémon was less of an encounter and more of a collision, like standing in the tide and getting hit by a wave that you weren't expecting. In the days following the release of its animated and video game forms in 1998, the entire atmosphere had changed in my school, my household, and my circle of friends. It became the focus of conversation, of debate, and of intense speculation. Then when Digimon arrived around a year later, we picked our sides and stood our ground, arguments about the merits of Pikachu and his hundreds of monster buddies echoing across the playground. However, it wasn't meant to last forever. *Monster Kids* is about that, too.

Pokémon never truly went away, and neither did many of its competitors and compatriots. Most of the initial claims that it would crash and burn, disappearing from our cultural consciousness as quickly as it arrived, were proven quite wrong. But it's undeniable that Pokémania did eventually wane. Theaters became emptier, cards that once sold with stock market heat went to the clearance section, news broadcasts that warned parents of Pokémon's impending effects on their children (and their wallets) moved on to new things. Pokémon was never over; instead it became so integrated in our lives that it felt like it was controversy becoming comfort food.

Monster Kids explores how that happened, how Pokémon got its start, how it spread, and how it created a trend of unimaginable size. It's also about the effects it had on media and marketing, many of which are still around now. Most importantly, though, it's about how a generation of us became Monster Kids and how the tagline "Gotta catch 'em all!" forever changed our lives (or at least our hobbies). Whether you were puzzled by it, lived through it, or wish to know what all the fuss was about, I hope you enjoy the story of these pocket-sized monsters.

Because trust me, experiencing it was unforgettable.

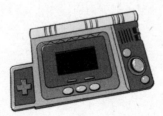

Chapter 1

BUGS ON A WIRE

The modern Pokémon franchise is almost too enormous to conceive. In fact, it's hard to find a medium that it hasn't permeated and thrived in. Go to your local Target or Walmart, and you'll spot it in the video game section, in with the movies, toy, clothing, and school supplies aisles . . . It's probably even in the grocery aisles, too. No, you can't eat Pokémon here in the real world (in the Pokémon world, it's a different story), but there's likely at least a box of colorful fruit gummies with shapes molded to loosely resemble some of the more popular characters. It's reaped billions and billions of dollars worldwide and was the pop culture tastemaker for millions of kids and young adults from Gen X to Gen Z. Pokémon isn't just popular—it's pretty much unavoidable.

And it all started with bugs.

Not the technological kind, though those tiny glitches and mishaps in code would become frequently associated with the debut *Pokémon* installments, often making for odd, memorable surprises. Some of them would even become the equivalent of playground folklore. We're also not talking about the "Bug" type Pokémon, just one type of the eventual fifteen elemental groups that Pokémon's creators would use to classify the magical critters. Bug types are another frequent presence in early *Pokémon* games, constructed in such a way that they often seem like six-legged training wheels that you practice with before you delve further into the games, where the beasts only grow bigger and more explosive. No, the bugs that provided the eureka moment for Pokémon are the very real creepy crawlers that probably leave most of the people you know disgusted at their mere presence. However, not for Satoshi Tajiri. Born in Machida, a city in the western Tokyo Metropolis, Japan, in 1965, Tajiri was a bug enthusiast to the extent that his friends nicknamed him "Dr. Bug." "Every new insect was a wonderful mystery," he told *TIME* magazine about gathering them. "And as I searched for more, I would find more." He even wanted to be an entomologist, which, luckily for Pokémon fans and this book, was a career path he didn't take.

It wasn't just bug collecting in the fairly rural areas near his home that enraptured the young Satoshi. He was also a fan of and inspired by Japanese comics (called manga) and the series *Ultraman*, an extremely influential character created by the special effects wizard behind the Godzilla film series, Eiji Tsuburaya. In the show, an intergalactic warrior collides with a member of the intrepid Science Patrol, the effortlessly brave and charming Shin Hayata. Hayata is given a "Beta Capsule" that allows him to transform into the hero Ultraman whenever earth is threatened by giant monsters much like the one that the warrior was chasing before his unfortunate crash.

And those giant monsters? Well, they are numerous and inventively designed with a new one coming to menace Ultraman, the Science Patrol, and mankind as we know it in almost every episode. If that wasn't enough of a hint of things to come, a later Ultraman series, 1967's *Ultra Seven*, would involve actual "capsule monsters." These were battle-ready monsters contained in a little box that could be used by the hero to fight for him. Remember that plot device, and the phrase "capsule monsters," because this isn't the last time you'll hear them.

"Everything I did as a kid is kind of rolled into Pokémon," Tajiri told *TIME*, but sadly, one of the ingredients of his childhood was quickly changing. Satoshi's hometown was already the location of massive growth when he was a child, and the construction of the Tama New Town development, and many other developments like it, would bring hundreds of thousands of people there. Then, in the years after World War II and the ensuing Allied occupation, Japan began swiftly urbanizing so, by the time Tajiri was fifteen, Machida's population had tripled, and the country's population had risen 20 percent. With the encroaching concrete apartment buildings and retail locations came fewer and fewer places for bugs to live. Real bugs, much like the ones in the *Pokémon* series, tend to prefer fields and forests over streets, sidewalks, and shoe soles.

Bug collecting is the hobby that Pokémon fans usually cite when discussing the origins of their preferred franchise, but it was only part of the reason. Tajiri was also getting older, and soon he was introduced to another hobby that would fuel his dreams. Arcades were booming in popularity around Tokyo, and attempts to paint them as hubs for juvenile delinquency likely only made them more appealing to a teenage clientele. Ironically, these arcades were probably built over some of the spots where Tajiri and his pals would have hunted for bugs a few decades earlier, but they made Tajiri a fan of video games, setting him on course to change pop culture history.

Such was his fascination with arcades and gaming technology that his pursuits leaned toward the self-made—as a teenager, Tajiri created dojinshi (which are self-published magazines) with a name that's familiar to anyone who's ever booted up a *Pokémon* game: *Game Freak*. Providing arcade game tips and strategies to eager players, *Game Freak* became a welcome resource for devotees who flocked to the magazine shop to learn the tricks necessary to help them master any of the games lining the arcade walls. Among *Game Freak*'s readers were future collaborators who would eventually become video game icons themselves, most notably longtime *Pokémon* designer Ken Sugimori. His interest in video games had overtaken his childhood obsession with cartoons and animation, so he decided to reach out to Tajiri to work on the magazine and, eventually, far beyond.

Despite going well past the efforts seen from usual fans, talking about video games and helping others out with them weren't scratching Tajiri's itch to be a part of the industry—he wanted to *make* games. The games available, typically variations of the same games that had littered arcades for nearly a decade at this point, "weren't very good" in his opinion, and he figured he could do better. So he took apart a Famicom, a Nintendo Entertainment System, which was at that time the best-selling video game console in Japan, to see how it worked. However, the home console wouldn't be the object of Tajiri's fixation even as he learned how to program games for it. Instead, he set his hopes on a handheld one—Tajiri wanted the Game Boy.

Sometimes Simple Is Best

Originally beginning as the producer of playing cards, Nintendo evolved over the course of the twentieth century into a video game development and publishing powerhouse. Their console releases included heavy-hitters like the Famicom, the Game & Watch, and then, in 1989, the Game Boy. Though it was the pride and joy of Nintendo's legendary Research & Development No. 1 team, the Game Boy of 1989 is a far cry from the handhelds of today. It was a sizable, thick, gray rectangle, more closely resembling a cheap toaster than a Nintendo Switch. And even in its initial heyday, it was easily outpaced in terms of power by its handheld competitors. Systems like the Sega Game Gear and Atari's Lynx were capable of better graphics, better sound, and less toaster-ness.

On paper, the Game Boy didn't stand a chance. Kids would see its simple-looking games and flock literally anywhere else, since video games are a medium where popularity is very often based on looks. Even though, time and time again, a great design does better in the long run—take, for example, Nintendo's Mario, who hasn't changed all that much since the mid-nineties, and yet we treat every new *Mario* game installment as the pinnacle of our species—having the most lifelike graphics possible is better in the short term because it's seen as a progressive artistic achievement. So if the space marine that you control looks more realistic when tearing the heads off demons than the other guy's space marine, you win.

Despite being outmatched in power and graphics, the Game Boy crushed its competition thanks to its ability to, one, give players the *experiences* they wanted and, two, give them these experiences for a *very* long time. The Game Boy's battery life was hard to beat, and, considering that these handhelds were designed to offer kids a chance to play games outside of the confines of their living rooms, this was a huge factor. The user manual claims that, depending on the "Game Pak and temperature," the four AA batteries could power up to fifteen hours of gaming. That's borderline eternal when you put it next to the Sega Game Gear, which lasted from three to five hours with an army of *six* AAs before bidding players adieu. A Sega Game Gear died an ugly death on a too-long car ride, while a Game Boy laughed at its mortality.

The console also had a more consistent library than others, which is kind of an easy win when the catalog includes things like *Super Mario Land* and the block-stacking phenomenon *Tetris*. A quick aside: If you take anything away from this book, aside from the deeply necessary and positively vital knowledge about monster-collecting series from the late nineties, it's this: when in doubt, package your gaming system with *Tetris*. Classic titles like that made every Game Boy a treat and left the act of unwrapping a Game Gear under the Christmas tree on the wrong side of history.

These were all good reasons to become interested in the Game Boy's hardware, but Tajiri was focused on something else: He admired the console's link system, which allowed players to "link up" to another Game Boy through a cable that was plugged into a port on the console's upper left side. Today, this sounds about as archaic as making a telephone out of two cans attached to opposite ends of a string, but the link cable allowed video game players and their friends to connect and compete, most famously on *Tetris*. Plus, the cables were packaged with the Game Boys, so every household that bought the system was bound to have at least one lying around somewhere.

It's because of the link cable that Tajiri's fantasy took form. He envisioned bugs crawling back and forth along the cables with kids playing the Game Boys engaged in fierce competition but also in "interactive communication." This dream laid the framework for what would become "Pokémon trading," an action that has been with the franchise since the very beginning and, in the early days, was its prime selling point.

Tajiri's amateur study of game design (along with the knowledge of his friends) led him to scrap *Game Freak* as a magazine and transform it into a video game development company. In the years to come, he continued to write for various other magazines from time to time for extra money, but his main focus now fell on actual game creation. And it didn't take long for Game Freak's inaugural effort to be released; the puzzle game *Quinty* was born in 1989 and was later renamed *Mendel Palace* when it was released in America on the Nintendo. While a far cry from the revolutionary role-playing game that would be Game Freak's magnum opus, *Quinty* (and other games developed in the early nineties) are important to the history of *Pokémon* because they essentially helped keep the lights on as the team got their feet wet in the trials of game development. A puzzle game where the player flips tiles to deal with enemies, *Quinty* doesn't have much in common with *Pokémon* except being fun to play, which is really all that matters.

From Capsules to Pockets

Okay, the name *Pokémon* has been used a lot already, but that wasn't always the game's title. Remember those "capsule monsters" used by the hero in *Ultra Seven*? Well, *Capsule Monsters* or "Capumon" was the original title that Tajiri and Sugimori pitched to Nintendo in 1990 when they presented their grand monster-collecting adventure. They were pretty set as the name of the franchise, too, until trademarking it became troublesome, so they changed it over to *Pocket Monsters*. No real loss, though. Thankfully, both "capsule" and "pocket" do similar jobs of conveying a vibe of "Hey, these are handy monsters that you can just carry around!"

The premise of *Capsule Monsters* should be familiar, not just to people who know the history of the franchise, but to anyone who's been within spitting distance of a *Pokémon* game. The game focuses on creating and trading a team of monsters as you travel around a fictional world, and it shouldn't be too much of a surprise that the early monster and setting concepts are reminiscent of what would eventually come down the line. According to Sugimori, now classic monsters like the armored Rhydon, the cuddly Clefairy, and aquatic Lapras, which are all staples of the first *Pokémon* games, were originally meant to be included in *Capsule Monsters*.

That said, this game isn't a 100 percent clean Poké-prototype. For instance, it was set to contain 200 creatures, a third more than the 150 that would, officially, make it into the first *Pokémon* games. Also, trainers, the title given to players and all those who have decided to make raising these monsters their life's purpose, were supposed to fight alongside their Pokémon.

If this sounds baffling to you, you're not alone. "If you could fight on your own, what's the point of having Pokémon?" Sugimori said in an interview with Nintendo about the abandoned concept. And that's understandable. If given the choice between getting the stuffing punched out of you by a total stranger in the woods or letting combat-hardened dragons tussle in your stead, most would go with Option B.

Another difference between the games lay in the way the players acquired their monsters. Tajiri wrote in the planning documents that "rather than defeating them in battle, as you've done in RPGs up until now," you were going to gain Pokémon allies through a kind of "charisma" statistic. Basically, you had to get monsters to think you were cool if you wanted them to hang out with you. This definitely resonated with the idea

7

of trainers and their Pokémon being best friends and travel partners, rather than players simply being monster-kidnapping warlords.

Kindred Spirits

With our modern knowledge of Pokémon and what it would become, this all sounds like a no-brainer, right? Collecting monsters and battling with them? Seems like Nintendo president Hiroshi Yamauchi should've just backed a dump truck full of cash up to Tajiri's office and waited for success to roll in. However, Nintendo wasn't exactly thrilled when the game was first pitched. In fact, they didn't quite *get it*, and despite the success of role-playing games like *The Final Fantasy Legend*, which would influence *Pokémon* and its visuals, executives weren't sold. It seemed like Tajiri and his friends might not get the funds they needed, and Tajiri wasn't about to embark on his legend-in-the-making journey.

That is until another legend-in-the-making stepped up to bat for him.

If there was a Mount Rushmore of video game creators, then Shigeru Miyamoto would be on that sacred monument for having helped create ridiculously successful series like *Mario*, *Donkey Kong*, and *The Legend of Zelda*. He'd worked with Nintendo since 1977 and was well liked by its president and well-respected by his peers, so if Miyamoto vouched for you and your ideas, it meant *a lot*. And he liked Tajiri and found promise in the idea of *Pocket Monsters*, so, with Miyamoto's support, the idea was accepted. Nintendo hired Game Freak to develop the game.

Looking at their backstories and interests, it makes sense why Miyamoto would be drawn to *Pokémon*'s creator. As a child, Miyamoto also liked to explore nature and often wandered the caves and forests near his hometown of Kyoto, Japan, and relished the sensation of childhood discovery. This thrill of entering unknown locations with nothing but scant supplies and your own bravery was a feeling that would inspire the creation of *The Legend of Zelda*, a series that, like *Pokémon*, thrives by invoking the rush of an adventure.

This also wouldn't be the last time that Miyamoto made a call that would alter the trajectory of the franchise forever. According to current *Pokémon* producer Junichi Masuda, it was Miyamoto who suggested putting different Pokémon on different game cartridges, giving each of them a handful of their own unique monsters. This would turn the need to trade in order to "catch 'em all" from a fun aspect to a necessity and is a practice that has stuck around to the present.

Despite Nintendo's immense status, having the support of Nintendo didn't mean having unlimited resources. Game Freak had around ten employees for most of the making of *Pokémon,* and that making lasted . . . nearly six years. Late nights and later paychecks were the norm as Game Freak team members pulled double and triple duty. Meanwhile, Tajiri, who was directing, writing, and helping to design the game, lived with his father to save money. Even still, Game Freak employees often had to take side jobs to make ends meet and laid their hopes in hired gun projects like *Yoshi* to keep the enterprise funded. Some even quit when told about just how little money Game Freak had to work with at certain points in the process.

THE LOST DECADE

It likely didn't help Game Freak designers' stress levels that, if their careers in video games didn't pan out, hope was scant elsewhere. Japan's swift urbanization came with lengthy economic prosperity in the middle parts of the twentieth century, but a financial bubble had also been steadily growing thanks to intensely optimistic amounts of spending, speculation, and record-low interest rates. Despite the efforts of the Bank of Japan and other financial institutions to avoid bankruptcy and escape quickly rising debt, the bubble forcefully exploded in the early nineties. A vast recession, later dubbed "The Lost Decade" due to its long-lasting effects on both the Japanese economy and society, left many without work and without career prospects. Over ten years, the unemployment rate nearly tripled.

For decades leading up to the Lost Decade, young people had felt assured that, when school was over, they'd join the legion of "salarymen," an idealized role that entailed leaving your well-taken-care-of family each morning to join countless others on the way to work at a job that you were very unlikely to ever be fired from. It was the very definition of a "safe bet." Sadly, a record number of people never saw that goal met, with businesses increasingly relying on more part-time workers, which left a demographic primed for traditional success quickly facing a sense of existential hopelessness. A need for escapism was all but assured. Luckily, Japanese pop culture, especially in the area of video games, was more than able to provide.

The employees that stuck around pushed to develop a game quite unlike any that had ever come before it. The bulk of this work involved the creation of monsters, hundreds of them.

Filling Out the Ranks

Monsters have always been a staple of video games, especially in Japanese role-playing games. Creatures like Slimes, Cactuars, and Orcs litter the locations of *Final Fantasy* and *Dragon Quest*, another series that would inspire the look and feel of *Pokémon*, providing opportunities for the players to slay something and earn experience, both in game technique and in the points necessary to upgrade your character to stronger forms. Rarely, though, did they look like something that might be your best friend.

The main characters of *Pokémon* aren't really the trainers, but the bountiful titular pocket monsters, many of which are easily identifiable regardless of your knowledge of the games. The process of designing and redesigning each monster was a long one, with the polished creatures of today being preceded by some rough-looking abominations. Early Pokémon designs are sometimes clunky, often a little terrifying, and usually ride the line between cartoonishly appealing and morbidly obnoxious. To make the finalization process even tougher, the game designers couldn't just create a bunch of them randomly and hope that kids would be compelled to coach them. Instead, they had to design them to fit into certain types, like the Bug type mentioned at the beginning of the chapter.

In the first pair of games, *Red Version* and *Green Version*, Pokémon could be one of fifteen elemental types: Normal, Fire, Water, Grass, Ground, Electric, Rock, Psychic, Bug, Fighting, Ice, Dragon, Ghost, Flying, and Poison. As you can imagine, many of the designs visually represented the elemental types—Fire Pokémon are typically red or somehow on fire, Fighting Pokémon are shaped like weight lifters and martial artists, and Rock types look like, well, rocks. The benefit for players was obvious: If you can guess that the fish-shaped organism is a Water type as soon as you see it, you can start to devise the tactics you need to catch it right off the bat.

Since these elemental types would need to have advantages and weaknesses to one another in a kind of rock-paper-scissors system—Fire beats

Grass → Grass beats Water → Water beats Fire, etc.—Game Freak had to develop a certain number of each type so that one wasn't more available than another. Of course, this didn't always work out as planned. For example, the first pair of games only included three Dragon and three Ghost types, and Water types outnumbered Fire types two to one. But, oh well, chalk it up to growing pains.

As involved as Sugimori was in creating and polishing the looks of this monster parade, he actually wasn't the one to design the most famous critter of all, the one that came to serve as a sort of brand ambassador for the franchise, and the one that you're probably thinking of *right now*. Yup, Pikachu, the friendly yellow mouse with a lightning-bolt-shaped tail that's been emblazoned on almost all the Pokémon merchandise ever released, was the creation of a young artist named Atsuko Nishida.

Queen of the Monsters

Despite being the visionary mind responsible for the designs of some of the most iconic Pokémon in the franchise, which pretty much sold the game to millions of children, Nishida doesn't crave the spotlight. In fact, she is notoriously shy, and if you watch interviews with her, you'll mostly see her talking while holding large Pokémon plush dolls in front of her face and torso. Thus, it's kind of fitting that, when she was called to help with the *Pocket Monsters*, she was attached to an entirely different game.

One of the other projects that Game Freak was developing around the same time as *Pokémon* was *Pulseman* for Sega's Mega Drive system. Directed by Sugimori himself, it looks very akin to the popular *Mega Man* games, in which you control a cyborg through various colorful, side-scrolling levels, blasting away at enemies. It is no surprise that *Pulseman* would also evolve into a kind of cult classic, considering that the Game Freak dream team of Tajiri, Sugimori, Masuda, and others had also worked on it. And who was working on character designs as part of that team? None other than Nishida.

In fact, she was working on the designs for them when she got the call from Sugimori: He needed some adorable monsters for *Pokémon*.

Sugimori had grown tired of creating *tough*-looking monsters, so he tasked Nishida and a fellow designer named Koji Nishino to come up with monsters that were cute and had two evolutions. A major selling point of *Pokémon* is that if you raise your Pokémon to a certain level, they "evolve" and rapidly transform into a new, stronger form, which is tons of fun for players, but hellish for a design team. But Nishida and Nishino were up to the task. They based their concept on squirrels, and after many discussions back and forth between the two of them and Sugimori, they finally landed on the design for Pikachu, who absolutely *radiates* joy.

There was just one question: Would people want Pikachu? Nishino had already planned to make Pikachu a little harder to find than most other monsters, meaning that players would have to crawl around in the weeds of the digital forest for way longer if they wanted to nab one. In a game that is full of twenty-foot water dragons, four-armed fist-fighting experts, and birds that leak ice, fire, and lightning, would an adorable, reclusive electric mouse feel valuable to players? Compared to the might of some of the other Pokémon, asking kids to consider Pikachu almost seemed like an ironic request.

However, all fears would be set aside when Sugimori printed out pictures of the monster designs, including Pikachu, and asked his fellow Game Freak employees to choose the ones they preferred the most. Pikachu was the very clear winner. Always bet on Pikachu.

Of course, we know that Pikachu would go on to become *Pokémon*'s global emissary, a superstar who, to this day, retains a prominent role in nearly every branch of the franchise. RJ Palmer, who served as an artist for 2019's *Detective Pikachu* film, claims that a lot of Pikachu's success is due to the creature's extremely identifiable shape and characteristics, as well as the fact that "Pikachu" sounds a lot like "Pokémon." While that phonetic similarity doesn't sound like a big deal, it probably makes a world of difference to a confused and frustrated parent desperately trying to tell a GameStop employee that their child wants "that Pikachu thing."

If you remember the name *Pokémon*, you can probably remember the name Pikachu, and vice versa.

Nishida was also responsible for the designs of Charmander, Bulbasaur, and Squirtle (or Hitokage, Fushigidane, and Zenigame as they are known in Japan), the three little starter Pokémon that players choose from at the beginning of the game and that basically serve as the invitation into the game's wider world. It is for Pikachu, these adorable starter Pokémon, and for the other character designs she provides in many, many subsequent games in the franchise that Nishida's role in the history of the franchise cannot be undervalued. She gave us some of the most iconic pop culture icons of the late twentieth century, and monsters that Game Freak—then later Nintendo and the Pokémon Company—could build a whole brand around.

Crash and (Nearly) Burn

The process that led to the release of the franchise's first installments, *Pokémon Red* and *Green,* was challenging enough, but creating an appealing game with hundreds of diverse varmints that would revolutionize role-playing adventures as we knew them wasn't the full extent of it. We haven't even gotten into the computer crashes yet. Late in the game's development, as current *Pokémon* producer Junichi Masuda recalled in an interview with *Polygon,* one such crash nearly ended the entire project. It was a disaster that would have rendered years of work completely useless, and it all started with a bug.

At the time games were developed on Unix computer workstations called Sun SPARCstations, which ran on proprietary hardware. The problem with this was that each company had a specific operating system, meaning that if something went wrong, you couldn't just ask the local tech support to drop by and take a look. Unfortunately, when the computer workstations failed, they failed very uniquely.

And, as luck would have it, they failed and crashed, apparently, all the time.

One such crash ended up disconnecting the team from ". . . the game, all the Pokémon, the main character, and everything" they had worked so hard on. To Masuda, who'd been working on the games as a programmer and musical composer for about four years at this point, it wasn't just a backward step. It was a Game Freak apocalypse, with the likely outcome either being a redo of mountains of previous work or calling it quits completely. So he did what anyone in the eighties could do when your computer crashed: He dove frantically into computer research.

Having previously worked a job dealing with computers, he exhausted every option, calling up his former employers for assistance, and asked an internet service provider for help. He even submerged himself in English-language books about computers, just to ensure that the years that they'd spent making *Pokémon* weren't a waste and that all their work wasn't gone forever. Eventually, they managed to get everything running again, but it left the team a little shaken. For a moment, it seemed like *Pocket Monsters* had ended before it even had a chance to begin. Then again, if some predictions were correct, it wouldn't even be a beginning worth surviving for.

Bad Timing

In the five and a half years that *Pokémon* had been in development, the Game Boy had aged from a refreshing piece of mobile hardware to suddenly seeming to be on its last legs. Most video game consoles, including Nintendo's, tend to last around six years, and the Game Boy was no exception. In Japan, its sales had seen a steady decline, going from nearly 3 million units sold in the 1990 fiscal year to only a million in 1995. In other regions, the numbers were a little more uneven, but the downward trend was still noticeable. In the United States and other countries, 1995 was the worst for sales since its debut year. It was clear the Game Boy had seen better days.

Watching the declining sales of the console, Nintendo and Game Freak feared that they'd sunk more than half a decade into something destined for a dying, soon-to-be-replaced system. At that time, half of Game Boy's top ten titles ever sold had already come out. Little did they know that there would soon be a time when the rest of those games would one day all be versions of *Pokémon*.

Pokémon Red and *Green* were originally set to come out in October 1995, though the release date would be pushed to February 1996. According to current Pokémon Company president Tsunekazu Ishihara, the new date was the "worst time" to sell a game because it was far past the end of the sales season, and effectively doomed *Pokémon*'s debut to a time when not many people were interested in buying new video games. Still, Nintendo released and promoted the series, most notably with a commercial featuring a young girl asking baffled senior citizens in a park if they wanted to battle monsters. This is followed by short clips of people of all ages playing *Pokémon Red* and *Green* together, their Game Boys linked by a cable. From the very beginning, the intention was clear: *Pokémon* wasn't something that you played alone. To get the full experience, you needed *other people* to play with. Possibly the elderly. Preferably within a few feet of you.

This commercial was smart marketing, but it also solidified the ideology of the entire series. *Pokémon* is about forming relationships between beings, whether they're Pokémon or people and, by marketing it as a game best served in pairs—a game that kids could play with their friends and parents, or young ladies could play with octogenarians in public—it cemented that ethos. *Pokémon* is for everyone.

On February 27, 1996, with *Pokémon Red*'s box emblazoned with the fire-spitting dragon Charizard and *Pokémon Green*'s box lavished with the blossoming dinosaur Venusaur, the pair of games hit store shelves. The "Before Pokémon" era of civilization was over and now the "After Pikachu" one could now begin.

Only . . . it was pretty slow going at first.

Chapter 2

WHAT COMES AFTER 150?

Pokémon *Red* and *Green* weren't bombs, but they didn't exactly ignite immediate demand either. At first, Ishihara recalled in an interview, they just kind of hovered "around the edges of the top 10" video games being sold. Meanwhile, *Famitsu*, a popular Japanese gaming magazine, gave the games reviews that were fair, but not extraordinary. With the magazine using the combined scores of four critics grading the pair of games on a ten-point scale, *Pokémon Red/Green*'s score amounted to 29/40. Another magazine found that out of the top ten most anticipated games, players voted *Pokémon* into fourth place.

However, word of mouth was strong, and internet message boards eventually began to swarm with talk about *Pokémon*, with one creature grabbing people's attention in a way that others, even the ever-lovable Pikachu, couldn't. To make things even more interesting, it was a Pokémon that wasn't supposed to be in the game at all: Mew.

151

Mew's spot in the Pokémon universe has always attracted an amalgam of fact and rumor. Ask any millennial about it, and they'll regale you with stories of the "Mew under the truck," which was a fake game tip about the creature's location that eventually turned into a piece of *Pokémon* legend. It was also frequently given to us by our friend's cousin's uncle's brother who *definitely* works at Nintendo.

Here's what we know that is fact. Invented by Tajiri and placed into the game by Game Freak programmer Shigeki Morimoto, Mew wasn't supposed to be added into the game when it was. In fact, nothing was supposed to be added, taken away, or altered at the stage of development when Mew was implemented. With only a short time left before its planned debut and a few hundred bytes of space left in the game's memory—it was already close to bursting with all the monsters and monster-based adventures—it was time for the team to step back from the game and wait. After all the crashes, there was no need to test the game's fragile code.

Even with the precarious situation, Game Freak wanted the mystical cat creature in the game, so Morimoto added it in with the idea they wouldn't be using it at the time of launch. Best case scenario, the character could serve as a nice little surprise for particularly intrepid fans. Worst case scenario, it would be a fun Easter egg—a special 151st Pokémon in a lineup of 150; the kind of developer secret that only gets discovered years later. While the game does mention the tiny, catlike Mew in various bits of lore—assembled diary entries found in an abandoned mansion tell the story of scientists discovering Mew in a jungle and the experiments in which it gave birth to Mewtwo— there was no location for players to find Mew in the game itself. Unlike the other legendary Pokémon, Mew isn't hanging out in the back corner of any labyrinthine dungeon, nor can it be discovered by ceaseless wandering in forests and caves. As far as the game's story is concerned, Mew exists, but that's about it.

Fans would ensure that it wouldn't stay like this for long. Intent on peering into every nook and cranny of a game and its capabilities, someone *did* find Mew. By exploiting a glitch based on certain Pokémon stats and basically fooling the game into thinking that Mew had already been unleashed from its coding prison, players could run into the miniature demigod. News quickly spread, and soon people all over Japan were desperate to figure out just how to nab Mew themselves. Suddenly, the "secret" was out. And the number 150 plastered all over the game was a lie.

Taking advantage of this sudden interest, Game Freak, along with a manga magazine called *CoroCoro Comic* (published by major Japanese publisher Shogakukan), launched their "Legendary Pokémon Offer" sweepstakes, where out of a pool of entries, twenty winners would be chosen to mail in their *Red/Green* game cartridges and have Mew officially given to them. Like the link cable, mailing in your game and having it mailed back to you in order to acquire a new character sounds absolutely prehistoric by modern standards, but it was an exciting chance for ravenous Japanese *Pokémon* fans back in May 1996 and 78,000 entries poured in.

After that first sweepstakes, more Mew giveaways would follow in the coming months, with *Pokémon* rising in sales on a near week-to-week basis. Its constant growth stunned an industry that was used to the typical pattern of major sales at launch, followed by diminishing returns. In the wake of *Pokémon*'s popularity, Nintendo also released its new home console, the Nintendo 64. This new hardware, combined with the success of the *Pokémon* games and the resurgence of the Game Boy, must have seemed like good omens for the future. And the games were just the first wave. *CoroCoro*, a publication that would become synonymous with the franchise because of its promotions for it, had also just created the first Pokémon manga, *Pokémon Pocket Monsters*. By the summer of 1996, the Pokémon empire was ready to be unleashed upon the masses, though it would come with way more poop jokes than you might imagine.

Brand Name

If you've never heard of the *Pokémon Pocket Monsters* manga, don't worry, because there's a very good reason why. In *Pokémon Red* and *Green*, you play as a silent, stoic ten-year-old venturing from his hometown for the first time in order to catch Pokémon and eventually earn enough gym badges to challenge the Pokémon League. Along the way, you save the world from the notorious terrorist group known as Team Rocket, meet a variety of helpful, Pokémon-obsessed people, and gain a better idea of the strength and friendship it takes to become a true Pokémon champion.

Pokémon Pocket Monsters is *sort of* about that. The manga was much more comedy-focused, with the goofy protagonist named Red, a naming option in the game, teaming up with a talking Clefairy, a short pink Pokémon with huge ears. In fact, all the Pokémon can talk with one another and with humans. It's like a Pokémon sitcom, only instead of your new pals being neurotic New York City residents, they're tiny, endlessly crude monsters.

That said, though the manga was popular and eventually became a long-running series, it never made its way to America and thus tends to be ignored in larger conversations about Pokémon's various early branches. Created by mangaka Kosaku Anakubo, the stylized designs often clashed with the family-friendly counterparts from the games and, later, the anime. Similarly, the humor, which includes Pokémon and human genitalia, and all manner of scatological gags (if you got into Pokémon to see Pikachu taking enormous dumps, this is for you) doesn't mesh well with the gentler image that Pokémon and Nintendo were trying to project in their upcoming international efforts. The bond between *CoroCoro* and Pokémon was established very quickly. A few months (and a few Mew giveaways) after the initial launch of *Red* and *Green* and what would seem like a very off-brand manga, *CoroCoro* became the home base of an actual game release: *Pokémon Blue Version*. Less than a year after the original games, *Pokémon* was getting an enhancement.

Earlier I mentioned bugs in the technical sense, and there were plenty to be found in *Red* and *Green*. So, to address the issues, Game Freak decided to give the original entries a major cleanup, but keep the same story, starter Pokémon, and goals, and then give it a fresh package—*Pokémon Blue*. While the original goal was to fix the glitches and errors, the biggest change for the brand-new *Blue* was the Pokémon designs themselves, which received an overhaul from the ones seen in both the *Red* and *Green Version* just eight months earlier.

These artistic changes stemmed from the fact that during the development of *Red* and *Green*, Sugimori and company weren't, for the most part, basing the in-game artwork off any larger out-of-game drawings. Of course, there were sketches and concept art, but when Sugimori helped create the looks for the Pokémon sprites, he did it with the limited number of pixels that he had available on the Game Boy screen and simply hoped the image did a good job representing each creature. This left a lot of the *Red* and *Green* designs looking a little . . . wonky.

Established *Pokémon* fans can tell what monsters the sprites are *supposed* to be, but many were hard to recognize with their squashed and distended bodies stuck performing weird poses. For the initial launch, all Sugimori's now-classic illustrations that appeared on the video game boxes, strategy guides, and merchandise packaging were adapted from his pixel art. This provided a weird cohesion, however, as in the case of *Pokémon Blue*, Game Freak now had the ability to work in reverse order and design the pixel monsters based on their popular artwork.

The good news was this would effectively "normalize" most of the creatures' designs. It also meant that when it came time to export *Pokémon* around the world in 1998, Game Freak didn't adapt *Pokémon Red* and *Green*. No, instead America's *Red* and *Blue* was an adaptation of . . . just Japanese *Blue*—though with some adjustments to allow for trading different monsters between the games.

But before it was adapted, in October 1996, subscribers to *CoroCoro* were given the exclusive opportunity to own *Pokémon Blue*. It would be almost three years before retail customers were able to nab it in Japan, and served as the first upgraded "third" version of a *Pokémon* game. *Blue* set a franchise template for years to come, offering a slightly overhauled version that was marketed, to an extent, like a whole new game.

In October, the official trading card game was also launched in Japan. Developed by Creatures Inc. and featuring now iconic art from artists like Mitsuhiro Arita, Keiji Kinebuchi, and, of course, Ken Sugimori, the trading cards adapted the video game's battle mechanics—where monsters were strong and weak against one another based on their various elemental types—and added some *Magic: The Gathering*–esque elements (a card game that had found an unofficial home in Japan in the mid-nineties and a huge fan in then Creatures CEO Tsunekazu Ishihara). *Pokémon*'s card game also carried with it the legacy of "Obake Karuta," or "monster cards," a game created hundreds of years earlier that involved collecting various cards with monsters from Japanese mythology printed on them. Further supporting the brand, *CoroCoro* magazine continued to promote the trading cards as it had with the games, helping to ignite an interest that became a major pillar of Pokémon's expanding franchise as it moved forward.

In 1996 Pokémon evolved from RPG underdog into a red-hot title, then into a full-blown franchise. And it would repeat this success the next year with the help of a cartoon starring Pikachu and a young boy named Satoshi.

Triple Threat

Pokémon's debut year would only serve as a teaser for the ambition to come: manga, anime, and plans for a gaming future lay in 1997. Other merchandise, including the quickly proliferating trading cards, was flourishing as well, providing a solid foundation of support for the growing franchise. New deck expansions were released, and people absolutely loved them, which meant trading Pokémon became almost *too* easy, because now you could do it just by passing a playing card to someone within arm's length.

While a lowbrow comedy manga might have come first, the manga series that most people associate with the franchise, *Pokémon Adventures* (or *Pocket*

Monsters Special in Japan), debuted in March 1997, written by Hidenori Kusaka and illustrated by Mato. In comparison to the crass and madcap *Pokémon Pocket Monsters, Adventures* is a much more straightforward telling of the games' narrative, even if it does take some creative liberties from time to time to develop the world and the main character. In the games, Red is a silent ten-year-old who has whatever strengths and flaws the person playing him has. In *Adventures,* he's a capricious yet determined wannabe trainer whose talent and empathy always impress those around him.

The manga was a hit with fans and Pokémon creators alike, even garnering Satoshi Tajiri's endorsement: "This is the comic that most resembles the world I was trying to convey." And while that's likely not a slight on the previous manga's juvenile comedy, it does give you a better idea of the world that Tajiri conceived from the beginning, one that began in the limited confines of the Game Boy and expanded into the player's imagination.

The manga often answered questions that many people had when playing *Red, Green,* and *Blue:* Can a Pokémon trainer get hurt by the Pokémon's explosive attacks? Yes. Are trainers often in danger due to living in a world with these massive, elemental beasts? Oh, yes. Pokémon get hurt, but do they get hurt like physical beings in the real world get hurt? All you have to do is see the manga panel where the snake Pokémon Arbok is gruesomely sliced in half and you'll have an answer to that question. In short, *Adventures* acts as an unofficial companion piece to the games, illuminating aspects of the universe that people wondered about without complicating the games' respective plots. And they had no shortage of material to draw from.

Golden Goose

Having only gathered more notoriety and esteem in the year since the games' debut, Game Freak and Nintendo felt that it was the perfect time for a follow-up. In their eagerness, plans for a sequel to *Red* and *Green* were put in motion, and they intended for an early 1998 release. Continuing the naming convention of having two colors and symbols, one to represent each game, they were originally titled *Pocket Monsters 2*, and later *Pocket Monsters 2: Gold and Silver.* Shown off as a demo at the 1997 Nintendo Space World trade show later that November, these follow-up games would take everything that worked in the first games and make them even better.

This meant all the rough elements or issues that people had with *Red* and *Green* would be smoothed out, but it also meant that any additions that Game Freak hadn't had the time, money, technology, or manpower to develop for the original games would be added. New monsters. New rivals and gym leaders to tackle. New locations to explore. The main character might even listen to the radio and ride a skateboard around. Rad!

In fact, Nintendo and Game Freak were so confident in this release schedule that Ho-oh, an extremely rare, legendary Pokémon that would have a huge role to play in the *Gold* and *Silver* games, was placed mysteriously into the climax of the first episode of the *Pokémon* anime. Surely this was a great way to drum up excitement for the games, and kids would be figuring out what was up with that colorful bird in less than a year's time, right?

Wrong. Unfortunately, Game Freak and Nintendo had both acted a little hastily. The development team at Game Freak, which had, thankfully, been expanded a bit due to the success of *Pokémon*, was still far too overworked to deliver the new *Gold* and *Silver* versions in time. Thus, the planned spring 1998 launch date was postponed indefinitely, giving the *Gold* and *Silver* teams the necessary time they needed to fulfill the inevitable and incredibly high expectations following after *Red*, *Green,* and *Blue*'s smash successes.

The third piece of the franchise's domination would be an anime. *Pokémon the Series* began as a runaway success and remains a seemingly unstoppable animated show that, in some ways, has proven to be more famous than the games it was based on. Its origin story also illuminates the plans that all of Pokémon's partners had when it came to safeguarding what had become a very lucrative property.

Pokémon . . . The Musical?

Takeshi Shudo's knowledge of the Pokémon franchise was fairly limited when he was approached by his friend, director Kunihiko Yuyama, to write the anime. A screenwriter most famous for his work on *Magical Princess Minky Momo*, Shudo wasn't nervous about taking on the project—nor did his prospective bosses give him much room to be. In fact, the decision to create a Pokémon anime had already been made. According to its producer, Takemoto Mori, in an interview with *Animerica* magazine, a "Mr. Kubota," the managing editor of Shogakukan, had created the proposal for the series. The anime's creators had decided to "take the Pokémon world that kids already knew and put it on film," so now all they needed was a head writer.

Shudo had been writing anime for almost thirty years when he joined the team to flesh out the *Pokémon* anime and was thus well versed in taking the reins on series and guiding them creatively. However, from the very beginning, the atmosphere surrounding this project was different from his previous ventures. *Pokémon* was tightly structured, and "anything that might harm the image of the franchise" was inspected and controlled, while, according to blog posts that Shudo wrote later about his career that "animation in Japan tends to be produced in a very informal way." Another thing that struck Shudo in particular was the message given to staff that they should play the games and "Please love it." "That was the most intense line I had ever heard in the decades since I started writing scripts," Shudo recalled.

Shudo would never finish playing the game, citing that it gave him a headache, but he did appreciate the fact that it gave its fans so many different ways of telling their own stories. Inspired, he also opted for his own unique approach to the anime with his first version delivering the series narration through songs like a musical. Of course, the anime staff's reaction was about what you'd expect: "The idea of needing a song for every episode was overwhelmingly met with objections," and when the first two episodes were completed, the director asked him, "You were really serious about that first composition plan?"

Everything Shudo planned out had to fit in with the wider franchise's plans for quality control. The show was meant to last no less than a year and a half "without compromising the sales of the game." It was "not allowed" to bring down the rest of the Pokémon brand, and it would be unacceptable if it was an "inadequate adventure." It was important for the show to fit in with the competing offerings on TV, while also living up to the standards of the Pokémon brand.

In my opinion, this is where *Pokémon: The game series that got lucky enough to become other stuff* ends, and *Pokémon: The Real Franchise* truly begins. From now on, the video games and the anime would only be *parts*—very popular, lucrative parts, but only parts—of a larger whole. This is the moment when Pokémon has started or succeeded in expanding into nearly every medium, with each serving to fuel the brand, one that, in time, would no longer be contained only in Japan. The rewards were great, but so were the stakes. If one venture was to fail, there was a possibility it could hamper the growth of the rest. There were also whole audiences who would only interact with the brand through the anime or video games, never once touching the other, but both had to come away with the same impression and feeling that *Pokémon* is *awesome*.

There would be no promise of quality, though, if Shudo couldn't find a resonant theme that could carry the series and be a weightier emotional backbone than "look at all these collectible monsters from that game you like." Then he recalled the seminal coming-of-age film *Stand by Me*, a movie that is referenced on a television screen in the opening moments of *Red* and *Green*. From there, he understood what Tajiri was going for. Four kids on a coming-of-age adventure walking down railroad tracks is pretty similar to the anime formula of three to four kids on an adventure through the woods . . . with Pokémon. This feeling of being a young boy in a huge world where things are exciting and unknowable was what continued to drive Shudo's process throughout the anime's creation. Adults were scary, clumsy, and often strangers. Team Rocket, the villains, were seen through the perspective of children. The world did get old and remained firmly drenched in fantasy. Pokémon were not real animals, and the Pokémon world contained only Pokémon. According to Shudo (and the many fan theories to come after the anime premiered), real animals are extinct in the Pokémon world, now serving only as "legends."

Accompanying the young main character (named "Satoshi" after the creator of *Pokémon*) would be Pikachu, because Mori, Shudo, and others thought it was unfair to choose any one of the other starter Pokémon; players could only get one of these without trading and might feel excluded if Satoshi had different tastes than they did. A few years after Sugimori first showed the Game Freak designers the little electric Pokémon, kids around Japan crowned Pikachu the MVM, Most Valuable Monster.

Not only that, but it was decided that Pikachu would walk *beside* Satoshi, unlike every other monster in the series, which were caught in spherical devices known as "Poké Balls." This "electric mouse" Pokémon had far too much personality to be kept in captivity, so Pikachu would fight, have a sense of humor, and have more than a few whole storylines devoted to him. In short, Pikachu was now a *Pokémon* main character and was just as important as all the humans he hung out with. This opened the door to limitless merchandising options, too, because now any kid carrying a Pikachu plush or toy around would feel just like Satoshi on the trail with his favorite monster partner.

With animation by OLM Inc. and executive direction by Yuyama, *Pokémon the Series* was quick to find its footing with audiences upon release. It was during those early episodes that Shudo noticed one very disconcerting thing: When Pikachu did his electric shock attacks, the screen would flash very, very brightly. Maybe a little too brightly.

Chapter 3

FOR KIDS

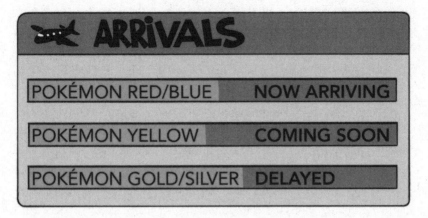

n December 1997, nine months before its American debut, *Pokémon* was mentioned twice in the *New York Times* in the span of just a few days. However, the articles weren't necessarily about *Pokémon*, but about *Pokémon*'s effects. Its reputation had preceded it, though definitely not in a way that its creators would have preferred.

The first article, published on December 8, marveled at the Game Boy's longevity, with the handheld now in its eighth year of life, and how, even when compared to its higher-powered contemporaries, "[the] Game Boy lives." After a price drop, a change in the size of the hardware, and the release of a game called *Pocket Monsters*, whatever clouds that once hung over the Game Boy's future had been cleared. Sales for the handheld had even shot past those of the Nintendo 64, Nintendo's main home console at the time, and one that had only been released the year before. Though *Pokémon*'s assistance in the handheld's achievement gets half a sentence, it was an inspiring comeback story, even if it was happening to a little block of buttons, plastic, and wire.

The second article, which was published eight days later, is much more serious, as the events reported within it would serve as a macabre signal flare for the franchise's imminent arrival. Nearly 700 Japanese children had been sent to the hospital for medical emergencies caused by the intense flashing lights of an animated TV show. Some vomited blood, some had seizures, some lost consciousness, and all the producers of the animated show were confused as to how an effect used "hundreds of times" could suddenly create such a violent and tragic reaction. It's not until the tenth paragraph that the *New York Times* mentions the show that caused the incidents: *Pocket Monsters*.

Hiroshi Yamauchi, president of Nintendo at the time, pointed a finger at TV Tokyo, the station that aired the anime, and TV Tokyo quickly announced that it would cancel all other broadcasts of the program. Police promised to investigate the event and, in the end, thanks to an episode called "Electric Soldier Porygon," the *Pokémon* anime was placed on hold for four months. However, the most interesting quote comes from a third grader, who, after talking about the episode making her dizzy, said, "I'd be sad if I could not watch the program anymore."

These two articles, one full of enthusiasm for the success of a product and the other full of anxious confusion, would set the standard for reactions to *Pokémon* in American news media. Though they weren't the first bits of info that people who lived in the US got about the franchise—the July 1997 issue of *Nintendo Power* magazine devoted four pages to *Pokémon* with the tone of "look at this *cool* Japanese series that you *might* get to play one day!"—they did help to firmly establish mainstream curiosity and uncertainty in it. What is *Pokémon*? And why is it so powerful? Meanwhile, as readers of the *New York Times* were just now hearing about this Pokémon thing, those who worked at Nintendo of America had long been preparing for it.

American-ized

Heavily involved in the creation of *Nintendo Power* magazine and Nintendo.com, Gail Tilden reinvented the way Nintendo communicated with its broad fan base. It was this expertise that led to her being asked to help introduce the

Pokémon video games to the rest of the world. Interested in the opportunity, any apprehensions that she had about the franchise weren't because of the negative PR surrounding the anime's seizure incident. Rather Tilden, at the time serving as vice president of product acquisition and development at Nintendo of America, was more concerned with the *game* because, as she stated to *TIME* magazine, role-playing games just didn't sell very well in America.

Unfortunately, a former RPG effort from Nintendo, *EarthBound* (known as *Mother 2* in Japan) had bombed in the United States a few years earlier, selling only half as many copies as it had in Japan even with a stunning $2 million advertising budget. To critics, it was a sign that American kids just didn't get it, and they preferred action games like *Mario, Donkey Kong, Mortal Kombat.* Bill Giese, a former game tester who was called on to be an early localizer for *Pokémon*, recalls a manager saying that, when it came to the games, "It's kind of a big deal over there. There's no way it's gonna sell over here. It's the next Virtual Boy." It is no surprise if you haven't heard of the Virtual Boy, since it was a lesson of what *not* to do. It was a portable 3D-based console that came with the infamous red headset. In the mid-nineties it was the go-to reference for the video game industry's most ambitious failures.

Tilden knew she had her work cut out for her. "The marketing team was looking at the game and wondering if it would be possible to re-create the popularity . . . what would need to be changed about it to capture the popularity of the game mechanic and engine itself, but maybe not the specific art style," she said. To address these concerns that the designs might estrange the game from potential fans, Tilden and her team tried out replacement designs in more of a "graffiti" style. When he saw the potential redesign, Pokémon Company CEO Ishihara recalled that it was an "unbelievable" overhaul with Pikachu altered to resemble a "tiger with huge breasts," something that looked straight out of the musical *Cats.* Thankfully, president of Nintendo of America Minoru Arakawa made the call, and the original art style would remain intact. There were movies, trading cards, TV shows, and more on the way, and redoing the art would not only be a waste of resources but undermine the brand's potential.

More important than the art style was making the series "culturally neutral," meaning that no matter who you were or where you played the games, you connected with it immediately. To an extent, *Pokémon* already is. While much of the lore and many Pokémon are based on Japanese folklore and many of the in-game environments and buildings are based on real locations and Japanese architecture, the story is intrinsically global in its harmonious tone and its themes. *Pokémon*'s core ideology of friendship, adventure, and collecting monsters resonates with anyone willing to accept it.

Translation duties would go to Nob Ogasawara, who was plucked from working on *GamePro* magazine to translate *Terranigma,* an RPG for the Super Nintendo that was never officially released in North America. Even before being given the assignment, Ogasawara had been aware of *Pokémon,* as he'd been sent tapes of the anime by a friend in Japan and eventually decided to buy the games. "I played it and was instantly charmed," Ogasawara said, admitting that he put nearly 200 hours into them. When he was being considered for the job, he was quizzed about the games and he even had to send in a creative writing sample, which was ". . . some nihilistic scene of a trainer visiting a Pokémon center," Ogasawara recalls as his plot. However, it was clear that his knowledge, talent, and enjoyment of the games made him the best fit for the job, though Ogasawara would later humbly call the events "a series of unlikely, dumb circumstance."

As part of the larger team working to bring the games to US audiences, Ogasawara would be responsible for traditional translation duties, but also removing "things like drunks, magic mushroom-taking, innuendoes about testicles," and anything that might fly in Japan, but could earn them a slap on the wrist from the Entertainment Software Ratings Board elsewhere. Also changed were the Pokémon's names, a duty left mostly to Bill Giese, Sara Bush (then Sara Osborne), and other localizers who, according to Giese, "sat in a dark writer's room" and would pitch ideas to one another about what each of the 151 creatures should be called.

It was their duty to piece together a product that stayed true to the spirit that Game Freak had imbued it with while also turning it into something that

Americans could grasp. "We had gotten info from Game Freak and they'd tell us the genesis of these creatures and what they meant and what they were inspired by," Giese said. Then the team had to do their best to honor the origins of the monsters, though Giese recalled that many times the technique would come down to "literally smashing two words together, writing it on the wall, and trying to say it fast and going, 'Is that a word?'" If you were wondering, this is how they came up with names like "Cubone" because "he wears a bone, he's a cub."

Hours were long and naming achievements were often notable, at least to Giese, simply because they led to a break. "Articuno, Zapdos, and Moltres. I remember those vividly because we were struggling with these legendary ones. And once I had in my head 'Uno, dos, tres,' I wrote it down on paper and I just put three elements together. And I thought 'Oh my god, this might work!' Not because it was creative but because it meant I had solved the problem and could now go home and have dinner."

Giese's love of pop culture helped him when naming Hitmonchan and Hitmonlee after Jackie Chan and Bruce Lee, and his affinity for *The Simpsons* gave the world Snorlax. "There's this episode 'Lisa's Wedding' where they go to this Renaissance fair in Springfield and Chief Wiggum has these medieval creatures that don't exist, like the Esquilax. 'It's got the head of a rabbit and the body of a rabbit.' And I thought it was funny, so I kept thinking, *Esquilax, Esquilax, Esquilax* and I don't know why that stuck in my head. And so, with Snorlax, you have 'snore' and 'lax.' I literally put that there because I like that joke on *The Simpsons*."

Sara Bush, who was also a game tester, had another memory of the creation of the Snorlax name, that it was a combination of the words "lackadaisical" and "snore." But unlike Giese, who had been given a kind of doomed prediction for the games, Bush's initial experience spoke to *Pokémon*'s global potential: "[My boss] gave me one of the actual Japanese cartridges . . . and I started playing them in Japanese. I do not speak or read Japanese. So, I started playing them and writing down my kanji, trying everything and then doing my translation into English. But even in Japanese, this game is a blast."

She worked with Ogasawara, Giese, and Hiro Nakamura, who helped provide context around Japanese meanings and importance that were behind the Pokémon names and story. Working on the *Pokémon* games was challenging, but Bush acknowledged, "This was like a living thing and really something so special. It was necessary to take diligence and precision."

However, the care they practiced didn't mean that it also wasn't an entertaining experience. "What a fun time that was," Bush said. "We were talking about the town names and the importance of the town names and the fact that they represented colors and shades and hues. I've also painted for years and years, and I was like 'It's like the paint colors!' So, we literally went to a paint store and we were looking at all those things."

The work involved a constant back-and-forth, not just between Nintendo of America and Nintendo of Japan, but with the licensor Shogakukan and Game Freak themselves. While the game studio was intent on ensuring that *Pokémon* be well taken care of in the US, the team commented on how easy the relationship and the "caretaking" process was. "All of them at Game Freak were so nice. It was exactly what you'd imagine an old developer to be. Everyone wore sweats, and they just kinda hung out and played and talked games," Giese remembered. Masuda was "incredibly kind," and when it came to Sugimori's artistic talents, Giese was "more in awe of him." Tilden referred to Tajiri as "a gentle and creative soul," with Bush adding, "He's just the neatest, nicest man."

"We decided to make an all-out effort to repeat the phenomenon in the Western world," Tilden said, hoping that the hard work that went into *Pokémon* would pay off with a replication of the phenomenon that had spread through Japan. The time and effort had been exerted, but now the question was whether North American audiences were ready to receive it.

Goodbye, Batman. Hello, Zubat

It should come as no surprise that the children's entertainment landscape of 1998 is far different from the one that exists today. In the years since, we've watched the downfall of brands that seemed impenetrable, along with the rise of titles and characters that went into the new millennium on the precipice of disaster. And for *Pokémon* to work as a franchise, it would not only have to rise above its kid-friendly peers of the time period, but also ward off the assumptions that would inevitably surround it. Namely, that it was a Beanie Baby clone.

The middle to late nineties had been the time of the Beanie Baby. These were stuffed beanbag toys that also relied on the collector's "it's better to try and get all them than just one of them" model, and during the nineties they quickly rose from a relative nonentity to a must-have item for all children and hobbyists. In the short amount of time, an entire scarcity-driven market was built around the collecting and selling of these small plushies, with fans and speculators furiously buying them in in the hope of a substantial payday when their future value increased. Some Beanie Babies were indeed rare, and many were costly, but in the end, the economy around this particular brand of beanbag doll would exhaust itself, burning out just a few months after *Pokémon* entered the scene.

Pokémon "clearly tapped into this kind of age old, especially Americana thing of collection, like baseball card collection, and all those things that go way back in our history," Bush said, but Nintendo of America believed that this brand would last because it offered more *options*. Like the Beanie Baby, Pokémon were made to be collected, but they weren't just collector's items. You could raise them, fight with them, and even release them back into the digital wild if you got bored with them. In this way, Pokémon differentiates itself from many collector's items in that your compiled assortment was built for more than just gawking at them from behind glass cases.

You could take these bad boys out of the box, play with them, and, most importantly, you could share them with your friends. This aspect allowed the games to effectively democratize collecting, a hobby that's usually reserved for those with the means, the money, and the space. With Pokémon, having the game and a friend to trade with meant gaining an equal chance of being the greatest collector in the world.

With its all-encompassing program of games, an anime series, a trading card game, and toys planned out and ready to launch, Pokémon wasn't likely to fizzle out in the same unceremonious manner as the Beanie Baby. This program also made it entirely unlike any other imported franchise in pop culture history due to its sheer variety and reach. While some brands might have had a popular cartoon and a popular toy line, or a popular movie series and a popular video game adaptation, most started with just one medium, then would build out if the original effort was deemed successful enough to be worth the risk of expanding. Pokémon was unique because it had it all from pretty much the start.

LIVING FOSSILS

Dinosaurs also played an important part in why *Pokémon* was immediately embraced by youngsters. Yes, *Pokémon* is fictional, but it still deals with a world filled with gigantic creatures that defy the modern genetic limits of biology and that beg for scientific explanation. Considering the explosion of interest in paleontology in the eighties and nineties, the blockbuster success of *Jurassic Park* and its sequel, as well as the availability of dinosaur movies on home video, plus the fact that multiple Pokémon were designed to resemble prehistoric beasts, kids around the country were already fit not only to enjoy the exploits of fabulous beasts roaming about, but to memorize their names, too. To the untrained ear, hearing someone say, "You have Pikachu, Squirtle, Ivysaur, Clefairy, and Zubat" doesn't sound all that different from "You have Baryonyx, Diplodocus, Troodon, Allosaurus, and Deinonychus."

While Pokémon might have needed to rise above the fad-status of Beanie Babies, its success was also helped by the growing void that superheroes were leaving behind. In 1998, enthusiasm about superheroes had waned, and they quickly lost their status as number one in children's pop culture. Though it may seem bizarre now, considering that the Marvel Cinematic Universe has made more money than the GDP of some countries, twenty-five years ago these characters were out of style thanks to declining comic book sales and the failure of big budget adaptations like 1997's *Batman & Robin*.

The audience was also shifting from younger viewers to a more adult audience. *Blade* received an R rating, barring it from the massive, and younger, crowds who, just three years earlier, had flocked to see *Batman Forever* and then migrated to McDonald's after for the Happy Meal toy tie-ins and the cool, special edition soda cups with the Riddler on the sides. In fact, that year, the freshly bankrupt Marvel Entertainment offered Sony Pictures the film rights for their entire roster of characters for just $25 million. To put that into perspective, Robert Downey Jr. earned roughly $1 million *a minute* to perform a side role in 2017's *Spider-Man: Homecoming*. He was in the movie for fifteen minutes.

On top of superhero films focusing on an older audience, the animated TV shows that had come to define certain characters, like *Batman: The Animated Series*, *X-Men*, and *Spider-Man*, had all recently ended their runs and, sadly, the comic book industry was in the pits, a victim of its own clumsy marketing tactics. Video games weren't much better off. The most high-profile superhero game released in the late nineties was *Superman: The New Superman Adventures*. But you might know it by its abbreviated name *Superman 64*, which was what was used when it was placed on more than a half dozen "Worst Games of All Time" lists. It would be two years before Bryan Singer's *X-Men* premiered and four years before Sam Raimi's *Spider-Man*, which would be the first film to make over $100 million in its opening weekend, rebuilding the foundation of the superhero blockbuster. *Pokémon*, on the other hand, arose, warmed up and ready for action. It was the evolution that children's entertainment had been looking for.

Friendly Advice from Aunt Hillary

"Gotta Catch 'Em All. Gotta Catch 'Em All."

Invented for the English language *Pokémon* debut, this phrase was eventually slapped onto nearly everything related to Pokémon outside of Japan and was repeated frequently during the *A Sneak Peek at Pokémon* promotional VHS tape. It's a catchy chant, one that you're bound to remember even if you can't recall any of the names of the monsters. And that is why it is so effective, as parents and kids didn't need to know the names . . . yet. All they needed to know was that it was best to have *all* of them.

Using the *Nintendo Power* mailing list, these promotional tapes were mailed around the country to sell its viewers on the franchise, a tactic Nintendo had previously used for the *Donkey Kong Country* cartoon. In the sneak peek are two adult narrators: one is a professor who spends the whole time explaining what a Pikachu and a Pokédex are, as well as affirming those watching that Ash Ketchum, the main character, has "class." The other narrator is Ash Ketchum's Aunt Hillary, who can't seem to decide whether they're called "Poke-uh-min" or "Poke-aye-mon things," but is very excited about the prospect of her animated nephew capturing hundreds of them.

Then, throughout the tape, kids show up to explain various characters or situations—including a preteen girl who seems to own nothing but Pokémon plush toys of various sizes—but, for the most part, it's up to the two adults in garishly lit rooms to try to convince you to find out what channel the show will be on. The tape also promoted the video games, along with the Pokémon Pikachu virtual pet and the trading card game, merchandise that would all debut a few months after the games' release. Then the sneak peek ends by telling viewers to keep an eye out for the "PokéCars," which would be driving around the country, showing off the anime and games, and even handing out free Pokémon stuff to any fan who happened to be way too close to the street at the time.

This whirlwind of information and products that lasts less than fifteen minutes was most likely a cacophony of nonsense to adults and an absolute thrill for the kids lucky enough to witness it. And this sentiment proved to be the biggest asset of the franchise during its early years: kids were the immediate experts in *Pokémon* and were on the "ground floor," if you will. It was something new, something entirely unfiltered by expectations or tastes established by series past, so parents had no clue how to change *Pokémon* because they had no comparison or reference to guide them. And kids had to get it *all*.

Nearly every month in 1998 *Nintendo Power* ran a new feature about *Pokémon* games, from articles about its effects on the resurgence of the Game Boy, to explainers that covered the ins and outs of its appeal, to six mini-magazines that guided you through portions of the game. While this was great for establishing a buzz around the game prior to its release, it was probably more than a bit exhausting for the *Nintendo Power* staff. When the review team finally did end up reviewing the game, their score was a 7.2 out of 10. Not bad, but also a far cry from the "this is the second coming" treatment that they'd seemingly been preparing for. Various other publications ran their own predictions about the anime leading up to its premiere. *Brandweek* listed the exhaustive amount of marketing Nintendo was doing, as did *Advertising Age*, which marveled at the more than $10 million spent on Nintendo of America's push to make *Pokémon* a success, but was also quick to remind readers that this indeed included the show that caused all those seizures. The *Wall Street Journal*, starting their piece with "Godzilla, shmodzilla," mainly focused on the toy potential and, yes, the seizures.

Overall, these were the two main takeaways: Nintendo of America was spending a lot of money on the show, so this franchise will probably make a lot of money in return, and the animated show causes seizures. Luckily, the negative press around the upcoming franchise would soften, mainly due to Nintendo's push to make it look as wholesome and exciting as possible. One way to do that? With wordplay.

On August 27, 1998, a month before the anime's official release, Nintendo held a special "ToPikachu" event in Topeka, Kansas, a city chosen because it was in the center of the US. As part of the event, the city officially renamed itself "ToPikachu," a change that tragically only lasted a day, and more than 2,500 lucky kids got the chance to play the games, watch some of the upcoming anime, and nab some t-shirts. "Pokémon 'Pretty Neat'" read the front page of the *Topeka Capital Journal*, alongside a picture of a seven-year-old embracing a gigantic Pikachu doll.

Seven hundred Pikachu plush were dropped from the air, along with ten skydivers who landed and drove away in the Pikachu-themed PokéCars. Then kids rushed into the field to claim the dolls—a mad display of energy for a product that hadn't technically been introduced en masse yet. "They came. They saw. They sold," continued the article, but to kids, it was extremely reasonable. It's *Pokémon*, remember? *Gotta catch 'em all.*

The games had been renamed *Pokémon: Red Version* and *Pokémon: Blue Version*, using the updates provided by the Japanese *Blue* version, while keeping the groupings of monsters found in Japanese *Red* and *Green*, respectively. The name and color change came thanks to the same Hiro Nakamura, who had been integral for the US team with localizing the games, and continued to be instrumental in figuring out how to ensure that *Pokémon* performed well across different markets. "It was his kind of experimenting with people and understanding that blue is the most popular color in America and that starting with *Red* and *Blue* would be better than starting with *Red* and *Green*. It wouldn't matter in the triangulation of water-fire-plant which two led," Tilden said of Nakamura's work.

Of course, everyone knows that fire and water don't mix, like, at all. So the games leaned into this dynamic by placing Charizard, the final evolutionary stage of little flame-tailed Charmander, on the cover of *Red*, and Blastoise, the final evolutionary stage of the tiny turtle Squirtle, on the cover of *Blue*. Kids would not only trade between themselves, but instantly understand the inherent competition going on. "Which one did you get? *Red* or *Blue*?" would be the prime opening line for elementary school cafeteria arguments for months and years to come. Despite this natural tension and competition, technically, no choice was better than the other, which is a theme that continues to run throughout the series even today. "The unique nature of the sheer size and variety of Pokémon," Bush said of the games, "means you can have your own special blend and your favorites. And nobody's was better or worse than another, just different. There was identity in that."

MONSTER MASHED

Prior to their release, there were two distinct commercials for the Game Boy games that were played almost constantly on television. The first was fairly chaotic, featuring a bus driver inviting a bunch of Pokémon on board, including a Pikachu, who greets him with a friendly "Pikachu!", to which the driver drolly and hilariously responds, "Yeah, whatever." It's all a ruse, however, and the driver hauls the Pokémon to a factory where the bus is crushed with the creatures visibly panicking inside. The demolished vehicle is then turned into a Game Boy, which the bus driver happily plays, with no thought to the numerous crimes that he must have just committed.

The second commercial was of a gentler variety, of two boys playing *Pokémon* in apartment buildings separated by a wide alley. Seeing that their owners are frustrated by their inability to catch the monsters found in the opposing game cartridge, their Pokémon pals leap to the rescue! Led by Pikachu, who, of course, was already anointed as the Monster Team Captain for the franchise's American reveal, the Pokémon escape the confines of their Game Boys and toss a link cable between the apartments. Then a handful of monsters make the precarious tightrope walk from one boy's Game Boy to the other, effectively echoing the image Satoshi Tajiri had had in his head of bugs crawling across a wire almost a decade prior.

This was the perfect encapsulation of the franchise—and remains so to this day. Amid the marketing maelstrom created not just to appeal to American consumers, but to overwhelm pop culture itself with *Pokémon*'s ubiquity, here were friendly monsters from a lush fantasy realm coming to life to help total strangers connect in the middle of a cold, urban setting. It is up to the viewer whether it's more of a capitalistic re-creation of nostalgic connection or humane bond formed by benign beings of supernatural biology. Regardless, the commercial is *Pokémon*.

Then, finally, the time had come. The anime was set to premiere on September 8, a strategic placement that would hopefully entice even more kids—okay, their parents—to go out and buy the games, which were following on the twenty-eighth. However, there is just one more player to introduce before we explore the shockwave that would follow *Pokémon* being unleashed into millions of homes across America. They're well known to *Pokémon* fans, some of whom remember them with childhood nostalgia, while others wish that they'd done things differently in their efforts to help make *Pokémon* as massive as possible.

They are 4Kids.

Slim Chances

The company Leisure Concepts began in 1970, and over the next two decades would make a name for itself by running the licensing operations for countless franchises to produce toys and tie-in merchandise. From James Bond to the Hulk, *Star Wars* to Farrah Fawcett—yes, they licensed the rights for products based on very real people, too—and various Nintendo characters, including the ones from *The Legend of Zelda*, all passed through Leisure's grasp at one point. The company's reach stretched beyond just licensing and it was even involved in creative ventures as well, most notably with the creation of the hit eighties cartoon *Thundercats*, so when Leisure Concepts began to produce television series in the early nineties, it wasn't like they didn't have any experience. The formation of subsidiary companies 4Kids Productions and Summit Media Group followed, and before the end of the decade, Leisure Concepts changed its name entirely to 4Kids Entertainment. And in 1998, 4Kids Entertainment got the rights to license *Pokémon* outside of Japan.

The partnership between 4Kids and Nintendo of America had been a long one by the time *Pokémon* hit their radar. 4Kids CEO Al Khan's connection with the gaming company dated back to the early eighties when he arranged for Nintendo's mega-hit *Donkey Kong* to be the pack-in cartridge for the short-lived ColecoVision console. "He pitched that he would become Nintendo's licensing agent for all the characters," Tilden said. This would include *Pokémon*, which Khan was eager to work on, especially since it would help improve 4Kids' financial status at the time. "He was really excited to watch what was happening and . . . that they would also be our licensing partner for *Pokémon*." Norman Grossfeld, president of 4Kids Productions since 1994, also immediately saw the potential of the franchise. "So, when I saw that there was something so popular in one country, my personal feeling was it could work everywhere," Grossfeld explained. The skepticism over the video game's RPG elements or the anime itself was not even a factor for Grossfeld: *Pokémon* was going to be a hit.

The biggest hurdle for him and the 4Kids team would be selling the anime to the networks and getting through their "preconceived notions or their snobbery for Western-produced animation over something from Asia." Luckily, thanks to 4Kids' prowess (and some of Nintendo's money), they'd at least be able to get it in front of eyeballs. "There used to be something called barter syndication," Tilden explained. "And what that means is you barter your advertising dollars with an individual station or a group that owns local stations. So 4Kids went out and shopped the show to eighty markets and bartered Nintendo's advertising dollars in order to get it on the air." This meant that 4Kids had to provide all the production costs up front, so if *Pokémon*'s first fifty-two episodes bombed, it could very well bring down 4Kids. The risk was so great that Grossfeld remembers that "some senior people at the company were saying, 'Let's farm it out to Canada, because if it doesn't work, we can blame them for screwing it up.'"

Grossfeld persisted in his plans for the anime, and Khan was already convinced that they had to place their bets on *Pokémon*. So Grossfeld presented this all-in approach to Shogakukan Productions at the 1998 NATPE television convention, saying, "What I think we need to do is make the show feel for German kids that it could be taking place in Germany. For American kids, it could be taking place in America. We don't want them to feel that it's from somewhere else. It's a local thing." After listing the various aspects that might not translate well from a Japanese audience to an American one, Grossfeld asked for "kind of carte blanche, to let me change the show as I think would work for this market."

And Shogakukan Productions agreed.

Chapter 4

PIKACHU'S BIG ENTRANCE

On September 7, 1998, children's television changed forever. Kids, some of whom had received the "Sneak Peek" VHS tape, saw Mewtwo leap into the sky, followed soon by Mew. Ash Ketchum stands alone in the middle of an arena. Various images of Pokémon and side characters like Brock, Misty, and Professor Oak flash by, all while singer Jason Paige croons a lyric that most millennials now know by heart: "I wanna be the very best." It's an animated opening theme that's grandiose, aspirational, and undeniably memorable. "It's like the Ten Commandments," Paige said of the song. Then the first episode began to play "Battle Aboard the *St. Anne*."

Wait, what? That's not the first episode, that's the fifteenth. Why did they start with that one? Well, the reason was likely because it's a pretty action-packed adventure, one where Ash has a full team of Pokémon, and it also includes the whole established cast, so it was chosen to preview what the show had to offer. There are a few battles, a big ship sinks—the fact that

Titanic had come out a year earlier and been the highest grossing film in history surely didn't hurt here—and the episode concludes with a cliffhanger. It's a much faster paced episode compared to the true opening episode, which is centered around the slow growth of the relationship between Ash and Pikachu. Instead of a more traditional introduction and story about friendship, *Pokémon* starts with a solid teaser for things to come.

So I guess, it was on September 8, 1998, that children's animated television changed forever. "Pokémon—I Choose You" was the name of the initial installment, and it laid out everything viewers needed to know to become invested in the universe. You learn what Pokémon are, you learn how their world functions, and you even learn how to get one in the games: head to Professor Oak's lab! Luckily, one of the world's most knowledgeable Pokémon experts lives within walking distance from you.

And, perhaps even more importantly, you learn who Pikachu is, and find that he's a spunky, rebellious little monster who does not like you and definitely doesn't like it when you tell him what to do. He eventually comes around, though, and by the end of the episode, he licks Ash Ketchum's face in a kind of "okay, we're cool now, bro" moment. Then they're friends for life.

In case it wasn't clear yet, Ash Ketchum isn't a direct translation of the character's original name, Satoshi. Instead, it is a pun-based moniker that, once again, took advantage of the "Gotta catch 'em all" tagline. In fact, the catchphrase was invented as a "positioning statement" by Grossfeld as a way to "keep kids engaged" while also just *barely* skirting Federal Trade Commission rules about directly influencing children through advertising. So while Ketchum was Grossfeld's idea, the decision to change the character's name from Satoshi to Ash was courtesy of Nintendo.

THE GODZILLA METHOD

Of course, creating a new character or altering one to be an American audience surrogate is nothing new for imported Japanese media. For example, the original 1954 *Godzilla* is a giant monster movie full of city-stomping and atomic fire-breathing, but it's also an extremely melancholic experience, one that reflects Japan's troubled relationship with nuclear weapons and the terror it experienced thanks to atomic warfare.

When it was released in the United States in 1956 as *Godzilla: King of the Monsters!*, it was heavily edited and an entirely new main character was added—played by Raymond Burr, who'd recently starred in Alfred Hitchcock's *Rear Window*—talking to stand-ins for the Japanese leads and basically providing commentary for the action. He gives a solid performance; but in the grand scheme of the plot, he is nothing more than a glorified sportscaster for the radioactive dinosaur's rampages. "We weren't really interested in politics," said US film distributor Richard Kay about the adaptation in Steve Ryfle's fantastic book *Japan's Favorite Mon-Star*. "At that time, the American public wouldn't have gone for a movie with an all-Japanese cast . . . We just gave it an American point of view."

While maintaining the core concepts of the original anime, all the adjustments came from Grossfeld and his goal to have it feel "local." Series producer Takemoto Mori told *Animerica* magazine that he actually liked the adaptation because "It was changed much less than I expected. Don't they normally change the plot right and left?"

Of course, typical things that you'd expect to be censored were, such as any rougher violence or hints of sexualization, plus a good portion of the score and the opening and ending theme songs were replaced, the former by the "Pokémon Theme" and the latter by the infinitely catchy "Pokérap." Featuring a man rhyming his way through all 150 monsters, the rap's verses were broken up by singing and shouts of, you guessed it, "Gotta catch 'em all! Gotta catch 'em all."

As catchy as the rap was, the opening theme, which was created by Grossfeld, songwriter John Siegler, and others, would become a hallmark of the series. Jason Paige, who had experience singing advertising jingles, imbued the theme with power ballad strength, fitting the "Bon Jovi meets Michael Jackson" requirements that he recalls the team wanted the song to have. Its popularity, according to Paige, may have had nothing to do with Pokémon. "They exist completely in a standalone way. Without the word 'Pokémon,' the song can be about so many things that are really important, powerful, positive, inspiring." It's an idea that has merit, especially because almost a third of the minute-long opening is over before Paige even says the word "Pokémon."

The reconstruction of the anime extended to its aesthetics, locations, and the way its characters interacted. Most of the Japanese writing, whether it was on signs or buildings, had to be scrubbed or replaced. When it came to the dialogue, jokes and even whole conversations were altered all for the sake of connecting with American children. Michael Haigney, who'd done voice directing work and had written anime localizations before becoming attached to *Pokémon*, unfortunately did not have the most positive first impression of the series when asked to join the team: "Is this the show that put all the kids in the hospital in Japan?" Watching some of the show didn't improve his opinion much, as Haigney felt that it was destined for swift cancellation. "We'll do this but you got to get at least half of the money up front, because this will not run for more than thirteen episodes. This show is a dog," Haigney recalled before remembering just how successful the show ended up being—to date, more than 1,100 episodes have aired in North America, and the number is still growing. "So that's how wrong I was. It was a good show. It came with good characters. It had heart."

Despite his reservations, Haigney joined the team and took on a role that he describes as "constant work." Because he was unable to add lip flap movements, the dialogue had to match the character's mouth on a syllabic basis. Combined with the job of having to write around the voice actors' recording schedules caused a sort of "patchwork" effect on the scripts and, as a result, his days sometimes ended at six a.m. the next morning. In his "spare" time, Haigney recorded the copious Pokémon voices necessary for the constant name-spouting monsters, though this led to another learning curve about the series. For instance, when he voiced Ash's Charmander for the first time, he had no idea it would be a recurring creature. "Wait, he keeps Charmander and now Charmander is in the next episode, too?" He had figured that it was a kind of "Monster of the Week" deal for the fiery little lizard.

While many of the changes and updates made to the show were hardly even noticed by most viewers who had no awareness of the original Japanese show, there is one that became infamous, at least as far as internet criticism of the dub is concerned. The backlash came when Ash's pal Brock, the former gym leader turned loyal friend, offers Ash an onigiri, which is a popular Japanese rice ball eaten as a snack. However, in a scene that's been recounted in countless memes, Brock calls it a doughnut, and so does Misty, Ash's other companion. In fact, in the span of eight seconds, it's called a doughnut three times.

Eric Stuart, Brock's voice actor, confirmed during a convention panel that the choice to call the onigiri a doughnut was done because the teams at 4Kids felt that more people across the world could recognize this as a pastry rather than as sushi. I'm not sure how *accurate* that claim is, but as a kid from rural North Carolina who didn't have sushi until he left his hometown for college, I can certainly understand the logic behind it.

How *Pokémon* would have fared in America if they'd altered less is anyone's guess. The fact remains that despite all these changes, American kids were enthralled from the start and kept ratings high, even beating the *CBS Morning News* in Los Angeles and once besting NBC's *Today* show. The characters and creatures that viewers had seen advertised through the dying days of summer and into the fall were finally available to watch every weekday. Often airing early in the morning, the program was the perfect way to start the day for a generation of monster kids who were too young to drink coffee, so they were energized through Ash Ketchum's quest. In no time at all, *Pokémon* became the highest rated kids-targeted show in syndication.

It also didn't hurt that the characters on *Pokémon* are genuinely likable and energetic because of the lively voice acting. Veronica Taylor's Ash Ketchum embodies the character's energy and stubbornness, while Eric Stuart provides a kind of brotherly goofiness and charm as Brock, as well as a genial clumsiness as Team Rocket's James. Rachael Lillis's Misty is endearing and bossy, while also providing Team Rocket's Jessie with an underrated sense of hilarious pathos. Haigney viewed Ash as "kind of like the straight man" while the rest of the characters "provide the comedy."

While many of the Pokémon were voiced by Haigney and other collaborators, there were two others who lent their voices to bring life to particularly notable pocket monsters. Ikue Ōtani is the only voice actress who worked on both the original Japanese and new American versions, and she was always adept at lending endlessly cute and feisty variations of Pikachu's "Pika," "Pi," and "Chu." And then you have Meowth, Team Rocket's catlike Pokémon, who is part mascot, part third wheel, and who was originally voiced with an embittered crankiness by Nathan Price and later with wonderful flair by the late voice actress Maddie Blaustein.

None of this was an easy task, but the main cast pulled it off with aplomb. For years, American dubs of Japanese media had been a source of ridicule— only good for a chuckle as you watched the mismatched lip movements and clumsy translations. This mindset was partly to blame for foreign media being unappreciated and why so many wonderful Godzilla films and Hong Kong martial arts films weren't seen as anything more than niche cinema, kid stuff, or camp. In order to succeed in America, *Pokémon* couldn't let itself be weighed down with those preconceived stereotypes. Instead, it had to prove that it was just like the other cartoons that it was airing alongside of, and luckily, it did.

Meanwhile, as Ash Ketchum built his Pokémon team, gathered a few gym badges, and traveled across the Kanto region with his pals, the clock slowly ticked toward the release of *Pokémon Red* and *Blue*. Recent sales for the Game Boy had been up from the previous year, plus the show was basically marketing the games to kids every morning, but would these things add up to a better chance at *Pokémon Red* and *Blue* hitting the ground running?

Instant Triumph

In the first two weeks, *Pokémon Red* and *Blue* had 400,000 retail orders. Games were selling out everywhere, with electronics stores like Best Buy handing out rain checks for as soon as November. In an interview in the *Los Angeles Times*, Sally Mendez, a parent desperate to find the game, revealed that she'd already looked for it at four different stores, to no avail. She was just one of many, proving that everything, from the marketing to running the anime a few weeks before, had worked. Nintendo was banking on selling a million copies by Christmas.

While parents went on desperate quests to find the game, critiques of it rolled in offering mixed reviews. *Electronic Gaming Monthly* called it the "definition of masterful game design," and deemed it "truly a social experience—something that's as much of a hobby as it is a game." However, while the commitment factor was a bonus for some, it was a turn-off for others. A writer for the *Los Angeles Times* compared his reaction to *Pokémon* to his bafflement at Beanie Babies, saying that both preyed on the "obsessive compulsive hiding in all of us." Some critics and players embraced the engaging gameplay that easily became part of your daily schedule before you knew what hit you. Others grimaced at a structure that seemed to grind your attention span into dust.

The strong response and high sales prompted Nintendo of America to take their efforts up a notch. Rather than follow the normal pattern of game promotion, they continued to push *Pokémon* weeks after its debut. "We made a new campaign and went back on air for . . . *Red* and *Blue*," said Tilden. "We were doubling down to get the install base going." The addictive and easily replayable qualities of *Pokémon* undoubtedly helped this extended promotion because it wasn't a game that fans would beat quickly and get tired of. This meant that when new fans joined in the community, they were met with open arms and eager link cables. For many kids, it was their first taste of the RPG genre, one that valued careful strategy and completist exploration over quick wins and blasting through levels. It was a game they could get lost in, on purpose or otherwise, from the "natural maze" of Viridian Forest, to the ladders and pitch-black, rocky floors of Rock Tunnel, to the teleportation pads that lead you around the Silph Co. office building, taking you higher and higher toward a confrontation with the boss of Team Rocket.

Following the success of the Game Boy games, November saw the release of the Pokémon Pikachu virtual pet, a tiny device that counted your steps and allowed you to interact with your very own Pikachu. Keeping true to anime form, this Pikachu was notoriously hard to please. And if you didn't show it enough attention, it wouldn't die like other virtual pets or leave feces around; rather, it would give you a disappointed look or just hide from you. It's an emotional letdown that is far worse in my opinion, especially since you'd have to shake it in order to apologize to Pikachu and take it for a walk.

Of course, then we had fast food tie-ins, which until the late 2000s were the ultimate sign that a pop culture movie or series was being primed for and or achieving cultural saturation. Everyone knew that if it comes in a Happy Meal, it must be big. Oddly enough, it wasn't the famous golden arches that would win the fast food licensing race and partner with Nintendo in a $17 million deal. As it turns out, Kentucky Fried Chicken, the famed dealer of cooked poultry, was *Pokémon's* first North American restaurant licensee. But you didn't get those Pokémon toys for free—at least not at first.

Unlike other toys that came with branded kids' meals, the first toys offered by KFC—stuffed beanbag renditions of Vulpix, Zubat, Seel, and, one of my favorites, Dratini—cost $4.99. So, technically, KFC wasn't just a vendor of fried food, but of Pokémon merchandise, too: a true example of product diversification if there ever was one. While they would eventually offer various free toys like little puzzles, non-permanent tattoos, water-squirting figures, and other standard fast food stuff—this original approach was extremely confident.

Would parents shell out five dollars, along with whatever they were paying for their bucket of chicken, for a Pokémon toy, one whose cloth exterior would soon be covered in greasy fingerprints? Some would, but whether or not parents bought the toys isn't the true point because, during those first few months, it was clear something far more critical was occurring. The KFC promotion saw Pokémon coming dangerously close to actually replicating the Beanie Baby fad that so many naysayers had actually accused it of being. KFC and Nintendo even played up the toys as bona fide collector's items, complete with little Poké Ball–shaped tags attached to them. The tags were most likely designed this way to remind consumers of a piece of distinctly late nineties wisdom: "Don't take the TY tag off the Beanie Babies, because otherwise they won't be worth any money at all."

The most fun part of the promotion was the accompanying commercial. In it an animated Colonel Sanders frantically plays a red Game Boy with *Pokémon Blue Version* in it and pronounces his game of choice "Poke-aye-mahn." He continues to shill for his new popcorn chicken and then threatens to start his own collection if you don't buy the beanbag monsters fast enough. The promotion ran for about a month and was ultimately a financial disappointment. Coming on the heels of the franchise's debut, it was a bit of a surprise. "They are the only people to have had a non-successful campaign," Tilden said. Bush, who moved from just being a member of the localization team to the team working on the franchise's massive marketing effort, said of the commercial, "[That] was before my time, or he would've been saying Pokémon correctly."

A lackluster performance from KFC did little to harm Pokémon's momentum, and it was still going strong leading into the holidays, where they appeared to have little true competition, and in hindsight, it simply looked like Pikachu trampling over a field of other creature toys. The virtual pet Tamagotchi was still on the shelves, but in 1998 it saw a drop in sales of around 80 percent from its heyday in 1996 and 1997. In many ways, *Pokémon* might have seemed like a more advanced version of the Tamagotchis, seeing as they were both predicated on tiny monster-raising, and *Pokémon* offered a wider plethora of options for that mission. Meanwhile, Sony's ill-fitted rendition of *Godzilla,* another Americanized version of a Japanese hit, never made good on the tens of millions of dollars spent advertising it. Though not going head to head with *Pokémon,* it's hard not to see the contrast between Pokémon's holiday success and the army of radioactive dinosaur toys lining the clearance rack.

While the offerings in 1998 would ultimately be dwarfed by the Pikachu-centric Christmas to come a year later, holiday catalogs were not completely bereft of Pokémon. A humorous and notable appearance came in the Sears Wish Book, which erroneously reported that *Pokémon Red* and *Blue* only had 75 monsters each and featured box art that barely resembled the real thing. "The latest overseas rage!" the catalog exclaimed, banking on the game's foreignness to provide some allure.

Many had expected *Pokémon* to succeed, and it was undoubtedly doing better than expected while proving both its harshest critics and stereotypes wrong. But this was nothing compared to what was looming on the horizon. Pikachu and his monster pals would soon show that they were here to stay, and 1999 was about to be the biggest year in the franchise's overseas history. Pokémon's takeover had barely gotten started.

VIP Treatment

Pokémon is "IN," declared the *Washington Post*, kicking off 1999, the year that is perhaps the most important in Pokémon's lifespan, at least in the United States. That year would be explosive, controversial, successful, and unceasingly chaotic. It started out as everything that Nintendo, 4Kids, and the other companies involved could've hoped for, but it would conclude with their worst nightmares.

January started with two huge developments. First off, the trading card game had made its official debut in the United States and was instantly a success of mammoth proportions. It did ten times better than the original projection, with one buyer for Electronics Boutique telling *BNET* that they'd "presold 50,000 booster packs before the first decks were even shipped," such was the hype. In a bit of business serendipity, the game was produced by Wizards of the Coast, the company that had brought *Magic: the Gathering* into the world in 1993 and, in doing so, had set the wheels in motion for the creation of the Japanese collectible cards that they'd now be adapting.

Just like with everything in Pokémon's early years, the excitement found complications. This "Base Set" and the cards released along with it would also, in just a few months, give school officials across the country a massive, mutual headache. Kids might not have been able to easily bring their Game Boys to school (trust me, *I tried*) but they could certainly smuggle in decks of *Pokémon* cards, and by April, schools began banning them.

The decision to ban the card game wasn't just about concerns around kids wasting time. Multiple principals claimed that this nascent Pokémon Prohibition Era was due to kids getting emotional over the game, after having been "suckered out of valuable cards" in unfair trades. This is, of course, a very humane way to say that they were tired of listening to kids complain about why Timmy should give them back their holographic Blastoise. However, one set of parents disclosed to AP News that they kind of liked that their kid was into *Pokémon*, with the father even adding that he appreciated the fact that in the Pokémon world, "boys and girls are equally powerful." Good on you, some kid's woke dad.

Following the card game came news about the anime, which after a drought of new syndicated episodes that had lasted since the previous October, it was revealed that the show would run exclusively during the Kids' WB programming block. This was a big deal considering that the

Warner Bros. branded lineup also included multiple DC Comics superheroes shows, the underrated *Men in Black: The Series*, and comedies like *Histeria!*. 4Kids had gotten caught in a bidding war between Kids' WB and Saban Entertainment/Fox, and decided to go with the former. "We made the deal and the deal points were written on a napkin at the hotel," Grossfeld recalls. Of course, this move did not come without its fair share of fanfare. In fact, the way that Kids' WB promoted *Pokémon*'s arrival remains a crucial part of the years-long process of basically turning Pikachu into an icon of Americana itself. They wouldn't just tell you that *Pokémon* was awesome. They'd have the most famous members of the Justice League do it, too.

"Hey, whatta'ya got there, a rabbit?" Terry McGinnis's Batman asks his mentor, the elderly Bruce Wayne. Both men are in the Batcave, and on the gargantuan Batcomputer is an image of Pikachu who, to be fair to Terry, looks like a rabbit. "It's a Pokémon," Bruce Wayne replies to his young protégé with the same matter-of-fact, "It's cool, you'll figure out this vigilante crimefighter thing one day" tone that came to define the *Batman Beyond* series. Five seconds later, Pikachu shocks the teenage Batman, sending him back and into another set of computers—which was an impact clip taken from a *Batman Beyond* episode called "Blackout," which would air just a few days later. And, though it's weird that Batman's first involvement with *Pokémon* was so needlessly hostile, this promotional commercial does do a lot to establish *Pokémon* as a worthy part of the Kids' WB lineup. They're so cool that even the Dark Knight seems to like them! That's got to count for something.

It also mirrors the promotions that ran two years earlier in which Bugs Bunny announced that *Batman: The Animated Series* would be coming to Kids' WB—a cartoon passing of the torch if you will. And Batman wasn't alone in his enthusiasm for Satoshi Tajiri's monsters. In the weeks leading up to the February thirteenth debut, promotional commercials featuring characters from different cartoons from the Saturday morning block were aired "celebrating" the arrival of *Pokémon*, as if they too knew that this Warner Bros. Television acquisition would be a godsend to their ratings.

For the *Pokémon* anime, the name of the commercial game was "enthusiasm," presenting a storm of enthusiasm that, like the events in Topeka or the Sneak Peek video, seemed only translatable to kids. You didn't have to tell people what it was about or why they should watch it because the monsters flashing on the screen did all the work. The commercial just had to make sure that everyone seemed excited about it. To make sure this point got across, one commercial featured kids tearing around on dirt bikes—which was late nineties shorthand for "Whatever this is, it's awesome!"—demanding that you needed to "catch 'em all" and then shouting Pokémon names at the camera. The message was clear: There is no single huge reason to tune in, but rather about 150 huge reasons.

While some might think that having a four-month hiatus would dampen the spirit and the appeal of the show, it did absolutely nothing to prevent Kids' WB's star attraction from blasting off again. The first episode on the Kids' WB lineup was centered around the unassuming Bug Type, Paras, a monster that's on no one's top ten list, with a plot that's not terribly interesting at all, but kids watched in overwhelming numbers. The first new episode of *Pokémon* was Kids' WB's highest ratings debut ever.

Continuing to harness the power of *Pokémon*, Kids' WB handily beat rival programming block Fox Kids in ratings, despite Fox Kids having recently debuted a new season of *Power Rangers*, whose viewership dropped 32 percent in only its second week. Kids, it seemed, had fled to Pikachu. A month and a half later, *Pokémon* was beating all Kids' WB's records, airing the highest rated episode in the block's history for kids ages two through eleven years old, and helping Kids' WB to trounce most of its competition on a weekly basis.

Along with Warner Bros. ordering more episodes of the show from 4Kids, they also began to broadcast the show more frequently, adding another new episode to the Saturday block, one for each weekday afternoon, and then another airing every weekday morning. In less than two months after the show premiered on Kids' WB, there were plans to show a staggering twelve episodes of *Pokémon* a week.

After seven months of exponential success for the Pokémon franchise, spring 1999 proved that it wasn't about to slow down. However, it was also an important season for another name in the monster-collecting genre, which was soon to become widely known as Pokémon's chief rival. Thanks to Japanese television, kids were being enthralled by a new type of beast, ones they'd previously known for years as tiny virtual pets. They were Digital Monsters, or Digimon for short.

Chapter 5

DIGITAL CHAMPIONS

During the Fox Family Winter 1999 Upfront, CEO Rich Cronin explained in a bizarre fifty-minute presentation to media reporters and insiders what to be excited for in the upcoming year of Fox Family and Fox Kids programming. Stepping onto a stage made to look like a garish pastel-colored kitchen, he thrilled the Toy Fair audiences with jokes like calling his dog Nielsen (after Nielsen ratings, of course) and then rattled off a Monica Lewinsky reference, one that the crowd could literally not be less enthusiastic about. Then he leaped into the new Fox Family offerings, which included a digital cable "Boyz Channel" and a similar "Girlz Channel," both of which would barely last a year.

But the most jarring aspect—aside from Saban Entertainment president Haim Saban, dressed up as a milkman, having to shoo a calf away from his backside and then sing "We Are the World" to close out the presentation—is what *didn't* get announced. In a few months, only a few of the cartoons advertised as the future pillars and selling points of Fox Kids would even be given a second glance. This was because by the end of 1999, those shows would be replaced or assigned a new slot because of *Digimon*, a show that Fox Kids would latch onto and never let go of.

Much like *Pokémon*, *Digimon* didn't come out of nowhere just to suddenly become a focal point of children's entertainment in the United States and then the world. In fact, it had been in the making for years, with its roots going all the way back to 1995 and a game called *Dogz*—spelled with a "Z" because it's cooler that way, obviously.

Developed primarily by a video game company called PF Magic, *Dogz* was the first ever virtual pet. It was a straightforward game that gave people the chance to choose from a few Breedz of Dogz and then raise one on your computer. You fed them, trained them, rewarded them, and tried to keep them from running away, all actions that would become trademarks of the virtual pet genre. It was successful enough for the company to create, you guessed it, *Catz*. But even with *Dogz* and *Catz*, the virtual pet options were still really limited, not technologically, this was still really cool for 1995, but in how your virtual pet filled in the role of an actual pet. For example, if you're the owner of a wonderful dog with no z, you'd likely say that one of the best things about having it is being able to go places with it, like taking it outside and for walks, among other things. So it is easy to see how a lot of the pet-raising experience is lost when you're forced to do it while you sit in a desk chair at the family computer. To progress, the virtual pet would have to become something that its owner could take out and care for on the go.

Enter Aki Maita, the Japanese entertainment company Bandai, and Akihiro Yokoi, a toy developer who also used to work at Bandai. Once Yokoi saw a commercial featuring a kid who wanted to take his pet turtle on a family trip, only to be scolded by his mother. Tragic, obviously. Someone please get that turtle to Disney World ASAP. Anyway, Yokoi was intrigued by this: What if the turtle-less nightmare was over? What if you could bring your pets with you, not just to places that allowed pets within their guidelines, but *anywhere*? He also wondered what would happen if you didn't try to eliminate the work that goes into pet-raising, but embraced it. According to Yokoi, "Pets are only cute twenty to thirty percent of the time, and the rest is a lot of trouble, a lot of work." He felt that the work helped one fall in love with a pet, and he took his plan to create a mobile, high-maintenance pet to his former employer.

Aki Maita agreed with Yokoi and realized that people would love a pet that they could take with them regardless of destination but saw some of the salesmen at Bandai grimace at the idea. Why would people be interested in a digital pet that you had to carry around and keep alive? "What's so fun about this?" Despite this less than positive feedback, Maita decided to work with Yokoi to develop what would become the Tamagotchi, a portmanteau of the Japanese words for "egg" and "friend," that lived inside of a device the size of a wristwatch. They even developed a backstory for the little creature: A scientist found a crashed UFO full of tiny aliens that could not survive on Earth due to its atmosphere, so he rushed them back to a lab and invented an egg-shaped case for them. Thus, the Tamagotchi was not just a toy, but a little creature in a little home. It's certainly an effective story because it reminded players that it wasn't just a protective toy case they were holding as they pressed those little buttons on the bottom. It was the Tamagotchi's only chance at life. *You* were the Tamagotchi's only chance at life.

While Bandai remained skeptical, feeling that the concept needed more work, Maita, who would eventually become the face of the entire operation and a leader in developing the Tamagotchi further, was more than up for the challenge. She took prototypes to the streets of Shibuya, a popular ward in Tokyo known for its liveliness and commercial footprint, where she tested the virtual pet on its eventual prime demographic. Most people seemed fascinated by the little monsters and their egg dwellings; however, high school girls absolutely adored them. Maita kept track of their reactions and feedback—the colors they liked best, the shapes they preferred, and the aspects they favored—and by the following year, on November 23, 1996, the Tamagotchi was ready for its official debut.

And people went wild over it.

Within two years, 40 million pets were sold. And even though some stores were initially hesitant to carry them, most likely because they were unable to see the appeal of a fake pet that you were forced to clean up after, soon they added the virtual pet to their stock and then could barely keep them on the shelves. In fact, the pets were so popular that a Tamagotchi black market emerged, with both authentic and knock-off Tamagotchi pets sometimes selling for anywhere between twenty and sixty times the store price.

Then, of course, once these millions of customers brought their extraterrestrial pets home, it was time for their relationship to begin. In some cases, it simply involved treating their new little alien pets as tiny time wasters, but others found a true connection. They agonized over their Tamagotchi, lost sleep, missed school, dedicated themselves to their welfare, and debated the merits of restarting them after they passed on. And this dedication and love wasn't limited to Tamagotchi owners who lived in Japan, but to owners all over the world. In fact, in 1998, a portion of a pet cemetery in England became devoted to providing a final resting place to little Tamagotchi, with people from around the world sending in their pets to be buried there. To each of them, the Tamagotchi was *not* a video game, but a creature that they'd loved and done their best to care for. It was sad that, as all pets eventually do, the Tamagotchi died; however, in refusing to replace them like you would a normal toy, people had decided to bid farewell to them, calling into question even further of what a pet can be.

Similar to the events that acted as a catalyst to the creation of *Pokémon*, the Tamagotchi and the attachment that some of its owners had to them stems from the rampant urbanization of Japan, which culminated into the existential depression of the "Lost Decade" recession. Studies have shown that, in times of financial crisis, people are more likely to be desperate for connection. Pushed into the cities and surrounding areas with the promise of economic and societal safety and then abandoned by the plummeting market, millions of people in Japan were now stranded with limited ways to take care of themselves and others. The concrete walls that surrounded them both inside and outside the cities seemed more like a tomb than a metropolitan oasis.

To cope with this loneliness, people often turn to pets like dogs, cats, lizards, horses, or anything that might relieve the mental and emotional burdens of isolation. However, owning and taking care of a pet like a dog, for example, becomes a bit complicated when you live in a city with few places for it to poop and sniff comfortably, so the option of having a digital pet that fits easily into your pocket is very appealing. Through it you're able to fulfill the very human need to take care of something and also feel companionship, all without having to figure out what your landlord's pet policy is.

Like how Satoshi Tajiri figured that people living in Japan might thirst for an adventure where you explored and gathered creatures, Maita and Yokoi struck a similar nerve and commercial gold, too. They realized that, no matter how far a person moved downtown, they still enjoyed keeping a pet. The Tamagotchi was the re-creation of nature and kinship through a digital space.

To this day, a thriving subculture remains around Tamagotchi with collectors still talking endlessly about them as well as discussing (and even modifying) them with new ways to lengthen their lives and improve their living situations. But, back in 1998, less than a year after they'd been released, with sales booming, toy producer WiZ and Bandai began to think about expansion and wondered if they could possibly tap into a side of the virtual pet that appealed more to boys. What elements were Tamagotchi lacking that this demographic would find entertaining? The answer was obvious: They didn't fight.

Battle Blobs for Boys

And so begins the story and the development of Digimon, a franchise credited to Akiyoshi Hongo, a person who technically doesn't exist. While you will see the name slapped on everything related to *Digimon*, it absolutely does not belong to a real person.

Rather, "Akiyoshi Hongo" is a pseudonym, representing two staff members at Bandai, the aforementioned Aki Maita and marketing director Takeichi Hongo, as well as the writer of the premiere Digimon manga Hiroshi Izawa. In short, Akiyoshi Hongo was a shortcut—crediting three people takes up a lot of space—and also gave the franchise a single "creator" to tie itself to rather than an array of businesses and studios.

In June 1997, Digimon virtual pets, developed by WiZ and marketed by Bandai, were released to the public. Since the Tamagotchi were a round, egglike shape, the device that the Digimon lived in would be square, literally a representation of the edgier elements of the little creature's lifestyle. The change in shape wasn't just for aesthetic or narrative purposes, but for utility as well because, in order for the Digimon to fight, you had to press them against each other to link the two devices together. Then, after three short rounds and a final blow, one monster was declared the winner while the other lost and sometimes got injured. If you ignored too many injuries, then your Digimon would straight-up die, a victim of both combat and your own callousness. It was pretty intense for a rectangle that's smaller than the average driver's license.

The initial hatched Digimon monsters closely resembled the more adorable, blobby Tamagotchi, but over time they evolved into a myriad of wildly fantastical and aggressive creatures, with many of their designs coming from WiZ's Kenji Watanabe. Watanabe is effectively the Ken Sugimori of the Digimon franchise but has unfortunately received much less acclaim for his work and talent. Heavily influenced by American superhero comics, he wanted the Digimon to be creatures that were "strong and cool" and would definitely appeal to boys who may have shied away from the gentler pet-raising of the Tamagotchi. The decision to focus and market to boys is a choice that would guide the franchise for the first few years of its existence, including how it was later sold overseas.

Over the next few months, more and more Digimon virtual pets were sold, and kids gobbled them up. As with Pokémon, the first major side project would be a manga spinoff entitled *C'Mon Digimon* and the first version of the *Digimon* collectible card game. This arm of the franchise would grow to such proportions in Japan that five hundred hobby shops eventually served as official stores for the card game, though it would never really make an impression in the American market, because, despite the beautiful card art, kids tended to find the rules of the game confusing. Meanwhile, new "generations" of the virtual pets popped up, each one progressing more and more toward Watanabe's "strong and cool" aspirations.

While *Pokémon* seemed relatively easy to advertise, at least in retrospect, early *Digimon* was even simpler. From the very beginning, *Pokémon* espoused friendship between man and monster, with the battles and the training reinforcing that ethos, even if forcing your creature pal to duel whenever you feel like it doesn't always seem very friendly. Digimon, on the other hand, were built for battle. If you felt a sense of partnership with the little rectangle that housed the battle beast in your pocket, great, more power to you. In fact, it wouldn't be until a few years later that Digimon became more than soldiers and transformed into actual vessels of human growth and connection. For now, they were very much meant to be fighters, not lovers.

This was, in part, due to the suffix "-mon," which was attached to every Digital Monster's name. Unlike Pokémon, which would give each of its creatures a distinct title, Digimon would partially erase its monsters' sense of identity with names like Agumon, Gabumon, Devimon, Angemon, Seadramon, etc. While their designs were wildly creative—again, Watanabe does not get enough credit for supplying the franchise with all manner of dragons, bugs, warriors, and machines—their purpose was singular: to train, to fight, to evolve into something stronger, and then, one day, to die. If Pokémon were the Fellowship of the Ring, then Digimon were Conan the Barbarian.

Rapid Expansion

With the wide array of monsters confirmed as not only enjoyable but collectible, 1998 took the series to new heights in a variety of ways. First, in January, the Digimon virtual pets made their debut in the United States, with one commercial featuring two boys yelling in a basement while shadows of fiery monsters brawled against the wall behind them. It's a far cry from the *Pokémon* commercials, in which kids were connected by a link cable and were aided by their Pokémon to complete a common goal. If a Digimon were to escape its game, it seemed likely to devour you.

In Japan, Bandai was also publishing the first video game based on the series, called *Digital Monster Ver. S: Digimon Tamers*. If in *Pokémon*, you're a trainer, then in *Digimon*, you're a tamer, though your title really depends on what particular series you're in. While important to its history, the video game was extremely underwhelming and basically served as an upgraded version of the digital pet, a far cry from the game changers that *Pokémon Red* and *Green* were a few years earlier. Combined with the fact that the games were released for the Sega Saturn, a console that was never really able to gain any momentum and was rapidly eclipsed by the PlayStation and Nintendo 64, in hindsight it is easy to see how this game was destined to be lost to time. But no worries, the game that would come to define the series was not far behind it.

The longest running Digimon manga, an adventure series written by Hiroshi Izawa called *Digimon Adventure V-Tamer 01,* was also released in 1998. Having written the previous year's *C'Mon Digimon*, Izawa was extremely involved in creating the look and spirit of the snowballing franchise, especially when it came to the spiky-haired, goggles-wearing protagonist Taichi Yagami.

At first glance, Taichi might seem like *Digimon*'s attempt at replicating Ash Ketchum, especially because he's loud, brave, and painstakingly excited about the monster franchise that he's the figurehead of. However, while Ash Ketchum is built to be a character that each new generation of *Pokémon* fans can relate to, Taichi became a character for children to grow up *with*. If you haven't noticed, Ash has, since the late nineties, remained in eternal *Pokémon* stasis as a ten-year-old, with all the problems and feelings to match. On the other hand, *Digimon* fans were watching as Taichi did a lot of learning and growing over the years.

He would prove to be so popular that his name, appearance, and pieces of his personality were taken and used to construct an entirely different Taichi! An animated show was in the works, featuring him and seven of the other "Chosen Ones," and it was set to debut in the early months of 1999. During the spring and summer of 1998, writer Satoru Nishizono, director Hiroyuki Kakudou, and producer Hiromi Seki were gathered to form the team that guided the first *Digimon* anime titled *Digimon Adventure*.

Perhaps due to the quick expansion of the Digimon franchise at this point, very little was set in stone for these key creative roles when it came to developing the anime. All director Kakudou knew was that Bandai and Toei Animation Studio, which was hired to produce the series, wanted an anime based on the virtual pet. Producer Seki had to be sure that their creative team was allowed to add human characters, which seemed like a reasonable request given that most of the franchise thus far had revolved around Digimon combat.

Nishizono knew that they wanted a different version of Taichi and Agumon, the little yellow dinosaur that commonly served as Digimon's monster captain and, effectively, the Pikachu of the franchise. Aside from that, he was given the green light to craft characters and situations as he pleased. One source the creative team eventually did revolve around was Jules Verne's novel *Two Years' Vacation* in which a bunch of schoolboys find themselves stranded on a deserted island. However, this is no *Lord of the Flies* scenario intended to show the hidden evil of man, and instead the children band together to save themselves from all sorts of nefarious Digimon.

Tasked with filling out the cast with eight regular characters, plus a Digimon partner for each, in order to diversify the possibilities of the story, Seki, Kakudou, and Nishizono also invented the island where the adventure would start. Unfortunately, they didn't have the luxury that the Pokémon series did where an entire region had been copiously laid out and explained in a video game prior to the show. They also decided early on that, in the final episode, the kids would separate from their monster pals. Given a year's worth of weekly airings to tell the story, the team devised a narrative that promoted "courage and friendship," where each main character, through the help of each other and their Digimon pals, would come to conquer some hidden insecurity and unlock some kind of internal strength.

With such a relatively large cast of central characters and a seemingly infinite number of monsters to work with, certain goals had to be set to make sure that everyone had equal time to shine and grow. For example, Seki wanted even the monsters who weren't very cute to be "cool" by the end of the series, which meant giving them a chance to fight and prove themselves through heroics. Although many episodes are devoted to Taichi, Kakudou made sure to frequently separate the Digi-Destined in order to tell more stories all while they were separated without the fear of losing viewers. The reason for this? Aside from making sure the characters all had equal time on screen, he just "really hates" shows that only let one central character do anything.

And this is the greatest strength of *Digimon Adventure*, the affinity you feel for its characters and the way that, by the end, every single one of them feels authentic, important, and like the main character. This was accomplished through many, many scenes where the characters interact and joke, worry and grow, with each given a fulfilling yet distinct personal arc. Sure, viewers might have tuned in for the cool new monster evolutions and the explosive battles, but they stayed for the hangouts and the feeling that, no matter who you are, you and your friends related to brave Taichi, troubled Yamato, helpful Sora, candid Mimi, intelligent Koushiro, fearful Joe, naïve Takeru, or curious Kari.

It's with the anime that Digimon truly came into its own, moving from a Tamagotchi alternative centered around fighting to a franchise capable of extraordinary things. Pokémon, in a sense, had always been this way. Its broad story and advertising always plainly stated that *Pokémon* was something to be enjoyed by everyone. Plus, it didn't hurt that games were released on the Game Boy, a console with a large ratio of female users—in 1995, Nintendo claimed that female gamers made up 46 percent of their audience—which allowed it to break away from the sad stereotype that video games were a "dude's medium." Now *Digimon*, with its wonderful cast of animated characters, could claim the same.

But before *Digimon* aired on the small screen, it got a big-screen treatment. Mamoru Hosoda was a promising young animator at Toei Animation Studios when he was called upon to direct the *Digimon Adventure* short film, which debuted on March 6, 1999, the day before the anime aired on TV. Running at only twenty minutes, it tells the story of young Taichi and his little sister, Kari, and their first experience meeting a Digimon. Hosoda, not yet knowing exactly how much Toei wanted to connect the film to the upcoming anime and growing franchise, directed it as a standalone, with each character and monster having its own arc.

If you haven't seen it, then go do that, because it is really great stuff. It's a tour de force that's equal parts coming-of-age tale, kaiju mystery, fish-out-of-water comedy, and big monster battle royale, which Hosoda directed with all the visual flair and atmospheric beauty that would come to define his whole career. Hosoda, who would later be nominated for an Academy Award for the Best Animated Feature Film of 2018, has always excelled with this kind of science fiction, something that finds a way to ground characters in bigger fantastical concepts, and this animated short was no different. *Digimon*, the toy-selling anime series, would have downright auteur beginnings.

A New (Digital) World

After airing on March 7, the anime was a consistent success, usually landing in the top ten TV episodes being broadcast in Japan each day. It would even be a competitor network-wise as well, *Pokémon* was on the anime-centric station TV Tokyo, while *Digimon* found a home on Fuji TV, where it resides to this day.

WORLD BUILDING

The anime served as the first part of a one-two punch with *Digimon World* for the PlayStation, the first in a long series of *Digimon* games. *World* is an extremely interesting game, blending the creature-raising mechanics of the series' virtual pet past with the role-playing elements that would come to define its future games. That said, it's also the kind of game that only gets made early on in a franchise's history, a weird stab at trying to establish just what its point of view and mission are. In this way, it resembles the quirky atmosphere of *Pokémon Red* and *Green*, but it would only sell 250,000 copies by 2000, which was considered middling sales when compared with *Pokémon*'s eruptive performance.

The show would not remain in Japan without an American introduction for long either. Unlike the *Pokémon* anime, which had a gap of a year and a half between its Japanese and US debuts, *Digimon* only took a few months. There is an argument to be made that the shorter adaptation time could be because *Pokémon* had already laid the foundation for it but, either way, the show was soon found by Saban Entertainment, a company that, like 4Kids, holds a complicated spot in the history of anime localization.

Saban Entertainment had been in business with Fox since the mid-nineties and had worked with talented TV producer Margaret Loesch to find a home for not only Marvel's soon-to-be-classic *X-Men* cartoon in 1992, but also a localization of Toei's *Super Sentai* series. The show was about a team of Ultraman-influenced Japanese superheroes who, when their city is threatened, don colorful outfits and pilot rad gigantic robots, topped only by the fact that the robots usually combine to form an even bigger, radder robot. And for years, TV executives had passed on it, thinking it was too violent, too corny, or a combination of both. But by replacing the Japanese heroes with young American actors and dubbing over the monsters' voices, Saban and Loesch managed to get forty episodes green-lit, with many more to come, after good test screening reviews.

The new version, now titled *Mighty Morphin' Power Rangers,* was a massive hit, despite the constant criticism that all that alien monster punching wasn't great for its young audience. Toys sold out each holiday season, with one mother telling the *New York Times,* "I've never seen such a terrible show in my life, but my boys just love it. They are possessed, and so am I." *Power Rangers* remained a staple of the Fox Kids programming block for years to come, and combined with seminal superhero cartoons like *X-Men*, *Spider-Man*, and *Batman: The Animated Series*, Fox Kids had a winning formula.

However, as we all know, those days were ending. *Batman: The Animated Series*, which had been so critically lauded that it earned a spot on primetime TV and aired against CBS's *60 Minutes* for a short time, had departed after five years to be exclusively shown on Warner Bros.'s competing programming block, Kids' WB. The Marvel cartoon series like *X-Men* and *Spider-Man*, which had formed an interconnected onscreen universe long before the Marvel Cinematic Universe, were winding down. Fox Kids maintained good ratings, but it needed a new show to be *the* show, the one it could build its entire brand around like it had with *Mighty Morphin' Power Rangers, Batman, Spider-Man,* or *X-Men* in the past. Enter *Digimon Adventure.*

Saban had acquired the rights to *Digimon* and its story about a team of child heroes fighting an escalating monster force with their own monster force, a perfect fit for the Fox Kids Saturday morning lineup. Jeff Nimoy, who'd previously worked for years with NFL Films and ESPN, auditioned for the show as a voice actor. Thanks to his previous ties with Fox and his experience with his own production company, he was soon moved up to writing, editing, and directing the localization. "Who's gonna watch this piece of shit?" he said, recalling his initial reaction to the first episode.

According to Nimoy, the money wasn't great, and he wasn't completely sold on the show's premise, but the ability to "just do what we wanted" sounded great to him and his business partner, Bob Buchholz. "They went nuts for it at Fox Kids," Nimoy said, and the team took the "existing footage to do something new with it." Haim Saban, eager to repeat the formula that had worked so well with *Mighty Morphin' Power Rangers*, approved of this direction. The goal "was just to make it as funny as possible," Nimoy said about the Fox Kids version. "Really, we wanted to be a young, hip show on Saturday morning."

Meanwhile, *Pokémon* had been on the air for almost a year at this point, and though the media was quick to point out their similarities when *Digimon* debuted, Nimoy insisted that no influence was taken from the Pikachu brand. Honestly, it was hard to even find time to notice them anyway. Localizing *Digimon* so soon after its Japanese release meant that Nimoy and his team only got the scripts "two or three months ahead of time." And though they'd alter the character's personalities and add copious jokes for the American audience, the stories stayed consistent, mostly out of necessity, because they "didn't have the luxury of planning ahead."

But even without trying to copy any of *Pokémon*'s tactics, *Digimon* still inherited some of its difficulties. The issues with matching lip movements affected *Digimon* in the same way, forcing actors to adjust their approach to voice acting. Laura Summer, who'd previously worked on the Saban localization of *Tonde Burin*, named *Super Pig* by Saban, found this to be a particular challenge when she voiced the cute *Digimon* underdog Patamon. "In original animation, you just get to act and then they do the art work to your voice, rather than match flaps. You really have to serve the technical side first, and you have to act within the technical part."

The final hurdle and change came in finding a new title. Although *Digimon Adventure* is a perfectly suitable name for an adventure series about Digimon in any country, Saban and Fox decided to change it to *Digimon: Digital Monsters*, possibly to remind kids of what *Digimon* was an abbreviation of. Oddly enough, to promote these new Digital Monsters, we got something that would jog the nostalgia centers of any sentient person who existed around the turn of the millennium: a promotional video featuring two kids who, in just a few months, would be the stars of *Malcolm in the Middle*.

Thirteen-year-olds Frankie Muniz and Justin Berfield were no strangers to commercials, though they'd never had the chance to promote tiny computer monsters. In this instance, they'd sit together in a room with a gaggle of other children and watch Fox Kids cartoon teasers. From the looks of the kids, the promo was hinting that *Digimon* would be perfect for the preteens who already felt Ash Ketchum to be a little childish. One promo, featuring other animated series to come, ended with Berfield asking, "Is that all the tapes?" before a kid named Zack—who earlier dubbed himself "The "Zackman," so you can put two and two together—revealed one more. He put it in the VCR and Frankie Muniz shrugged toward the camera for no particular reason before *Digimon: Digital Monsters* was revealed.

When the commercial is done briefly explaining the plot and hyping up the arrival of "TV's hottest new heroes," every kid in the room bursts into applause, which is the unsubtle antithesis of what every middle schooler would likely have done: hide their excitement and pretend to be too cool to care. However, the promo was loaded with fireballs, giant bugs, and kids just barely dodging danger, so it did its job of looking like it was worthy of a spot on Fox Kids.

Sadly, just as *Pokémon*'s approach had been thoughtlessly compared to the Beanie Babies that preceded it, comparisons between *Digimon* and *Pokémon* were inevitable. Within two weeks of its debut, the *New York Times* likened it to a "blatant imitation," with Donna Friedman, who served as senior vice president of Kids' WB at the time, throwing down the gauntlet by saying, "We have the number one franchise with *Pokémon*, and the formula for creating such a phenomenon is so far unknown to man or producer. So, although many people will try to copy *Pokémon*'s success, it will not be easy to do."

Though one promo touted the tagline "Gotta catch our fall," an obvious and less catchy spin on "Gotta catch 'em all," time would show that *Digimon* was not a *Pokémon* copy, but an alternative. Joshua Seth, voice actor for lead character Tai in Saban's English dub, believed that the franchise might have been appealing because it almost foretold the future. Back when the series debuted, "the internet was pretty new . . . Not everybody had email yet. The themes that [*Digimon*] was talking about at the very beginning of the very first episode were about the battle to come between the real world and the digital world," Seth said. "It's a battle that we all face now—how to find balance between our real lives and our virtual lives. I find it fascinating that it's actually become our reality now, kinda like *The Matrix*." Whether it was because of its forward-looking themes or not, overall, *Digimon* could not have come at a better time.

Audiences had already been taught to look out for series like *Pokémon* and were quick to accept a story in which elementary schoolers befriend cartoonish creatures. Plus, those who had spent the last year with *Pokémon* and felt like their attention was waning now had a new, vaguely similar anime to dive into. For clueless parents, it also gave them one more shopping option when all the Pokémon toys were gone, while for lovers of arguments, it was no longer "Do you like *Red* or *Blue*?" It was "Do you like *Pokémon* or *Digimon* more?" A riddle of the Sphinx if there ever was one.

Agumon Versus Spider-Man

Digimon still had to make up for lost time. Its American release had already started off at a disadvantage. There was an anime, one that turned Saturday mornings into a competition between Kids' WB and Fox Kids for monster battle supremacy, but after that, what then? When kids got done watching *Pokémon*, they could go play the game or break out their toys or eat the fruit gummies with Pikachu on the front of the box, his little yellow arms raised as if congratulating them for having impeccable taste in snacks. They could go read one of the manga adaptations, the most prominent of which in America was *The Electric Tale of Pikachu*. Helmed by former hentai—a type of Japanese illustrated smut—artist Toshihiro Ono, it would become the first comic issue since 1993 to sell more than a million copies. It was also the manga that broke the slump that the American comic book industry had seen in the mid-nineties and proved that American mainstays like Batman and Spider-Man would have to up their game if they wanted to keep pace with Ash and Pikachu.

Fans could research Pokémon on a tiny toy Pokédex or spray themselves with Pokémon cologne—though one YouTuber said, "It smells like a KFC wet wipe." Or, if they were lucky, they could even learn how to save their money with a talking Pikachu piggy bank; money that would inevitably be spent on packages of Pokémon cards or other merchandise. A circle of life if there ever was one.

In short, the *Pokémon* anime was the big tip of a very huge iceberg. But when kids got done watching *Digimon*, that was about it. The Digimon virtual pets, while available, didn't quite have the synergy of the *Pokémon* anime's relationship to its games: One was a commercial for the other. An uphill battle was in store for the "Digi-Destined."

First, *Digimon* would need to win back the attention that the Fox Kids programming block had lost to *Pokémon* when children had migrated to Kids' WB in droves. For Fox, this meant the delay or indefinite hiatus of shows that would have shown at least some promise in a pre-Pokémon world. "It was all due to the success of *Pokémon*," said Fox Kids' vice president of programming at the time Roland Poindexter, who was eager to try to replicate *Pokémon*'s success in any way possible. "Clearly this kind of show is a phenomenon where if we can't be number one, we can at least be a strong number two. That's just the business."

So Poindexter spoke to AnotherUniverse.com about "dropping the ball" with *Pokémon*, but it was clear that he wouldn't make the same mistake twice. Staples of the Fox Kids' lineup were pushed to the wayside, including the remaining Marvel cartoons, which Saban had helped to produce earlier in the decade. The release of *The Avengers: United They Stand*, the latest in an animated universe, was postponed and then all-out cancelled by February of the next year. In another reality, *Spider-Man Unlimited*, which saw the wall crawler fight crime in an edgier alternate "Counter Earth," would have been a Fox Kids tentpole but, instead, it was cancelled after three episodes, with the rest of its single season pushed out until December 2000. Even lower on the list of priorities, but in no way any safer, was *Big Guy and Rusty the Boy Robot*, a cartoon based on a comic by industry legend Frank Miller. It survived six episodes before it was replaced by *Digimon*, leaving the remaining twenty-six episodes to air over a year later in a mismatched schedule. But this all made sense to Fox Kids. *Digimon* quickly became a contender in the top ten on Saturday mornings, a ranking where *Pokémon* often held the top two spots. More airings of *Digimon* meant more chances to dethrone *Pokémon*.

Also high on the list for Fox and the other companies involved in the animated race was what was called "aggressive introduction." This meant Fox had to fast-track copious *Digimon* merchandise, from clothing to home video to toys to trading cards to school supplies, before the 1999 holidays, and then have even more to come. Originally, their plan had been to move the show to weekday afternoons after a sort of Saturday morning primer, but *Digimon*'s success caused them to drop it. It would be on Saturday mornings and on weekday afternoons. Fox was happy with *Digimon* for sure, but they also *needed* it. It was their primary anti-Pikachu weapon.

Getting a late start wasn't all bad, though. In a way, because it didn't have tons of branded merchandise, *Digimon* almost felt like the "indie" cousin to *Pokémon*, one that wasn't hampered by ceaseless marketing noise. Plus, it helped that the characters were a bit older and their personalities a bit rougher. The rivalry between the two lead male characters, Tai and Matt (the American renaming of Japan's Yamato), who often were at each other's throats, each concerned that the other wasn't a strong enough leader, was a far cry from the "we'll work it out in the end" attitude of Ash Ketchum and his friends. "A lot of people have found Tai's journey to be particularly poignant and relevant to their own lives," said Joshua Seth, Tai's voice actor, "because we're all the hero of our own story, and we see that reflected through characters like Tai." Kids who had been *Pokémon* fans in the spring could graduate into *Digimon* fans in the fall, channeling all their potentially newfound angst through its characters.

Preferring the *Digimon* anime to the *Pokémon* anime was a matter of almost invulnerable personal choice, but it was in a particular line of toys that *Digimon* cornered a part of the monster-collecting market that *Pokémon* never really tried to exploit: evolution. Evolution, or Digi-volution in the case of the *Digimon* dub, was a big part of both series, signifying growing, a fresh new creature form, more explosive powers, and also an achievement in personal prosperity.

When a Pokémon evolves in the anime, it isn't just because it's just gotten stronger, but usually because it's overcome some taxing obstacle like a gym leader match or a particularly robust monster. Same goes for Digimon, as the little creatures were able advance to the next level—going from Rookie to Champion to Ultimate to Mega, thanks to some emotional breakthrough that they shared with their human partners. In short, Digi-volution is like the eureka moment at the end of a therapy session, with the therapist being whatever enemy behemoth wanted to crush them at the time. One of the biggest differences between the two was that, while a Pokémon evolution was permanent, the transformed Digimon reverted back to its little, hungry, child-sized form after the battle. Anime fights are exhausting!

At that point, Pokémon had generally shied away from toys that displayed these evolutionary lines unless it was in the form of a package that included all the forms as separate figurines. Having a single Pokémon figure change from one stage to the next was pretty rare because, though fantastical, their progression was treated as ultimately natural. But Digimon weren't constrained by any evolutionary logic. For example, when Greymon evolves into MetalGreymon, it becomes part cyborg, its head suddenly encased in metal and one of its arms is replaced by a robot claw. It might not fit into any of Charles Darwin's theories, but this type of thing is perfect for an action figure that, with a few twists, snaps, and bends, can transform.

So perhaps one of the most interesting Digimon concepts ever put into toy form is their continued line of transforming creatures, which were first introduced to the US and became instantly comfortable in the hands of any kid who had ever held a Transformers toy. And now, thanks to Bandai, kids could take the little talking lizards, wolves, and bird friends that they saw on Fox Kids and maneuver their working parts into more powerful and ridiculous forms. Despite *Digimon*'s status as a massive money-maker, it would likely never be able to keep up with the sheer force of *Pokémon* and Nintendo. But it was little areas, like the toys and the surprising emotional depth on display in the anime, that allowed it to carve its spot.

Still, while *Digimon* was performing its opening act in the US, many still had their eyes on *Pokémon* because, after a year spent enrapturing millions of kids through television, Pikachu was finally going to the big screen.

Chapter 6

BLOCKBUSTER

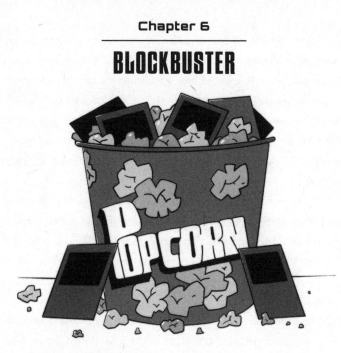

They called it the "Pokéflu."

This is the term used in the *New York Times*, though its exact origin remains unclear, to describe the wave of kids that deliberately missed school to see *Pokémon: The First Movie*. Earning $10.1 million on its opening day—a Wednesday, no less—it was the biggest opening day for any Warner Bros. animated film in history. To this day, it also remains one of the highest grossing anime films.

Debuting in Japan in the summer of 1998 and written by anime head writer Takeshi Shudo, *Mewtwo Strikes Back*, titled *Pokémon: The First Movie* in the US, focused on the story of Mewtwo, the most powerful monster of all. Tucked away in a cave that you can only enter after you've beaten the *Red* and *Blue* storylines and become Pokémon Champion, Mewtwo is a genetic experiment, the clone and child of the secret monster Mew. Scant details were available throughout the game, and it's easy to imagine that if you played it without watching the anime, in which Mewtwo makes an appearance in the opening theme song, you might not even know it was there.

The movie follows a *Frankenstein*-inspired plot: Mewtwo is created, lashes out in confusion, and is then taken under the wing of Giovanni, the leader of Team Rocket. Upon realizing it's being used to further Giovanni's nefarious plans, Mewtwo escapes and decides to "strike back" by creating a lavish flying castle and tricking Satoshi (Ash) into attending a fancy party there, where his and his friends' Pokémon are then stolen and cloned. Luckily, Satoshi (Ash), his friends, and Mew find a way save the day, with the former eventually sacrificing himself to show Mewtwo that not all humans are bad and that Pokémon and humans can be friends. Then, Mewtwo waxes philosophic about recognizing "the gift of life"—though in the Japanese version, his motivation is even more cryptic—and flies off with all the cloned Pokémon to live their lives in peace. Oh, and Ash comes back to life, reborn thanks to the tears of Pikachu and the other Pokémon. That seems worth mentioning.

While the film's creation was a big deal, its success was even bigger. Generally, anime tie-in movies tend to be easy to discard in the long run, and often their plots are created in small pocket universes, so they don't affect or connect to the narrative of the TV show. However, *Mewtwo Strikes Back* was different because its plot was teased in little bits of various episodes and its lead monster was shown in the opening theme that played before every episode. While the plot of the film doesn't have a major impact on the show, somehow it manages to ride the line between being an extension of the story and a grand special event film. In all honesty, that was a fine place to be, since it made it a must-see.

Still, some studios just didn't get it. Norman Grossfeld shopped the film around to license and distribute the release, and while they got a few offers, they ultimately went with Warner Bros., who owned the programming block that the anime appeared on. "In one studio," Grossfeld recalled, "it was like a very classic Hollywood meeting. They were saying 'Oh, you know. Go with us. We'll have Leonardo DiCaprio play Ash. This way we'll be able to market it with big names.'" Obviously, Grossfeld turned this approach down, knowing that, at best, anime-loving kids would find it rather jarring if they went to the theater and suddenly heard the star of *Titanic* as Ash.

For fans, the allure and excitement of seeing Pikachu and pals on the big screen was overwhelming. A Warner Bros. call-in campaign to win movie-related prizes crashed the phone lines in Burbank, California—and this was just one example. Pikachu was a celebrity, Pokémon's Chosen One, a creature whose status as series representative had only grown since *Red* and *Green*'s release. That could be because it's a hard character to get tired of— cute, funny, goofy, huggable, but always up for a fight—and few other mascots can cover all those bases. You'd never see Hello Kitty in a gym battle, nor would you want Mickey Mouse to ride on your shoulder.

So, to replicate Satoshi's enviable experience of having an adorable yellow Pokémon follow him everywhere and act as a tie-in product for the new movie, Game Freak developed *Pocket Monsters Pikachu*, known more commonly in the United States as *Pokémon Yellow Version: Special Pikachu Edition*, the longest title in the main game series to date. There was so much text on the box for the North American edition that Nintendo had to cut out the usual "Gotta catch 'em all!" slogan. No worries, though, kids already knew what they had to do.

In *Pokémon Yellow*, Pikachu is your starter Pokémon and, as in the anime, it absolutely abhors you until you get on its good side. Your character can turn around and interact with Pikachu and, in a tinny sound using Pikachu's voice actress, Ikue Ōtani, the monster will say its name with an enthusiasm that matches how much you're in its holy favor. It also has a variety of expressions, ranging from "disappointed to be in your presence" to "feeling sick from a poison attack" to "shockingly elated over recent accomplishments," that it shares with you as, with all your Pokémon, you try to keep Pikachu healthy and happy. In short, Game Freak didn't give players an aesthetic alteration of the original set of games—though Ken Sugimori and his collaborators did redesign the in-game monster images to correspond more to their anime appearances—instead, they had efficiently inserted a virtual pet into the *Pokémon* experience. Part game, part Pikachu-themed Tamagotchi.

Meanwhile, the Tamagotchi itself had been seeing a drastic descent in sales, thanks in part to *Pokémon*'s saturation. Similarly, the Giga Pet, created by Tiger Electronics mostly to capitalize on the Western market, had a roller-coaster-esque rise and fall. Starting with basic pets like a dog and cat, before moving to creatures like the baby T. rex from the recent dinosaur bonanza *The Lost World: Jurassic Park*, and then landing on bizarre ones based on properties like *Batman & Robin* and World Championship Wrestling, the Giga Pet line burned very brightly thanks to its simplicity and its copious licensing partnerships. You could bathe Batman! Train with a tiny "Hollywood" Hogan! It seemed like less of a measured effort or thoughtful plan and more of a series of blind dart throws, a company hoping that if they released enough miniature "pet" versions of pop culture names, kids would want to nurture at least one or two of them. Sadly, the Giga Pet never found the pop culture creature or icon to help keep it afloat, and sales plummeted.

Though the virtual pet genre seemed to be waning, it is interesting to see how the further amalgamation of virtual pet aspects into the Pokémon franchise game firmly combined, and in a way strengthened, each of their comparative ideologies. Both Pokémon and Tamagotchi dealt with encapsulating a sense of nostalgia for the natural world that had been lost, at least in the minds of their creators. Both were about fostering fantasy creatures that were entrusted into your care because you were fit and capable enough to provide for them. And though *Pokémon* and *Digimon*, the Tamagotchi stepchild, added a heavy battling aspect, in the end, a lot of these gentle central concepts remain. *Pokémon Yellow* was a game meant to cash in on the success of the anime, but it also managed to synthesize the notion of Pokémon being "companions" more than any game before it thanks to this new Pikachu addition.

Of course, the game was another huge success, and *Yellow* pretty much became the "must-have" game in the series. Gail Tilden knew it was a great idea because it established a way to connect and expand the audience with a single cartridge. Now those who only knew the franchise from the anime or perhaps had never played the games or previously owned a Game Boy had an easy entrance into the whole franchise. Perhaps most importantly, the opportunity to work on one more game that was built on the framework of existing ones gave Game Freak more time to fine-tune *Gold* and *Silver*, the set that they intended to be the "ultimate" Pokémon games.

Though *Yellow* was released two months after *Mewtwo Strikes Back* in Japan, it preceded the American film's release by a month. So, in a way, *Yellow* hitting shelves marked the end of an era, as it was the last game to be released in North America for the original Game Boy. By now the Game Boy was over nine years old, its life expectancy surprising everyone, especially since its twilight years had been spent as the fruitful playground of the *Pokémon* franchise rather than in dull, outdated decline. But though this was the end of the original Game Boy, it was certainly not the end of the Game Boy line. Heck, it wouldn't even be the end of the Game Boy shape.

Its successor was the Game Boy Color, slightly smaller in size, but more powerful and now able to take handheld adventures from the realm of black-and-white into beautiful color. When inserted into the GBC, *Pokémon Red*'s world took on a tone of copper red, *Blue* received a navy wash, and *Yellow*'s assortment of colors made it look like you were practically playing the anime—well, by 1999 standards, of course. The GBC had been on store shelves in Japan and North America about a year when *Yellow* gave its progenitor a well-deserved send-off in October 1999. It is interesting to note that the evolution between the two consoles mirrored *Pokémon*'s status—still popular, but now with a broader appeal and potential for new audiences than ever before.

Yellow and *Pokémon: the First Movie* went hand in hand, and allowed kids to play through their own version of Ash Ketchum's journey before experiencing it on the big screen. It was an experience that they loved and that caused critics to throw their hands up in defeat. Reviews on game websites found *Yellow* to be fun, but also little more than a stopgap, a rehash to hold eager longtime players over until they could get a brand-new fix. This wasn't all bad, though, because, as we said before, kids who were getting into the series a year after it debuted could catch up and dote on Pikachu in the latest style.

As for the movie, multiple reviewers poked holes in the logic of a story about finding peace with your existence in a franchise about using your team of monsters to beat up your opponent's. The *Guardian* called it "boring" and "impenetrable"; CNN deemed it "low budget Japanimation"; Common Sense Media found it "excruciating," and the *Hartford Courant*, in a common theme among these opinions, pitied the parents who had to take their kids to it. "It is going to cost you," the article reads, as if the *Pokémon* movie was some kind of karmic retribution for being unable to get your kids into sports.

However, *Pokémon* fans were absolutely unconcerned with these takes, as were the teams behind its localization. Coming a little over a year after the anime and games' release in North America, the movie served as a symbolic victory, its premiere at the historic Grauman's Chinese Theatre representing *Pokémon*'s journey from underdog to icon. It was a red-carpet affair full of huge posters, children bearing countless bits of merchandise, like shirts, hats, and toys, plus actors in Pikachu costumes cavorting around in front of photographers while the film's soundtrack blared in the background. Celebrities including Rob Lowe, Virginia Madsen, and Laurie Metcalf showed up along with a good number of others who had their children in tow. "The boys wouldn't let me sleep unless I figured out a way to get us here today, *so here we are*," Lowe cheekily told the press. "Pikachu is my favorite movie star. It used to be Mel Gibson, but now it's Pikachu."

The event only got grander once everyone moved into the theater itself. "It was packed. It was crazy," Michael Haigney remembers. "Like three rows ahead of us was David Hasselhoff. And a lot of people had brought their kids, and when that Poké Ball came on, they went nuts." Many other key figures from 4Kids, Nintendo, and Warner Bros. attended, both to celebrate and to gauge just how well the movie would be received, like Bush, who said of the throngs of fans and celebrities piling into the theater to watch the fruits of their labor, "It was surreal for me . . . It was nothing that I ever thought would happen. But it was a beautiful day."

Grossfeld remembered the explosive delight of the children, the joy that erupted around their clueless parents. Of course, they were more excited than anyone to see Ash Ketchum and Pikachu on the big screen, and the teams involved were deservedly elated by their reaction. "As soon as the movie ended," Grossfeld said, "the lights were just coming up and the kids were screaming. They loved it. And someone in our group, all they said was 'Ka-ching!'"

Hitting the number one box office spot, *Pokémon: The First Movie* would beat out *Mortal Kombat* as the highest earning movie based on a video game. Its $85 million box office gross in America also meant that it toppled the hopes of more established purveyors of children's media as well, including Walt Disney Company's *Bicentennial Man*, which faltered with $58 million and their remake of *My Favorite Martian,* which fared similarly. And in the duel of movies with "first movie" in the title, Pikachu handily dismantled *Doug's 1st Movie*, proving that some characters and stories, especially that of sheepish Doug, were better left on TV.

But was that box office number due to families and kids wanting to see the movie . . . or was it because of something else? The question comes up because, along with a ticket, audience members received one of a handful of collectible trading cards, which might have helped more than a just a little with achieving those gross numbers. "We definitely had a hot opening weekend, and then it tailed off really quick," pondered Tilden. "So, in hindsight, nobody knows how many of the ticket sales were people who just went and bought four tickets to get four cards and didn't actually care about the movie."

And, knowing how hot the trading card game was at the time, it's not unreasonable to think that was actually what happened.

Card Crisis

Tommy Priest had experience with card games. He helped lead events for Wizards of the Coast to promote the new *Magic: the Gathering* decks and, eventually, he'd get the call to work with WotC to develop a *Pokémon Trading Card Game* mall tour. The *Magic the Gathering* tours had been successful, and since, by the spring of 1999, *Pokémon* had shown no signs of slowing down, there was reason to believe that a series of mall events would strengthen the brand, promote some merch, and get kids enthusiastic about the cards. What Priest never could have anticipated was just how enthusiastic they would be.

After successful events in Miami and Atlanta, Priest and his team headed to the largest mall in New Jersey where "over 10,000 people showed up, stood in line," Priest remembered. "As the crowd grew, the fire department arrived, shut down the event, and closed the mall for exceeding fire capacity. We had to hide out in the mall management office until the crowds were cleared. Some people were in line for five hours and not happy about the shutdown." Like the games and the anime before it, the trading card game had taken on a life of its own and one, perhaps, that took the brunt of *Pokémon*'s backlash, at least in America. Its accelerated rise into notoriety would cause it to become the scourge of schools across the country. Accessible, collectible, and portable, the cards were brought by kids to school en masse, and teachers and other school staff would spend most of the 1999 school year trying to plug the holes in their ship, the openings leaking Pikachu, Charizard, and 149 others into the cafeteria.

While the game had come out the year before, as the franchise grew so did the card game's popularity, making it an escalating issue that carried throughout the year, as cards were banned in schools in multiple states as early as April 1999. Wizards of the Coast was extremely pleased with its performance—"It's just turned into this hottest thing," said spokeswoman Carol Rogalski to the Associated Press—but by the fall, suddenly phrases like "trading pits" were used to discuss the fervor with which kids approached their new extracurricular obsession, bringing to mind black market dealings rather than a circle of children shouting about cards near the bus lot. One principal, not sensing the irony, said, "It just became such a monster" when discussing the pocket monster panic.

Booster packs of the cards ranged around three dollars, not extravagant enough to prevent them from being bought in bulk by parents desperate to keep up with their kids' insatiable appetite. But was it just an appetite, or had it spiraled into an actual addiction? There was an argument that before kids opened the packs, they didn't know what cards they would be getting, which falls under certain definitions of gambling. They just had to hope that they would get a rare card every once in a while, a roulette to nab something either tinted with holographic art or powerful enough in battle that would make their trip to KB Toys worth it. It's not exactly casino-level thrills, but there was the potential for trouble.

And trouble would be soon found. While there were the general "the prices are getting higher and they're outselling *baseball cards!*" anxieties reflected by some hobby shop owners, there was also actual crime making its way to the Pokémon world, crime that even Team Rocket likely wouldn't have been competent enough to manage. From May to December 1999, $20 million worth of bootleg Pokémon merchandise, much of which was trading cards intended to be sold to clueless parents and kids, was seized by authorities. Then there was a million-dollar fake *Pokémon* card operation—though it wouldn't be the last. A teenager in Canada was stabbed over a dispute involving the cards, and there were multiple reports of the game causing fights. One young boy stayed inside of a store until after it closed in order to steal dozens of packs of cards, only to call 911 when he realized that being locked in meant that he couldn't get out.

Critics and pundits were decidedly unable to come up with measures to cut down on *Pokémon* card–related hijinks, so attempts at reassurance were offered. *New York Times* articles from around the time had titles like, "Coping: Who's Afraid of the Pokémon Monster?" and "Learning From Pokémon." Each repeated the basic mantra that Pokémon non-believers had been spouting for a year: Don't worry, eventually a new fad will come, and Pikachu will disappear in the rearview mirror along with Furbies, Beanie Babies, Tickle Me Elmo, and every other "must-have" toy of the recent past.

But that time wasn't now, and Pokémon was a must-have item with the holidays looming. The Charizard trading card was the number one most wanted Christmas gift of 1999, an odd situation for a fan considering that your chances of unwrapping it on December 25 were purely random. It illustrated the pure hunger fans had for more Pokémon stuff in general. "We're making them as quickly as we can," said a Hasbro spokesman of the toy company's sound-making Pikachu dolls.

While concerns that the ethics of buying packs of cards in hope of randomly being granted something worthwhile ran rampant, most people didn't take it so far as to accuse Pokémon of dooming their children to a fourth-grade gambling addiction. That is until two moms did just that, filing a lawsuit against Nintendo of America for getting their kids hooked on buying *Pokémon* cards. One of the mothers had spent more than $2,000 on cards and used this as the foundation of her argument that buying *Pokémon* cards was no more redeemable than putting an elementary schooler in a casino. Lawyer Alan Hock, who'd watched his son become interested in acquiring baseball cards, built his case around the rare cards' scarcity. "Make no mistakes about it—these kids are gambling," he told the *Arizona Daily Wildcat*. "Our experts tell us that when the kids buy the cards, they act just like a gambler in a casino. They act nervously, they perspire, when they open the pack of cards, they squeeze them like a poker player trying to squeeze a flush. And worst of all, they can't stop." Hock eventually went on the *CBS Evening News* to argue this, but Nintendo of America was mostly nonchalant in its response: "To our knowledge, none of these cases have been successful."

Thanks in part to the cards, the amount of money Pokémon made in the first half of 1999 was almost double everything the franchise had earned in 1998. Hundreds of licensors brought merchandise to store shelves. The games made their way to the United Kingdom. The anime dominated its demographics and time slots.

This was the year of *Pokémon* and no one could escape it.

Pokémania

"Isn't this that cartoon that gives you seizures?"

Bart Simpson and the rest of the Simpsons stare at a TV in Japan while a show called "Battle Seizure Robots" plays. Seconds later, they're all convulsing on the floor thanks to the flashing effects in the show. The episode, "Thirty Minutes Over Tokyo," is full of multiple references to Japanese culture, with *Pokémon* now so prevalent that even one of its grimmer moments was seemingly ripe for satire.

Not only was there more *Pokémon* on TV in 1999, but there was plenty of TV *about Pokémon*. *Saturday Night Live* commented on the dilemma of children being duped for cards in school with a skit in which *Friends* star Jennifer Aniston lambasted her son over some bad trade deals—"But Charizard is the coolest Pokémon!" she pleads to her misguided kid. And *South Park* was nominated for an Emmy award for an episode where the main characters become obsessed with "Chinpokomon." The most intricate reference, though, probably comes in the short-lived sitcom *The Norm Show*, in which comedian Norm Macdonald tries to manage a kid named "Ash" who wants to catch Pokémon. This leads to an oddly detailed battle between Norm, the boy, and Team Rocket, with the monsters played by apathetic people in Pokémon costumes—"Actually, I have a rash and it hurts when I Squirtle," says the man in the ill-fitting Squirtle suit, his depression overwhelming his battle spirit. It plays like a late nineties fever dream.

By the time that *Pokémon* celebrated the first anniversary of its arrival in America, the atmosphere surrounding it—the bewilderment, the excitement, the sheer amount of Pikachu—had only grown thicker. The front of the November 1999 issue of *The New Yorker* showed a bunch of costumed children on Halloween night staring in awe as a Pikachu drags a bag of money down the sidewalk. Depending on your view of Pokémon, Pikachu could very well be outright robbing people; however, taking into consideration that one of the kids is dressed as the Sith Darth Maul, a character from the recently released *Star Wars Episode I: The Phantom Menace*, it is also a cute bit of pop culture commentary. No other film released that year would come close to its $431 million domestic box office haul, but when it came to pushing merchandise? It seemed that Jedi and Sith lords were neck-and-neck with Pokémon masters—and it would take more than the Force to topple Ash Ketchum.

In the late nineties, before its print sales plummeted due to factors that would shake its entire medium, *TIME* magazine was a triumph of the industry with a print and online presence and prestige that seemed miles ahead of its competitors. And in the later days of 1999, it became home to Pokémon, with an issue that is by far the most comprehensive attempt to explain Pokémon to the general public of North America that a major news publication had ever attempted by that point. The issue captured the wide-ranging response to the franchise, featuring judgmental opinion pieces, feature articles, and an interview with Satoshi Tajiri, the man who started it all.

And the cover? You've probably seen it even if you've never read *TIME* in your life. Emblazoned with the title "Pokémon!" and 3D models of six of the creatures leaping into the air, it asks the question, "For many kids it's now an addiction: cards, video games, toys, a new movie. Is it bad for them?" It is certainly an alluring bit of text, one that would get you to at least take a second glance as you saw it in the news rack at the grocery store checkout, but it answers itself by saying it's an addiction, which is inherently harmful, right?

Inside, the editorials were mostly spent agonizing over whether Pokémon makes children better people, and why one reviewer just didn't understand the appeal of the recent movie. The main attraction, though, was the "Beware of the Poké Mania" feature, which was frankly mistitled, because it was Satoshi Tajiri's first big interview with an American magazine, and he isn't someone that people needed to be wary of.

Tajiri, maintaining his usual humbleness and remaining consistently reassuring, approached the franchise that he gave birth to with no hand-wringing or attempts at brushing away bad PR. In fact, he seemed content to talk about why he enjoys *Pokémon*, what caused him to create it, what he thought of its success, and, most importantly, why he thought others should enjoy it. The article also featured comments from other influential *Pokémon* figures like Masakazu Kubo, an executive at Shogakukan, and Gail Tilden, whom Kubo refers to as the "Dragon Mother of Nintendo," but overall the interview isn't meant to scare readers, unless the mere existence of Charmander and Squirtle makes them shudder.

At the end, the article compared the ethos of the games to men in World War II training crickets to fight and kill one another. It's a likely unintentional callback to Tajiri's original influence of bugs peacefully crawling across a wire, and it's also a reminder of the violence that many thought *Pokémon* stood for at the time. It's an accusation that, despite twenty-five years' worth of in-game messaging that "no, these creatures are our pals and they also really like to compete," *Pokémon* still grapples with. Released at the same time, an interview for *TIME* Asia titled "The Ultimate Game Freak" almost seemed published to refute those claims specifically. Described as tired, with his eyes "bloodshot" and his hands and lips trembling from exhaustion, Tajiri managed to dive into what attracts him to gaming and his efforts to instill a certain playful gentleness into *Pokémon*. "I'm not interested in creating violent effects," Tajiri says, effectively shooting down the allegation that *Pokémon* was invented to program a generation of bloodthirsty youngsters. In fact, when it comes to the kids playing the games, his mission is the opposite: "I want to make their lives better."

Unfortunately, the assertion would be bigger than any one interview could assuage and catapulted *Pokémon* to prime-time news. The MSNBC news report about "Pokémania," hosted by news anchor Brian Williams, who pronounced *Pokémon* a different way no less than three separate times, featured both a psychiatrist and a "self-proclaimed toy guru" to offer their takes. The "guru" had a desk stacked full of Pokémon figurines, plush toys, and home video items, and did have some kind of conversation with Williams, though it was fairly one-sided. Most of their chat centered on Williams talking about how his kids seemed to like the franchise, while the guru tried to both provide a messy exegesis of the anime while also shilling a half dozen different products. But previously in the conversation, the psychiatrist informed viewers that parents should basically play goalie between their kids and *Pokémon*, and that "the message is violence" before her interview is mercifully cut short.

Today, it might sound rather outlandish to make the connection between *Pokémon* and violence, but at the time, we were barely half a year removed from the Columbine massacre in which two youths murdered nearly a dozen of their classmates at a Colorado high school. The media, parents, and professionals were desperate to dig up any meaning or catalyst behind the event, and video games were a prime target—unfortunately, the boys responsible for the tragedy had enjoyed playing titles like *Doom*, a video game that's had more than its fair share of fingers pointed at it. Combined with the copious battles over video game censorship and their moral impact, the technological angst over a potential turn-of-the-millennium Y2K disaster, and easy comparisons to things like dog-fighting, *Pokémon* being shuffled onto the chopping block seemed inevitable.

The attempts to reflect some kind of culture war with the MSNBC segment, between those aware of Pokémon's more innocuous features and those who feared it was an introduction to brutality, were betrayed by the clumsiness of this segment's construction. Instead, the culture war aspect was overshadowed by Pokémon's awe-inspiring status as a mover of merchandise. The toy guru's desk of potential Christmas list items, the B-roll consisting of kids in line at the store, fans playing the games with one another, and buyers hunkered over their recent Pokémon acquisitions—it did not matter what morals you ascribed to it. It was invincible.

Then tragedy struck.

Darkest Hour

In the eight weeks surrounding the release of *Pokémon: The First Movie*, Burger King dispensed multiple kinds of Pokémon toys with its standard menu items, including 151 special cards—not trading cards, just cards with art of the monsters on them, which were only slightly less coveted than the official things—and 57 different Pokémon plush toys. Burger King planned to distribute roughly 25 million of these toys, and, to house them, they created tiny plastic Poké Ball replicas that were about three inches in diameter. They came apart in the middle, just like the real thing, so you could either choose to keep your toy in them or take the toys and just leave a bunch of Poké Ball halves lying around your home and in the backseat of your mom's car. The promotion was worth around $22 million.

It should come as no surprise that the promotion was a hit, and parents often talked about how they'd got the Burger King toys on the way to and from the theater playing the *Pokémon* movie. With the toys offered in both Big Kids Meals and Kids Meals, the partnership paid off with a 30 percent rise in Burger King sales. The commercials followed the common themes of previous Pokémon advertising with kids doing cool stuff before congregating in shared Pokémon enthusiasm or adults just trying to weather the frenzied storm. More than 1,000 Kids Meals were being sold a day in some locations. In others, inventory grew scarce and Burger King was forced to apologize for the frequent shortages. On December 10, 1999, E! Online ran the headline "Pokémon Crowns Burger King."

Then on December 11, 1999, a thirteen-month-old girl was found to have suffocated to death in her playpen. The cause had been the Poké Ball toy.

Little did Nintendo or Burger King know, when the ball was split in two, there was a groove in the top half, which allowed it to lock into the bottom. This groove, though small, could easily fit around the bridge of a small child's nose. In the twenty minutes that it took for her mother to take a shower, the toddler had gotten the ball stuck to her face and had been unable to remove it. Her sisters, only four and five years old, were helpless. The US Consumer

Product Safety Commission asked for a recall of the toys and for the promotion to cease. In response, Burger King claimed that all safety guidelines had been met and that "it was not concluded that the ball was the cause of death," and the toy giveaway continued.

While it was heartbreaking that it happened even once, sadly, it would not be the last accident. An eighteen-month-old was barely saved in time by her father after he found her, blue in the face, with a Poké Ball half stuck to her. So, after one fatal accident and one close call, Burger King finally relented, and on December 27, 1999, they announced a recall. But, by that point, most of the eight-week promotion had already happened and millions of toys had been distributed. It took over two weeks for them to put an end to it, and the recall ended up being the largest in history. Notices were not only put on television, including a segment on the *Today* show, but were also sent to thousands of Burger King locations, over 50,000 pediatricians' offices, and websites that were known to be commonly visited by Pokémon fans. For each returned toy, Burger King offered a free small order of French fries.

Burger King destroyed millions of unsold Poké Ball containers, along with a huge number that had been given back. It was reported that many more were discarded by parents, though the toys that came inside of them were often kept, as their safety was never called into question. However, this effort wasn't 100 percent preventative. In January 2000, a four-month-old suffocated to death in his crib, another victim of the Poké Ball toy. With this came even more attempts at a recall, and while this one came much quicker than the original effort, the attempts at PR management from Burger King felt hollow and unsatisfactory.

Dissatisfaction with Pokémon suddenly reigned. News segments that covered the tragedies whiplashed between urgent calls for the toys to be destroyed and callous "where were the parents?" finger-pointing. In one, two siblings—one of whom holds the toys up to the camera and shouts the names of the respective Pokémon, reminiscent of the early commercials— throw their toys away in a trash can while their mother tries to reconcile what happened and reassures the reporter that it wouldn't happen under her close watch. Just before the broadcast returns to the table of newscasters, the boy, who dropped the balls into the bin, muttered, "Don't worry. We can have them back after the weekend."

2000

Pokémon would be the last pop culture triumph of its kind of the millennium, the last franchise to saturate grandly and in a global fashion. While its success would continue into the next, arriving as the undisputed Game Boy Heavyweight Champion, ready to defend against all challengers, a little piece of it would remain. For there's a part of Pokémon that will always be locked in 1999, before the Burger King tragedies and before the scandals over the trading cards. It was a specific kind of enthusiasm that the franchise has never quite been able to capture in the same way since.

The year 2000 would mark the end of the first era of Pokémania, both the good and the bad. Its American wave had started with a blend of confusion and enterprise, with parents and pundits warning of the medical emergency caused by the anime's effects while also marveling at the sheer amount of money that Nintendo was throwing at its Western debut. So it's only fair that it would conclude with the same mixture. All the fears and speculation about the impact of *Pokémon* had come home to roost, whether apt or exaggerated. The anime, the games, and the cards, none of these major pieces of the franchise came through without varying measures of success and controversy. Though one question lingered: *Pokémon* had become one of the most popular franchises in the world, so where would it go from here?

Well, two ways at once: First, it would evolve, then secondly, it would head to war. First, *Gold* and *Silver*, after a long gestation, finally made their debut in November 1999 in Japan. With them, any lingering fears that *Pokémon*'s formula was a one-hit wonder were put to rest for good. With a new story, new lands, new monsters, and new options, this set of games provided a smooth, memorable experience that remains, arguably, one of the best that the series has ever offered.

And that war? While *Digimon* had been added to the mix in the late summer of 1999, numerous other players were preparing to join the fray, each one eager to at least nibble off a slice of the pie that Pikachu had made. Or, if they were able, topple the *Pokémon* reign for good. The landscape was about to be filled with even more monster-collecting franchises, some capable, some bizarre, some ready-made for success, and some that would be victims of their own producers' hubris. Could they assail *Pokémon*'s impenetrable branding and range of electronic experiences? After all, by the end of 1999, *Pokémon*'s opening theme song in America shouted, "We all live in a Pokémon world!" True as that may be, they weren't alone, nor would they ever be again.

Chapter 7

FAILURE TO LAUNCH (A MEGA FRANCHISE)

When you look at Pokémania and its effects, it's hard to find any actual Pokémon "knockoffs," at least not in how we commonly think of the word. There were many different variations of the same core set of ideas, but true knockoffs—bargain-bin products meant to trick consumers into buying a "Pichaku" doll for their kids? Very few of those broke into the mainstream, and the ones that did exist were shoddy and doomed to a legacy of non-recognition, mainly because there were just too many series out there that were actually, well, *interesting*.

The notable franchises accused of being Pokémon knockoffs were either different series that debuted in North America around the same time as *Pokémon* or ones that emulated some of Pokémon's lucrative techniques. It would become quickly apparent, though, that it wasn't a one-size-fits-all situation. Various forces, both inside and outside of these franchises' control, would prevent them from taking the mantle.

So begins the tales of two anime series and a video game system that were often considered nothing more than "knockoffs": *Cardcaptors, Monster*

Rancher, and Bandai's WonderSwan handheld console. Each of them brought fascinating things to the table but, in the end, tended to be left out of the conversation around *Pokémon* versus *Digimon*. And they served to remind us that Pokémania was a maelstrom that changed nearly everything it touched, for better . . . or for worse.

Total Overhaul

Those who are fans of *Cardcaptors* might be saying, "It's actually called *Cardcaptor Sakura*!" And they would be correct! The work of an all-female group of Japanese manga artists called CLAMP, *Cardcaptor Sakura* debuted in 1996 as a manga series, which was another wonderful addition to CLAMP's already impressive resume. Previously, they'd created cult classics like *Tokyo Babylon*, *X/1999*, and a fairly short-lived but deeply important fantasy series *Magic Knight Rayearth*. "Talk about a group that never misses," said Anime News Network managing editor Lynzee Loveridge.

Cardcaptor Sakura was similar to *Sailor Moon*, another seminal series created by a female author from the nineties and part of the magical girl genre. The genre often focused on female protagonists who were tasked with defending the world with their amazing powers while also struggling with their regular everyday problems and relationships. Frequently overlooked outside of Japan, the magical girl genre not only gave its medium a wealth of amazing stories, but also helped to turn the worlds of manga and anime into an even more inclusive space—though women have always been into anime and don't let anyone tell you otherwise.

In fact, when the dub of *Sailor Moon* was cancelled in the United States thanks it to being given horrendously early morning time slots and weak marketing to match, thousands of fans rallied and petitioned for it to return. Which it would, eventually! For a larger number of anime fans who were growing up in the mid-nineties, there was a good chance that *Sailor Moon* was *the* series that kicked off their interest and obsession.

Sadly, *Cardcaptor Sakura* was not given the same chances as *Sailor Moon*. *Sailor Moon* was adapted, and many aspects were changed to make it more "palatable" for an American audience of teens, children, and those who had no clue what anime was. But at least it was given a chance to be itself.

The original manga story of *Sakura* centers around Sakura Kinomoto, a young elementary school girl who must use her powers to collect magical Clow cards that have been released into the world. The show follows Sakura as she defeats and recaptures the enchanted beings that have been released from their cards. Sakura is watched over and supported by Cerberus, more affectionately known as Kero, the guardian of the cards, who spends most of his downtime relaxing, eating, and playing video games while in his "false form" as a little, yellow, plush version of his lion beast form; and Sakura's best friend, Tomoyo, a wealthy, intelligent girl who often sews Sakura's many outfits and videotapes her adventures. Rounding out the cast is Syaoran Li, a challenger who also wants to capture the cards but later becomes a romantic interest for Sakura. The manga and anime would both win multiple awards for its well-crafted story that depicts genuinely playful, intriguing, and authentic characters and even outdoes *Sailor Moon* in some respects.

Well, at least it was all those things until Nelvana Enterprises Inc., a Canadian entertainment company responsible for both the production and licensing of various TV series and movies (much like 4Kids), got hold of it. Nelvana had been around since the seventies, founded because there were so few production entities in Canada. It was named after an early female superhero, Nelvana of the Northern Lights, whose adventures predated Wonder Woman's. Nelvana had a small-scale start, but they worked frequently and consistently, and by the end of the seventies, they'd even collaborated with George Lucas, animating the first ever official Star Wars cartoon as a part of the infamous *Star Wars Holiday Special*.

The eighties saw Nelvana work on more Star Wars series, titles based on the extremely popular Care Bears line of merchandise, *Inspector Gadget*, *Strawberry Shortcake*, and even a live action series that centered around the unmistakable eighties icon Mr. T. And the nineties were no different as Nelvana, boosted by animated hits like *The Magic School Bus*, decided to dive into anime for the first time and secured the rights to *Cardcaptor Sakura*. The late nineties were a felicitous time for anime, especially with the success of *Pokémon* and *Digimon*, along with the rising prominence of the anime-centric Toonami block on the Cartoon Network channel, plus the expanding home video market, and young fans were hungry for more. With a good time slot and solid advertising, things that *Sailor Moon* had lacked when it first made it to the United States, there was a chance for a hit.

Pokémon's localization had been designed to appeal to more global tastes, or at least what the producers thought they would be. But the core of the series, along with its themes and broader outlook, had not been edited. American *Pokémon* fans enjoyed *Pokémon* for the same reason that fans watching it in Japan did. *Cardcaptor Sakura*, unfortunately, was changed to a notorious degree, like renaming the show *Cardcaptors,* which was the first of many, many changes to things that Nelvana felt kids might find too alien.

Hope for *Cardcaptors* was scant even from the beginning. Michael Hirsch, an executive at Nelvana, had made the mistake of saying that it had "all the elements of a highly visible and successful merchandising brand" when promoting its debut, with few mentions of its inventive narrative or capable character work, except in reference to potential revenue and profits. The most damning bit, though, was the inclusion of the phrase "like *Pokémon,*" because *Cardcaptor Sakura*, aside from having magical creatures and a young protagonist, was not like *Pokémon* at all. It was an entirely different genre, a fact that was apparently an issue because of how much they edited and censored. The seventy-episode anime was cut down to thirty-nine episodes for its American release, and along with the standard process of censorship and renaming, the characters had most of their intricacies cut out and tossed aside. Sakura Kinomoto weirdly became Sakura Avalon and her quirks were replaced by stubborn action hero-esque readiness, while Cerberus became a kind of bro-ey Pikachu, his accent ranging from a nasally Brooklyn yell to clunky sidekick grunt. The romance between Sakura and Syaoran, who was now named Li Showron, was almost entirely gone, and he became little more than a rival stock character, the Gary Oak to Sakura's Ash Ketchum.

Perhaps the biggest change was that the series would be reframed to focus more on the Clow cards and their magical beings, creatures that Nelvana likely hoped could be turned into action figures or slapped onto the side of lunch boxes and t-shirts and sold like *Pokémon*'s zoo of monsters. The first seven episodes were skipped, eliminating many of the little character beats for Sakura and fast-forwarding her journey to the first time she met her rival, Li, just as both Ash Ketchum and his rival made their initial appearances in the first episode of *Pokémon*. The opening theme in English started with a chant of the names of the cards—"Wind, Rain, Shadow, Wood, Sword, Thunder, Power, Sleep"—reinforcing them as something similar to the now widely recognized Pokémon types of Grass, Fire, Water, etc.

Of course, this overhaul did not go unrecognized. The *Chicago Tribune* ran the headline "Hot on the Heels of 'Pokémon,' Here Comes the Next Big Thing" six days after *Cardcaptors*' June 17, 2000, debut on Kids' WB. Aside from containing a proclamation that feels ludicrous in hindsight, the piece made little effort to explain the show's concept in a way that didn't hinge on *Pokémon*'s success, telling parents that if they were late coming around on *Pokémon*, they could invest in *Cardcaptors*. A Kids' WB senior vice president interviewed for the same article made it clear that it had a different "mythology" and "quest" from *Pokémon*, which was a solid start, but had a lot of the same "core elements." Which it did *now*, but that was only after it was changed a bunch.

Though *Cardcaptors* was called "a sort of *Pokémon* for girls" by Kidscreen .com, the massive reconstruction of the series was clearly anything but focused on girls. Instead, much of it came across as the opposite, an attempt to temper down any overly "girly" qualities to appeal to the boys that shows like *Pokémon* were typically aimed at. Sakura's personality had been whittled down to its Ash Ketchum basics, whole romantic subplots had been thrown out, and anything that could remotely be considered homosexual subtext—which is one of the most discussed and frequently applauded parts of the original manga and anime—was forced out. Instead, Sakura and her pals now went around fighting different monsters, and a groundbreaking story created by an all-female team had suddenly been reduced to "*Pokémon*, but worse."

However, the haphazard quality didn't prevent its success on Kids' WB; it was regularly among their top shows in its early run. But unlike *Pokémon*, thanks to the vast trimming done to the episode count, *Cardcaptors* could only appear in spurts, filling in the latter half of 2000 and then returning in the fall 2001 to finish off what remained. The tie-in products, ranging from a too-late Taco Bell promotion in early 2002 to a dub of a movie that never got a true theatrical release, were muted in their popularity. In the end, *Cardcaptors* would go down as a triangle anime peg forced to fit into the square hole left behind from *Pokémon* franchising. Less a new series than a retention effort for Pikachu enthusiasts.

Has it gotten better since then for the magical girls? A little. Thanks to the rise of home video, anime streaming services, and a consistently growing Western fandom, the magical girl genre has managed to ascertain its legacy. However, things are far from perfect. "Despite it being a well-established subgenre that goes back to anime's early origins," Loveridge laments, "licensors in the States can't seem to figure out how to engage with its audience so it can experience the same level of success it has in Japan."

Spice Girls' "Wannabe" Creates a Tiger Plant Warrior

If you insert Paula Abdul's *Spellbound* album into your PlayStation, it will resurrect a golden plant warrior. Try David Bowie's *Earthling* and a horned wolf will appear, ready for battle. Got a copy of comedian Jeff Foxworthy's *You Might Be A Redneck If…* lying around? It will spawn a full-blown dinosaur, one desperate to be trained for combat. Such is the beauty of *Monster Farm*, a series built on the idea that people probably had a lot of CDs lying around in the late nineties and that there was a high chance they were also interested in monster duels.

Monster Farm, which would be named *Monster Rancher* when released in North America, is a time capsule of a series and one that was destined to be popular during a very specific era of media and possibly never reach those highs again. Obviously, its video game developer, Tecmo, didn't plan for it to be pushed toward extinction. For a short while, it was popular enough to be mentioned in the same breath as *Pokémon* or *Digimon* before it ultimately succumbed to the medium that made it unique in the first place.

Unlike Game Freak, Tecmo had been in the video game business a long time before throwing their hat into the monster-raising ring. Founded in the sixties, Tecmo had a hand in developing entertainment equipment and then, finally, video games in 1981. Their run from the late eighties to the mid-nineties is perhaps what they're best known for, unleashing franchises like the football game *Tecmo Bowl*, the action-packed *Ninja Gaiden*, and the fighting series *Dead or Alive*. By the time they started *Monster Farm*, they were an established hit-maker. However, unlike those prior games, *Monster Farm* was built on a very unique gimmick.

The metadata of a compact disc consists of a few things: the artist, the track numbers, the length of the songs, the International Standard Recording Code, etc. If you happen to have a CD player in your car and you pop a CD in it, the metadata is what causes something like "6. 'Toxic'—Britney Spears—In The Zone (2003)" to show up on the little screen. By using the PlayStation's ability to read the metadata of any CD, Tecmo was able to create an algorithm that generated different monsters. In the late nineties, CD sales were only on the rise, so there was a pretty good chance that anyone who bought *Monster Farm* would be able to spawn a fair number of creatures. Also, in case you were curious, *In the Zone* creates a cute little insectoid plant fighter, just in case you're a fan of Britney Spears.

The idea behind the game was pretty simple: You breed, raise, and train monsters on a little farm, and then you put those monsters in tournaments. In these tournaments, players battle other monsters to achieve higher ranks, gain access to more stuff, and eventually unlock more and more powerful monsters. Plot details are fairly scarce and, honestly, rather unimportant. If a new character appears to offer you something new or tell you about an intriguing development, it's rarely in the service of a broader narrative. Instead, the amount of joy you get from *Monster Farm* depends solely on how appealing the painstaking process of raising monsters is to you.

This wasn't an issue for the first game. Primed by the seemingly ever-increasing success of *Pocket Monsters* and the boom of the Tamagotchi, nurturing monsters was an easy fit in Japan. Released in July 1997, *Monster Farm* would sell over 500,000 copies before the end of the year. And unlike *Pokémon* and *Digimon*, which had to wait over a year before their main series of games hit American soil, the newly christened *Monster Rancher* ended up in the United States only a few months later. So, the question of "What came first in the United States: *Pokémon* or *Digimon*?" has an answer: Neither. It's *Monster Rancher*, where it enjoyed "brisk sales" according to GameSpot.

Why *Monster Rancher* isn't recognized as the ignition of the monster boom in the West is probably the result of a few things. First, being able to create monsters from the CDs you'd have lying around and seeing which one grants you the wildest designs is generally fun . . . until the novelty wears off. After that, the hours and hours you spend training for specific stats and employing your monsters to do various chores in preparation for local tournaments becomes a bit of a grind. The game's status may have also been hampered by its choice of mascot, the Suezo.

Pikachu is a clearly international-friendly design, its mammalian cuteness recalling both Winnie the Pooh and Mickey Mouse at the same time. Agumon, of *Digimon* fame, is a tiny dinosaur, a baby T. rex that looks feeble enough to trigger your paternal instincts, but with big enough claws that you know it can handle itself in a scrape. But the Suezo, a large yellow worm with a single giant eye and a gaping, toothy mouth, was neither cute nor apparently qualified for war. Though its species has cool psychic powers in the games, this strength is not visually apparent from the outset. Plus, at first glance, it looks like it would immediately topple over if it were ever turned into an action figure. Despite its questionable position as a leading man, Suezo can be found on the covers of ten different *Monster Rancher* games, usually with its giant tongue flailing.

One-eyed monster characters aren't very prevalent in American culture, with the most popular modern one perhaps being the wimpy Mike Wazowski from Pixar's *Monsters Inc.* series. In Japan, though, Suezo is reminiscent of a fairly well-known yokai (creature, spirit, monster, and other mythical being found in Japanese folklore) known as the Hitotsume-kozo. This unassuming thing looks like a little kid with a single giant eyeball. As bizarre as that sounds on paper, stories about it render the spirit harmless and even comical. It doesn't posit a one-eyed creature as an outright oddity like Western culture tends to.

Another reason *Monster Rancher* became known as a copycat rather than progenitor is that, unlike *Pokémon* or *Digimon*, whose video game debuts in the US were preceded by anime series that served as icebreakers for audiences, *Monster Rancher*'s anime showed up over a year after the game. Produced by TMS Entertainment, an experienced studio with more than three decades' worth of animation history by the time it began work on *Monster Rancher*, the anime dealt with the adventures of Genki Sakura, a young boy who himself is a talented player of Monster Rancher video games. It's the kind of plot point that popped up often over time in this genre: a main character of a story who is a devoted fan of the kind of merchandise that viewers could go out and purchase as soon as the episode ended.

After winning a special game, Genki is transported "to a faraway land, to a world where monsters rule," as the English opening raps. There, he meets a girl named Holly and her monster partner, a Suezo, who takes the wise-cracking, acerbic sidekick role, and they embark on a quest to resurrect monsters from stone discs, stop an ancient evil, and uncover the mystery around Holly's father. As an adaptation, it's a big leap from what most people know of the world established in the source material, and it adds copious lore, settings, and characters to a game series about running drills with your beast pals. It's also a pretty fun show, and the mix of personalities in the humans and monsters ends up giving it a kind of *Seven Samurai* vibe, if Akira Kurosawa had made that film about beasts you summon on a PlayStation.

Acquired by Bohbot Entertainment for the US release and dubbed by veteran production company Ocean Studios, *Monster Rancher* went through the typical translation and localization process. Its US debut happened around the same time as *Digimon*, but unlike *Digimon*, which immediately landed on Fox Kids, or *Cardcaptors*, which was basically tailor-edited to be a part of Kids' WB, *Monster Rancher*'s forever home wouldn't come until later. It first showed up in syndication and on the oft-forgotten BKN (Bohbot Kids Network) programming block, which found a place on the Sci-Fi Channel during the week.

Monster Rancher, which BKN president of network ad sales George Baratta told Kidscreen was an acquisition that was absolutely influenced by *Pokémon*, was poised to ride the Pikachu wave. BKN had taken worldwide merchandising rights and worked with TV stations on ways to potentially coincide with *Pokémon*, airing in time slots either coming just before or after the show, so that kids could flip over to *Rancher* as soon as Ash Ketchum left the air. That way, it wouldn't so much compete with *Pokémon* as (hopefully) feed off its energy source, a parasitic relationship to give the show a chance to establish itself.

Then, *Monster Rancher* was eventually thrown into the big leagues, taking a much-lauded Saturday morning slot and joining *Digimon* on Fox Kids. This was slightly before *Cardcaptors* entered the US market, meaning that in terms of series about young kids befriending monsters that they then watch fight one another, Fox Kids was up two-to-one against Kids' WB. With heavy merchandising plans, a *Monster Rancher 2*—though it would be known as just *Monster Rancher* in Europe, since the original had never been released there—and an anime in a prime spot, the franchise was set. While *Pokémon* had firmly established "Gotta catch 'em all!" as both brand ethos and mantra, the opening to *Monster Rancher* constantly included the phrase "Monsters rule!" reminding kids that *Monster Rancher* was the top dog among its competitors and the obvious fact that monsters *do* rule.

So what happened? Well, the show was solid, and the games have a pretty good amount of replay value if they fit your interests, but *Monster Rancher* was one of the first hints that the monster market was getting crowded. Along with rerunning episodes that had already appeared in syndication, the careful work that BKN had done to ensure that *Monster Rancher* would not be butting heads with *Pokémon* was undone immediately upon making it to Fox Kids. With *Digimon* already taking up at least one slot, although sometimes it was two or even three on Saturdays, *Monster Rancher* had slim pickings for when it could air. *Digimon* had become Fox Kids' People's Champion, but perhaps their roles would have been switched had *Monster Rancher* aired first. Then we'd all have had big "*Pokémon* vs *Monster Rancher*" debates during fourth grade lunch instead. So *Monster Rancher* was thrown into the eight-thirty a.m. and ten a.m. spots . . . which was exactly when *Pokémon* was airing on Kids' WB.

Pokémon obviously creamed *Monster Rancher* for months, and soon this double feature was reduced to a single show. By August 2000, *Monster Rancher* was gone from Fox Kids weekends and weekdays and, aside from a brief attempt at a weekday run in late 2001, its final resting place within Fox was on their unsteady "Made in Japan" Sunday anime block. All the changes in programming schedules, along with the fact that it was still airing in syndication while Fox Kids wrung it out, meant that any kid who wanted to get into its overarching plot was destined to be confused.

And it wasn't smooth sailing for the games, either. A common criticism about the games persisted: that not enough was done to differentiate all the entries in the series, and even though some remain memorable—arguably, *Monster Rancher 2* and *4* are the high points of the franchise—they suffered from diminishing returns. By the time *Monster Rancher EVO*, the fifth and final game in the main console series, came out, it seemed all but dead. Released in December 2005, its sales put it in the Top 500 best-selling games of 2006 . . . at number 491. Attempts at puzzle or card battle–themed games for the Game Boy Color, while cute, also failed to garner much interest.

Perhaps the biggest sign that *Monster Rancher* was not meant to have the same life cycle as *Pokémon* was the decline in the technology that had once made it such an interesting rival: CDs. Peaking in 2000, the number of physical albums bought dropped sharply on a nearly year by year basis afterward. CDs were quickly replaced by online retailers, streaming services, and devices like the iPod, and then, eventually, the common smartphone. Suddenly, a game series built to take advantage of the most prominent way to buy music was fossilized alongside them.

In later handheld games on the Game Boy Advance and Nintendo DS, players had to type certain phrases to create monsters or use the touch screen to draw simple images. These results didn't provide the same curious thrill, and attempts to replace the CD metadata summonings came off as shots in the dark on a mobile platform. Today, *Monster Rancher* is the very definition of a cult classic, with its golden age cut short by poor management and the downfall of the aspects that set it apart from the monster-collecting pack in the first place.

Handheld Rivalry

Gunpei Yokoi had invented the Game Boy, and now he had to kill it.

Okay, that's a little dramatic, but he did have to challenge it. Yokoi had been a leading member of that famous Research & Development No. 1 team at Nintendo, where he had created the Game & Watch device, produced a few famous Nintendo franchises like *Metroid*, and, eventually, designed the Game Boy, which was his crowning achievement.

The Game Boy was stunningly popular and, along with its later off-shoots like the Game Boy Pocket and the Game Boy Color, sold tens of millions of units since its debut in 1989. But the Game Boy wasn't just a popular handheld gaming device; for most of the world, it was *the* hand-held gaming device and the only one that truly mattered in the long run. Competitors came and went, but the Game Boy line stayed strong, out-selling them even as the device reached its twilight years. The Game Boy was Yokoi's monster, one that couldn't be stopped, especially now that it had a franchise like *Pokémon* attached to it.

Yokoi, though, had hit a rough patch the year before *Pokémon* was first released in Japan. His final major work for Nintendo had been the Virtual Boy, a headset-based system that the player would wear, allowing them to play games in a stereoscopic 3D style. He had been fascinated with the technology behind it for a long time, and if pulled off successfully, it would have offered something truly special and potentially revolutionary to the video game industry.

Sadly, the Virtual Boy wasn't meant to be and was rushed to the finish line by Nintendo, and it received terrible reviews. The system was clunky in nature, it didn't look great, and if played for too long, it could give you headaches and nausea, plus it came at a price that most consumers balked at. Fewer than a million units were sold, abysmal numbers for Nintendo, and it is widely considered one of the worst consoles of all time.

While a chairman of Nintendo of America would maintain in the *New York Times* that Yokoi always had a good relationship with the company, it's speculated that the creator took the failure of the Virtual Boy as a per-sonal blow. Leaving a legacy of innovation during his near three decades with Nintendo, he exited the company a year after the Virtual Boy was released. Yokoi started his own company, called Koto Laboratory, but it wouldn't take long for him to begin work with Bandai. A year after the toy and entertainment producer hit a gold mine with the Tamagotchi, they planned to enter the arena of handheld game consoles. And who better to design a competitor for the Game Boy than the man who had designed the Game Boy?

The WonderSwan would offer a range of improvements compared to the Game Boy, most prominently more processing power and an absurd battery life, where one AA battery was supposed to offer forty hours of play-time, even with the upgraded graphics. Thanks to extra buttons, users could even play the WonderSwan at different angles if they pleased. All the other handhelds released over the years had fallen short in at least one of the areas where the Game Boy excelled: either the batteries sucked, the graphics were underwhelming, the design was too clunky, or the price was too high, etc. But not the WonderSwan, which would effectively become the anti–Game Boy by taking everything the Game Boy did well and kicking it up a notch.

Sadly, Yokoi never saw its release, dying in a traffic accident in 1997. The WonderSwan was finished without him and remains his final gift to the gaming industry. But aside from its relation to the Game Boy, what makes it monster friendly? Well, considering that the Game Boy was now the hand-held home to hundreds of Pokémon, it made sense that Bandai wanted an answer to that. And so, launching March 4, 1999, on the same day as the WonderSwan, was *Digimon: Anode Tamer.*

Its plot was tied loosely into that of the anime, which would debut on TV a few days later. As a tactical RPG, it doesn't offer the same broad amount of monster collecting as *Pokémon* or even *Digimon World* for the PlayStation, which preceded *Anode Tamer* by a few months, but its enhanced graphics make it a curious substitute for Pokémon and the Game Boy. After this, the WonderSwan would become home to multiple *Digimon* games, ranging from RPGs to fighting games to enhanced versions of the virtual pets genre. That said, *Digimon*'s lack of a definitive game, one that the whole series could hang its hat on, plagued the franchise in the long run. Though the success of the WonderSwan did not totally rely on *Digimon*, the series never became a *Pokémon Red* and *Blue* phenomenon—the games that the entire franchise comes to revolve around. The WonderSwan catalog is surprisingly deep, hosting a solid variety of RPGs and anime-based titles (fans of the giant robot Gundam series could rejoice in it), but there really wasn't a backbone franchise for it, Digimon or otherwise, that would keep gamers' attention when releases seemed to dry up.

And attention was majorly necessary, for the WonderSwan had the unfortunate timing to be released after the Game Boy Color, which was not only the next step in the Game Boy legacy with Nintendo's brand recognition, but also had the entire catalog of the Game Boy behind it. Though it outperformed other competing handhelds at the time, the WonderSwan was only able to nibble admirably at the market that Nintendo had all but staked its claim in. By the time Bandai had worked to upgrade the WonderSwan with the WonderSwan Color, Nintendo had once again pulled their platform from under them, as attention had turned to the company's recently announced Game Boy Advance.

At one point, Bandai turned to toy giant Mattel for a United States release of the WonderSwan, but given that it was even harder to make a dent in Nintendo's handheld monolith in America than it was in Japan, any plans for this were quickly abandoned. After one more variation, the SwanCrystal, the line of systems diminished and was ended quietly by Bandai in 2003. It would be the company's final attempt at a video game console, though the WonderSwan's existence will forever serve as a great "What if?", a fine piece of technology that might have gotten a real chance at thriving had it not been almost poetically overshadowed by the earlier invention of its own creator.

And it's this invention, the Game Boy line, that we're going to jump back to, because it was about to see the true test of *Pokémon*'s success: Could the games and their success be accomplished twice? *Red, Green, Blue,* and *Yellow* and all their localized counterparts had been massive successes, but even with adjustments in artwork, technical fixes, and storyline alterations to make the product resemble its anime adaptation, they were still the same game with the same goals, the same quest, and very similar mechanical highs and lows. *Gold* and *Silver* would transport players to a whole *new* region with a gaggle of new monsters for fans to become enamored with. They would be a huge step forward, but also possibly the final one. There had been a severe underestimation of *Pokémon*'s shelf life, and if the original intentions of its creators had come to pass, they wouldn't have just been the RPG swan song for the Game Boy, but the end of *Pokémon* as we knew it.

Chapter 8

GOLD VERSUS *RED*

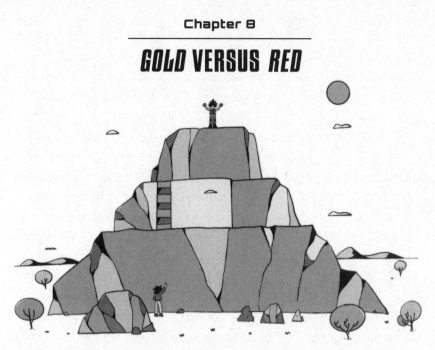

At the end of the games *Pokémon Gold* and *Silver*, you arrive at the top of a mountain. It's not just a physical peak, but also a narrative one. At this point, you've defeated the group of master trainers known as the Elite 4, dismantled Team Rocket's attempts at a terrorism comeback tour, won all the gym badges from both the newly introduced region of Johto and your old *Red* and *Blue* stomping grounds of Kanto, and you've likely assembled a team of all-star Pokémon. Now you've climbed up to the top of Mount Silver, the last location there is to conquer, and along the way you've heard whispers of someone, a boy who saved the world, became a top-notch trainer, and then vanished. His status is mythic, meaning that finding him would almost be akin to discovering the legendary Pokémon that hide out in caves, awaiting anyone brave enough to face them.

And then you see him . . . and he's you.

At the end of *Pokémon Gold* and *Silver*, the final "boss" of the game is Red, the same character you played as when you first booted up the *Red* version years earlier. His team is mostly mainstays from that first generation, including the beasts that graced the original games' boxes, Charizard, Blastoise, and Venusaur, along with the bulky powerhouse Snorlax, the effortlessly graceful Psychic type Espeon, and, finally, an absurdly strong Pikachu. The monster with the highest level ever to be found in a Pokémon game at that point would obviously be Pikachu.

The battle can be a tough one if your monsters don't have enough punch to demolish Red's, and when it's over, Red, never uttering a word, disappears. Then the credits roll, not just for *Gold* and *Silver*, but for *Pokémon* as a whole. Fighting and defeating the character you played as in the previous set of *Pokémon* games renders the two—both *Red* and *Blue* and *Gold* and *Silver*—a complete story. It also gives players the sense of growing up, for what could signify your advancing talent and confidence more than taking on something that embodies the previous pinnacle of your abilities and surpassing it?

Of course, this wouldn't be the end of *Pokémon*. The next two decades saw new games coming out on nearly a yearly basis; however, this was originally intended to be the series' grand finale. Tsunekazu Ishihara, who now serves as president of the Pokémon Company, stated in an interview with the late, beloved CEO of Nintendo, Satoru Iwata, that *Gold* and *Silver* would be the "finish line" and that he assumed that his "work as far as Pokémon was concerned would be over . . . I even thought that once we entered the twenty-first century, it would be time for me to do something else entirely."

It's why he'd worked to license so many products as an effort to ensure that *Gold* and *Silver* were a prime send-off for the series. That licensing explosion had been one of the main reasons why the Pokémon Company had been created. Originally established as a way to keep up with the new Japanese Pokémon Center stores in Japan, which were locations that existed solely to carry Pokémon merchandise, the company eventually went on to manage many aspects of the franchise. With the combined efforts of Nintendo, Game Freak, and Creatures, the organization was inaugurated to keep the branding of the empire going and in check.

And there was a lot to keep up with, especially in the medium of video games. What had begun as a handful of titles for the Game Boy had blossomed into a cross-system effort, with the Nintendo 64 becoming home to some of the most memorable (and weirdest) titles in Pokémon's history.

Out of the Game Boy

A lot of *Pokémon*'s original mystique lay in its main adventures being situated on the limited hardware of the Game Boy. That kids were so devoted to peeking into every nook and cranny to see if there was more is only a testament to just how big the adventure felt in their imaginations. Similar to the early rush over the discovery of Mew, another notable fascination that would contribute to this mindset of infinite possibilities was "MissingNo.," a game-breaking glitch creature that one could encounter after pulling off a specific series of actions.

MissingNo. could provide extra items thanks to its glitch, but it could also corrupt your game's file to the extent that your only option to reverse its presence was restart the entire game and lose all your monsters and progress. This didn't stop kids from checking it out, though, nor did it prevent them from developing a healthy diet for *Pokémon* fibbery, whether it was spreading rumors about a Mew hiding under a truck (it wasn't), or about the appearance of a "Pikablu" and "Pinkachu" (which were actually the Pokémon Marill and Snubbull, respectively, who would appear in the animated short that played before *Mewtwo Strikes Back*, but wouldn't show up in the games until *Gold* and *Silver*). They'd even attempt to unlock "Venustoise," a hybrid Blastoise and Venusaur that only appears once as a ghostly vision of a Pokémon for a few seconds during an anime episode.

It was these playground and internet rumors that have shaped the community and are almost intrinsic in how we approach *Pokémon* to this day. Every new release brings a round of fake Pokémon designs, forcing fans to constantly guess "Is it leaked data or someone's particularly solid fan art?"

in the months preceding a game launch. Even as the time between a game's Japanese and American debuts shrank, the allure stayed consistent, and gossip about *Pokémon* became borderline folkloric. There had to be more, even if that meant we were scrambling in the dark to discover what that "more" was. So we devoured every second of those Game Boy titles, immersing ourselves in a world we were desperate to know better.

That kind of interest and attraction is hard to re-create; however, the Nintendo 64, with its advanced graphics and lack of mainstay *Pokémon* titles, never really tried. Its *Pokémon* games are purely supplementary in nature, but in ways that also feel specifically designed to home in on the precise aspect that most attracts you to *Pokémon*. The games would initially form a quartet, *Pokémon Stadium*, *Pokémon Snap*, *Pokémon Puzzle League*, and perhaps the most niche title ever released for the series, *Hey You, Pikachu!*

With only forty-two Pokémon for players to use in battle, *Pokémon Stadium* was pretty bare bones—though those available monsters are definitely heavy hitters, ranging from Charizard to Gengar to Dragonite. Its initial incarnation, *Pocket Monsters Stadium*, never made it out of Japan after its release in the summer of 1998. But, as with the Game Boy games, it served as kind of a rough draft for its sequel, *Pokémon Stadium 2*, which was released in North America as *Pokémon Stadium*. It was a kind of "It won't hurt 'em if they don't know it's a sequel" move, but hey, whatever works.

Stadium, a turn-based battle franchise, gave players the grand battle experience the Game Boy games lacked. With all 150 original monsters available, it was a treat to suddenly see them in full 3D, blasting away at one another while an announcer repeated various incarnations of "Whoa!" and "Looks like a bad Pokémon choice!" and "What's next?!?" The voice actor tasked with playing *Pokémon* commentator was frequent 4Kids performer Ted Lewis, who recalled a Japanese representative in the recording studio urging him to give it *even more* spirit. "It was three eight-hour days, and I just remember being very light-headed," Lewis recalled. "That's what I remember from that time, being exhausted and light-headed."

Pokémon Stadium was an outlet built solely for fighting, and the game's mileage mostly depended on how curious players were to see what those little attacks on the Game Boy looked like on their TV set. That's not to say that it had limited potential, far from it, in fact, because it sold over a million copies in North America within a month of its release, but it was a Pokémon world that never left the arena. To get an idea of what Pokémon were like in the wild when not being ordered around by victory-hungry children, you'd need to get *Pokémon Snap*, a game that's not only one of the most beloved in the franchise, but in the realm of the Nintendo 64 in general.

If there's any phrase to describe the particular flavor of *Snap*, it would probably be "David Attenborough's *Pokémon*." In the game, you play as Todd Snap, a photographer who shows up in the anime as one of the numerous Pokémon-obsessed kids that Ash Ketchum hangs out with for a few days. Charged by Professor Oak to get some rad pictures of Pokémon, players set out on an expedition in a little high-tech trolley and document various bits of Pokémon behavior in their natural habitats. This boils down to watching Pokémon play around, interact with each other, and hopefully do something cool enough to warrant being subjects for an impromptu Nintendo 64 photography class.

While *Pokémon Stadium* was an elaborate look at what it was like to walk into a Pokémon Gym, *Pokémon Snap* was a replication of what you saw when you went back outside and into the fields and forests, caves and oceans. It was a study in Pokémon ecology. Your presence is felt—often you throw apples to get their attention or have them behave in a certain way, thus allowing you to snag an even cooler picture—but the tone of the entire game is calm and quirky. The fact that players have their photos graded by the flighty Professor Oak, a biologist who has inexplicably deemed himself qualified to be a photography critic as well, is almost an afterthought. The true joy of the game comes from seeing a gang of Charmander palling around, or a Pikachu chilling at the beach, or a Psyduck jumping out of a pond. It's peaceful in a way that no other installment of the franchise had ever managed to be . . . until *New Pokémon Snap* came out in 2021, which gave nascent and experienced fans a relaxing journey into what is basically a staff job at *Pokémon's National Geographic*. "It's another layer going back to Tajiri's original vision to present them in the wild," Sara Bush said of *Snap's* importance. "I just feel like it rounds out the story so incredibly. Not only are these something to collect and play with and manage, but they actually exist in their own natural habitat." The game's marketing was simple: You get to look at Pokémon, and *that's great*. One Japanese commercial even included a man dreaming of being a proud Pokémon photographer, only to abruptly wake up and realize that he fell asleep playing *Pokémon Snap,* Pikachu isn't real, and to live without Pokémon is to be miserable. The popularity of *Snap* also led to one of the most memorable promotions of the era, Pokémon printing stations in Blockbuster Video stores.

Partnering with the then video rental titan, Nintendo gave fans the chance to take their *Snap* cartridge to the store and print out the photos they'd taken of various Pokémon. "Mr. Arakawa [Nintendo of America's former president] was very excited about the sticker printers," Tilden remembered. "There was a greater vision that the stations could be used for other games and maybe create a collectible sticker craze." These bulky blue stations were incredibly hard to miss, stacked against the shelves of candy and copies of Eddie Murphy's *Dr. Dolittle* and *Shakespeare in Love* that were stocked at the time. If you were a parent trying to take your kid to Blockbuster for the chance at alternate entertainment options to *Pokémon*, well, good luck with that.

Then there was *Pokémon Puzzle League,* which was essentially Pokémon-themed *Tetris*, a block-fitting game with characters from the anime slapped in various places. The opening video does include Pikachu wearing sunglasses, though, and dropping them down his nose Ferris Bueller–style when Professor Oak, who is now in charge of recruiting for puzzle competitions along with being a photography expert and top Pokémon researcher, apparently, invites players to come shift some blocks. So, while it wasn't a particularly imaginative game, it's worth the purchase just to see that, really.

Finally, there was *Hey You, Pikachu!*, another stab at the virtual pet genre (remember the Pikachu virtual pet of 1998?) with a very interesting hardware extension. In this game, the player communicated with Pikachu via the Nintendo 64's Voice Recognition Unit (VRU), and it was the only game to use this particular hardware in the United States. It's never reached the nostalgia heights of *Stadium* or *Snap*, mainly because the technology was clumsy and often barely worked, forcing players to spend most of their time repeating themselves to an indifferent television monster. But the idea of being able to interact with Pikachu around your house in this way isn't totally lacking in charm. Considering just how broad the Nintendo 64 spinoffs and Game Boy side series were—which, oddly enough, included a video game version of the *Pokémon Trading Card Game*, pulling triple-duty as a card game tutorial and advertisement, as well as an alternative to the physical card game for those who didn't have the interest or money to collect all those darn cards—it remains memorably odd. It also says a lot about how much faith Nintendo had in Pikachu as a virtual friend and branding icon, giving it a platform where simply chatting with it is the ultimate and only goal.

On the other hand, while *Pokémon* continued to flourish in video game form, its animated adaptation would hit an obstacle. It had to answer the question, how do you keep the kid who wants to be the very best (like no one ever was) on that path without actually letting them become the very best?

Filler Arc

A few weeks after *Pokémon: The First Movie* came out and taught North American audiences that kindness conquers all, the anime series, still chugging along on Kids' WB, prescribed a different lesson. The show, which was now having to continue long past the boundaries of its original plan, had to come up with ways to keep viewers engaged, so they decided to show that while kindness was important, it wasn't all Ash Ketchum was going to need to get to the top. Sometimes you can want something so desperately, but that doesn't always mean that you are going to get it.

During the climax in a pivotal tournament, Ketchum is left weeping and begging his rebellious Charizard to continue battling. Instead the fiery dinosaur gives up, unwilling to listen to a trainer whom he doesn't respect. For the hero of an anime, it's an embarrassing loss. But it was a clever move to keep things interesting and, perhaps in some small way, it actually helped make Ash more relatable. Ash didn't win this time, but now kids would stay tuned to see if he'd become good enough to win next time.

The first chunk of the *Pokémon* anime had been based on the Kanto region, which was the same as the one found in the first set of games—*Red, Green (Blue),* and *Yellow.* Considering that *Gold* and *Silver,* along with the next new region, wouldn't come out in Japan until late 1999, and then October 2000 in North America, they had to buy some time. It is important to remember the purpose of the anime in the United States, Canada, and Europe was basically to test the waters for the upcoming games, with the show's popularity assuring Nintendo that the Game Boy version would be well received. With no new games to base the story on, would Ash Ketchum be left twiddling his thumbs until there were new products for his fans to play?

Obviously, the answer was no. Instead Ash, Misty, and Brock (and previously their Japanese counterparts) would head to the Orange Islands, an anime-exclusive location where Ash would compete in a big tournament. Well, Ash and Misty would, but Brock was replaced by Tracey Sketchit, a Pokémon artist with a pun-tastic last name to rival Ketchum's. He was voiced by Ted Lewis, the original actor for Team Rocket's James, who'd been replaced a few episodes in due to conflicting work. "I ended up leaving town. I got a theater gig," Lewis recalled. "And, of course, I was like 'Well, it's just this voiceover thing. Who knows how long it's gonna last?'"

In an interview with Pokebeach.com, anime director Masamitsu Hidaka revealed that Brock's swift departure was mainly due to fears that

US audiences would find his design racist—his eyes are fairly nonexistent, replaced by slanted lines, and considering the history and trends of xenophobic art, it was a very appropriate anxiety to have. So they made the decision to replace him with Sketchit, whose looks sort of resemble Ketchum but with a bad haircut—only to learn that everyone kind of liked Brock, especially when you compare his goofball personality to Sketchit's milquetoast hobbies. So when the Orange Islands arc ended, Sketchit was sent to hang out with Professor Oak for eternity, and Brock returned to re-round out the trio.

During the Orange Islands arc, fans saw Ash become regional champion but he affirmed that he wasn't a master *yet*. His rival Gary beat him handily after his tournament win, giving Ash and the show more reasons to continue, aside from blatant TV/video game cross-promotion. And though it had only been less than ten months since Ash's first big-screen adventure came to the US, he was about to show up again with *Pokémon the Movie 2000: The Power of One*. This time, he would be faced with a Pokémon with a creation story unlike any other: Lugia.

Shudo's Greatest Achievement

According to the *Pokémon* anime head writer, Takeshi Shudo, the Pokémon films were "lucky films to work on from the perspective of a screenwriter." The seizure-inducing sequence from the early anime episode had diverted attention from the production company to the anime, leaving Shudo with an enviable amount of creative freedom. This meant that the first film's narrative, focusing on the story of Mewtwo and his desire to take vengeance on humanity, didn't have a lot of cuts or edits made by executives or higher-ups. It was exactly the story that Shudo wanted to tell, for the most part. Then, because of its massive success, he was granted similar freedom for the sequel. All he had to do was include

"Explosive Birth" in the title—though it was a title that would never make it to the United States because it doesn't mean anything in the long run.

For *Mirage Pokémon: Lugia's Explosive Birth* aka *Pokémon the Movie 2000*, he created the concept of Lugia, a gigantic flying Pokémon that lived in the sea, though its appearance and various traits would be fleshed out by the film's other creators, Ken Sugimori, and members of Game Freak. This was the only time that a person outside of Game Freak would ever create a Pokémon. In fact, when Lugia later showed up in the *Pokémon Silver* game and as the mascot on the box, no less, it surprised Shudo. The second film was written a few years before the games even came out, so Game Freak must have grown pretty attached to Shudo's new monster.

However, while writing the film, Shudo was troubled by the fact that Satoshi (Ash) wasn't growing up. In fact, in his first few drafts, he didn't even include Satoshi or any of the main cast, and it was only after a committee meeting that he revised it and added the characters back in. Satoshi (Ash) was merely repeating the same formula from episode to episode, movie to movie. This was a growing concern, which eventually turned to distaste, that he had with the product he was working on, but it was also a problem that is often echoed among former fans of the anime. So, when Shudo was eventually told that the anime might last ten more years, it caused him even further dismay.

Of course, the reasoning for keeping Ash Ketchum as an eternal adolescent is pretty logical from a business standpoint, as every new season and story of the anime becomes immediately accessible to new fans as they're effectively starting their journey into the franchise with Ash. But from a writer's perspective, it must have been fairly frustrating.

Shudo later admitted in a blog post that his writing process included copious amounts of alcohol and drugs, usually tranquilizers, which he'd buy at a pharmacy. He claimed that it "helped him make sense of the lines of dialogue spinning in my head." Regardless of his creative process, he did want *more* for Satoshi (Ash). In fact, he planned for multiple endings for the overall narrative; one included Satoshi aging and dying, while another showed Pokémon revolting against their former human masters. They were strikingly ambitious ideas, but considering the plans for the anime to potentially keep circulating until the heat death of the universe, they were ultimately futile.

Shudo remained with the anime until 2002 and wrote the third film, after which he departed the series. The writer worked on a giant robot anime called *Dancouga Nova* a few years later, but he never saw an ending to the *Pokémon* anime that he'd been pivotal in helping to develop. Experiencing a subarachnoid hemorrhage at a train station in 2010, Shudo passed away at the age of sixty-one.

Pokémon The Movie 2000 carried over many of the messages from the first movie—Lugia, like Mewtwo, struggle with the ramifications of their existence as literal gods in a world of imperfect humans who mostly wish to control them. However, instead of a Pokémon being the prime antagonist here as it was in the first movie, the villain this time is a rare Pokémon collector named Lawrence III, who flies around in an awesome airship and has the traditional anime bad guy spiky hairstyle. This change likely helped the film score higher among critics, who no longer had to look past the thematic leap of "Why are these monsters instructing us about peace when they mostly want to fight each other?" which had weighed down the first film in their view. Here, all they had to understand was that some jerk was being awful to Pokémon. Easy enough.

That said, reviews remained, for the most part, lackluster, with the Rotten Tomatoes Critical Consensus including the phrase "Doesn't match up to virtually anything out there," which might be one of the harshest things ever written about movies in general. Critics panned its animation and storytelling, this time with the added burden of the film being a sequel, plus a good number of negative reviews came with a tired revisit of how much the reviewer disliked the first film, too. Of course, no one really expected Pokémon movies to be critical darlings. They were made for Pokémon fans, who would surely flock to the theaters once again for this new big-screen adventure.

Which they did . . . at first. *Pokémon The Movie 2000: The Power of One* had a strong opening day in North America, only scoring 1 million less than *Mewtwo Strikes Back*. It also had the added bonus of opening on a Friday, while the first film came out on a Wednesday. Friday releases mean weekend-ready crowds, kids and families no longer hamstrung by getting up for school or work the next day, while a Wednesday tends to doom you to a few days of irrelevance among children. This time, the film wouldn't have to rely on another outbreak of the Pokéflu in order to draw a crowd. But even despite its advantages over the first film, in the end, *The Power of One* made a little over half of the previous film's domestic gross in the United States. *The First Movie's* quality as an event film had obviously not carried over to its sequel. Little did the franchise know it at the time, but this would be the first sign that they would never reach those heights again.

On TV, ratings were still good, but a concerning drop of about a million viewers happened between the first and second quarter of 2000. There were a few factors that could have played into this, ranging from kids going on summer break to an extended gap between new episodes on Kids' WB, or fans growing bored with watching Ash sail around the Orange Islands. Regardless, time would tell if this was a trend or merely a small dip before a whole new adventure began. However, Ash finally heading to the new Johto region wouldn't be the most interesting anime escapade of 2000. Instead, that honor would go to *Digimon* and a movie that is the very definition of a cult classic.

Three-for-One Deal

The most oddly inescapable song of the late nineties and early 2000s was "The Rockafeller Skank" by DJ Fatboy Slim. Usually known for its continuously repeated hook, "Right about now, the funk soul brother," it's found in the prom dance sequence from *She's All That*, the scene in *Bruce Almighty* where Jim Carrey uses his new god powers to make Jennifer Aniston orgasm in a bathroom, *American Pie*, multiple *Sex and the City* episodes, and, surprisingly, countless other places. And one of those other places is *Digimon: The Movie*.

If we're being honest, it might be surprising to hear that song in an animated film, but truly the whole soundtrack to *Digimon: The Movie* is kind of an incredible time capsule, and one that seems like an expensive licensing nightmare. However, writer and voice director Jeff Nimoy was delighted. "I couldn't believe it! I thought they were just gonna give me an original score. They got the hits of the day!" Along with the explicitly Digimon-themed songs that were introduced in the show, it has LEN's "Kids in America," Barenaked Ladies' "One Week," offerings by Less Than Jake and The Mighty Mighty Bosstones, and even a pre-*Shrek* use of "All Star." With all these memorable tracks combined with dueling digital monsters, it all feels a lot less like a film and more like a piece of pop art. And actually, it kind of is, because *Digimon: The Movie* isn't technically even a movie. Instead it's *three* films crammed into one.

Less than a year after Pokémon unleashed its first feature film on the United States, 20th Century Fox had plans to do the same with Digimon. The only problem was the fact that Digimon didn't actually have a movie to do this with. What it did have was the delightful *Digimon Adventure* short by Mamoru Hosoda, a forty-minute action epic called *Digimon Adventure: Our War Game*, also directed by Hosoda, and the long-winded *Digimon Hurricane Touchdown/Transcendent Evolution! The Golden Digimentals*. The last one had a different director, and none of the art styles in any of the films quite matched one another, but all the groups involved, from 20th Century Fox to Saban to Toei Animation, wanted a movie—and someone wanted it to include all three films.

The hurdle facing them now was that no one seemed to like the last film very much. Its pacing was pretty slow, and Saban's founder, Haim Saban, said, "It took me a week to watch that third movie last night." Regardless of whether they liked it, the team had to use it, and so Jeff Nimoy and his writing partner Bob Buchholz filled the script with copious jokes, while attempting to edit the whole thing together in a way that made it feel at least a little bit cohesive. It was a full-time job in addition to the full-time jobs they had working on the *Digimon: Digital Monsters* series, meaning that by the time the film was finally done, Nimoy was more than exhausted. "Twenty hours a day, six days a week," Nimoy recounted.

The end result was, to say the least, a bit chaotic. It includes some memorable bits of funny dialogue, and watching the various Digimon fight with fluid animation not seen in the TV series was a sight to behold. As a narrative, though, it barely gives the viewer any time to breathe. The last portion is little more than a skimming of the original product, introducing a whole new batch of kids, though ones who had been introduced a few weeks earlier on TV on *Digital Monster*'s second season. If you hadn't checked in with the show recently, the jarring leap to a new central cast was a frustrating addition. Critics latched onto this aspect, and many articles were sympathetically aimed at the parents taking their kids to see it: "Parents, if you don't want to compete with pop culture to raise your children," wrote a critic for Film.com, ". . . this is where you draw the line in the sand."

Preceded by a short featuring characters from the *Angela Anaconda* cartoon, another series from the Fox Family brand, *Digimon: The Movie* wasn't a flop and even made back its budget and then some. The blockbuster status of *Pokémon: The First Movie* eluded it, though, and a lackluster ad campaign—one that included a sweepstakes to send entrants to Hollywood, erm, I mean "Digiwood"—led to the film topping out at around $16 million. "They didn't advertise the movie," Nimoy lamented. "They didn't do it, even on *Digimon* [the show]. They didn't want to have to eat that $40,000 in advertising revenue for a thirty-second spot."

Of course, this was a true missed opportunity, because the aforementioned new set of kids that appeared in the second season—which was adapted from *Digimon Adventure 02* in Japan—would be introduced alongside older versions of the kids from the first season. This meant that audiences saw something that didn't happen too often with animated characters on American television: the effects of growing up. And that wasn't all.

Intent on exploring the relation between *Digimon* and adolescence, this new season introduced Ken Ichijouji aka the Digimon Emperor, the anime's first villainous human character. An embodiment of the kind of loneliness that's all too frequently found when you feel misunderstood as a youth, Ken is one of the best examples of *Digimon*'s poignancy.

Adventure 02 remains underrated as a sequel. The main manga series *Digimon Adventure V-Tamer 01* was solid, but never made it out of Japan. The *Digimon World* games seemed confused in their focus, with the first *Digimon World* release in America promoted with a poster that read, "CAUTION: MAY NOT BE SUITATBLE FOR PEOPLE WHO SUCK AT VIDEO GAMES," and the second game opting for a complete change in genre. The virtual pets had never been considered a truly vital piece of the franchise in America.

Thus, the anime stood alone as the best representation of Digimon's global capabilities, and it was about to go through a major change. Putting it together was putting a strain on Nimoy, who felt overburdened and stressed. He left with only four episodes remaining in the second season, though he admits he didn't handle himself as well as he could have at the time. "I was burned out. I was, like, dying," Nimoy said. "So, there's a lot of fights over creative things. I was twenty years younger, I was a hothead. I was an asshole to work with, I'm sure. I was hard to work with and I was just tired of it all."

Gold and Silver

"But ya still gotta catch 'em all, and be the best that you can be!"

This needless—and needlessly catchy—reminder is part of the lyrics to the opening theme for *Pokémon: The Johto Journeys*, the new season that would drop Ash Ketchum, Pikachu, and pals in the new region on October 14, 2000, on Kids' WB. Unlike the debut of the anime, which came three weeks before the games to provide a little teaser taste, the launches of this new entry in the *Pokémon* anime and the new set of games went hand in hand. *Pokémon Gold* and *Silver* hit store shelves the next day.

Mirroring the fleet of Pikamobiles that had been sent around the country to hype up the release of *Red* and *Blue*, Chrysler PT Cruisers overhauled to resemble Lugia, the mascot of *Silver*, were sent to perform similar duties. The color schemes and Pokémon featured on merchandise were switched up, though Tilden said that might have been a little misstep. "There were brands like Power Rangers that would come out every year with a new subtitle and toy packaging," Tilden remembers. "It didn't really work. You end up with a mix of things on the shelves and the consumer was really bought into the red, yellow, and blue branding." New packaging or not, 600,000 preorders were confirmed with two weeks left to go before release of the new games, while *Gold* and *Silver* had already sold more than 6 million copies in Japan in about six months. Six hundred thousand was a very good omen.

STAR POWER

Gold and *Silver*'s localization had been an interesting one, especially considering *Pokémon*'s status as a known commodity, rather than a plucky underdog with little brand awareness in the US. Jeff Kallas, like his friend Bill Giese, had worked as a gameplay counselor before teaming up with the *Pokémon* team, and he found it to be a fun experience with some interesting rules. For example, in *Red* and *Blue*, two of the fighting Pokémon had been named after famous movie martial artists: Hitmonchan (as in Jackie Chan) and Hitmonlee (as in Bruce Lee).

This generation would introduce a new fighting Pokémon to go with them, Hitmontop. But that wasn't the first idea for its name, as it was originallly meant to follow the action star trend with "Hitmonjet." "For Jet Li. And then someone in Legal caught on," Kallas explains. "They were more worried about people seeing the connection." And problems arising due to people finding their likeness in *Pokémon* was a very real possibility. Magician Uri Geller sued Nintendo in November 2000 over his alleged resemblance to the spoon-bending monster Kadabra, who was known as Yungerer, a play on Geller's name, in Japan. In fact, the lawsuit completely halted the creation of Kadabra trading cards for nearly twenty years.

A week after its American release, *Gold* and *Silver* gained the title of the fastest selling game of all time, an accomplishment it kept for two years until *Grand Theft Auto: Vice City* came along. Reviews were unanimously positive, and often rated the games a step above the originals. Famitsu's four-person combined score jumped from *Red* and *Green*'s 29/40 to 33/40. *Nintendo Power*, which had given *Red* and *Blue* a modest 7.2/10, championed *Gold* and *Silver* with an 8.5/10, while IGN had given the *Red Version* a perfect score and, well, that didn't change for *Gold* and *Silver*. "*Pokémon*? Still Fine" their headline might as well have read.

Were *Pokémon Gold* and *Silver* the "ultimate *Pokémon* games"? In a way, yes. Though the third version, *Crystal*, offered a player selection that would be the most inclusive step that the franchise had ever taken at that time, *Gold* and *Silver* represent the goodness of the relationship between man and Pokémon better than any other. At one point, just after visiting a farm where you help heal a sick Miltank, a cowlike Pokémon, with berries that you've collected, you're tasked with crossing the sea to get medicine for the Pokémon that powers the Olivine City Lighthouse. Of course, you do, and it is only after you've completed this task that you're allowed to fight the Olivine's gym leader.

This domino-effect video game quest—helping sick creatures that have integrated themselves into the necessary structures of the world by providing services to humans and then using the credibility earned by your generosity to nobly battle with these proud creatures—is an ultimate example of the player's role in the series as both shepherd, coach, and collector. After *Gold* and *Silver*, the debate over the clash between *Pokémon*'s themes of friendship and combat would seem old hat. The series had shown that the two could coexist and, in the case of these games, coexist beautifully.

With *Pokémon* solidifying all the things that made its tenure on the Game Boy great and *Digimon* further developing its treatise on angsty adolescence, it was time for the final major player of the era to join the show. It was time to unleash a series that, through a creator's burgeoning talents and ability to narrow in on his strengths, would break records and earn a spot in manga, anime, and trading card game history.

It was time to duel.

Chapter 9

HEART OF THE CARDS

After school one day, Yugi Muto and his pal Jonouchi head to Burger World, a fast food chain where their friend Anzu works. After Anzu reveals that she's working there to earn money for college, an escaped convict bursts in and takes her hostage. Harnessing the power of his Millennium Puzzle, Yugi becomes Dark Yugi, a taller, more confident version of himself, and challenges the convict to a game. In the Yu-Gi-Oh! universe, games are catnip for pretty much everyone, so the crook agrees to a competition where the two participants are only allowed to move one finger each. A cigarette, a lighter, and a bottle of vodka later and the convict's misstep causes him to be burned alive. He shrieks as he's engulfed in flame, and Yugi leads Anzu to safety.

The creator of this harrowing manga scene, Kazuki Takahashi, knew he had something interesting. Having freshly turned thirty-five, he was no novice, but he was also a few years removed from the "early twenties wunderkind" status that many often think of when they recall the origin stories of the most notable creators in manga. Running in the pages of *Weekly Shonen Jump*, perhaps the most famous manga anthology in the world thanks to over five decades' worth of popular titles, from 1996 to 2004, *Yu-Gi-Oh!* would end up being Takahashi's masterstroke.

By Chapter 4, in which the convict met his fiery demise, he just hadn't quite figured it out yet. Takahashi loved stories involving tense games and he had most of the major protagonists established; however, early *Yu-Gi-Oh!* included a different game every week, one that usually ends karmically and badly for whomever Yugi happens to challenge. It's an uneven but fun story, especially since readers get to watch Takahashi's art and writing become more refined on a near chapter to chapter basis.

Then Takahashi wrote Chapter 9 and introduced a card game called *Duel Monsters* and a character named Seto Kaiba. The game, a *Magic the Gathering*-esque competition based around defeating your opponent's monsters and warriors with your own, would call upon Takahashi's love of games and the fantasy genre. He, like *Pokémon*'s Satoshi Tajiri, had loved *Ultraman*'s creature-filled adventures as a child, and *Duel Monsters* and its many, many cards involved would test that devotion. Then there was the debut of Seto Kaiba, the perfect foil for little Yugi and a rich, cocky prodigy who can invent any games he wants and then beat everyone in the world at them . . . except Yugi.

Readers loved it, mailing in to *Weekly Shonen Jump* to let editors and higher-ups know that they wanted more *Duel Monsters*. Takahashi obliged and brought it back, and then, within a year, shifted the entire trajectory of the manga to focus on the constant card battles that Yugi and his pals contend with. It's honestly a great formula, combining the anxious strategy of a sports series with the explosive action and stakes of a fantasy adventure. His tale about *Duel Monsters* and the intensely passionate people who played it quickly made Takahashi extremely popular, and it kicked off a franchise that, later in the nineties, would branch off into a collectible card game and an animated TV series.

Oddly enough, the earliest incarnations of these were from the same companies that gave us *Digimon*. The first physical card game was licensed by

Bandai, publisher of the *Digimon* virtual pets, toys, and games—though the rights swiftly and solely went to entertainment developer Konami in 1999. And the first TV series was produced by Toei, the studio behind the *Digimon* anime, which covered Yugi's early stories, back when he tended to diversify his gaming interests outside of trading cards and could have reasonably been convicted for murder.

However, it was the second TV series, *Yu-Gi-Oh! Duel Monsters*, produced by Studio Gallop, that would capture the world's attention, falling much more in line with the monster-collecting shows that it would share schedules with. The premise was fairly simple: Yugi and his friends took on various challengers, most of them brandishing a themed deck of sorts—for example, Inspector Haga fills his deck with bug cards, Bandit Keith is a brash, conniving American with a ton of machines at his disposal, and Dinosaur Ryuzaki? You can put two and two together on that one. Just because the series had stepped away from Yugi's penchant for games with constant ironic punishment didn't mean that the series put aside darker subject matter. In fact, the series had a heavy emphasis on the supernatural, spiritual possession, and intricately designed dark fantasy monsters that older kids had no problem admitting their interest in.

Even though most of the drama comes from teenagers agonizing over a hand of cards or some other game, it was easy to see that the show would be a hit, one whose potential for merchandising combined with the increasing amount of anime on American television made it all but a shoo-in for localization. The only question was how soon, and what the market for its competitors would look like when it got there.

Overstock

There is no grand downfall for Pokémon, no moment of unstoppable peril that it would never come back from. Instead, if you look closely, there are certain dips and rises over time, something that it has in common with many franchises. The only difference is that Pokémon is much, much bigger, and in the dawning moments of the twenty-first century, it dwarfed nearly everything that could be compared to it. Any drop seems like a long one when it's from the top.

While *Pokémon Gold* and *Silver* eventually moved over 23 million units, sending the set into the top fifty highest selling games of all time, it was a step down from the 31 million sold by *Red*, *Green*, and *Blue*—and almost 46 million if you added *Yellow*. However, considering those astronomical numbers, the sequels could barely be considered a disappointing effort. The licensing extravaganza that Ishihara had implemented in order to raise awareness for the eventual *Gold* and *Silver* had paid off. Game Freak would not go down in history as a one-hit wonder, and with these two sets of games, instead built a foundation for the success that the franchise sees to this day.

The dip in TV ratings during the summer of 2000 did not cut the legs out from under the anime on Kids' WB, and 4Kids was able to sign hundreds of new Pokémon licensees before the year was half over. And more products meant more Pikachu face time. By September 2000, 4Kids ranked as number one on the list of *Forbes*'s fastest growing companies, a testament to their drive to get the Pokémon brand noticed by anyone with a pulse.

It was the *Pokémon Trading Card Game* where the real issue lay. Hasbro, now owners of Wizards of the Coast and thus responsible for the well-being of the card game in the West had, unfortunately, overshot their estimates. In December 2000, Hasbro announced layoffs of 750 people due to their misjudgment, with CEO Allen Hassenfeld telling CNN that while *Pokémon* cards were still on a bunch of Christmas wish lists, Hasbro had been too optimistic about their "forecast." Card prices, especially for those that were deemed extremely rare, suddenly dropped exponentially. The year 2000 had seen the release of five new trading card game expansions in the United States; then in 2001, they would dial it back to two.

PIKACHU'S JUKEBOX

One curious project that was scrapped was a pop band that would represent the Pokémon brand. Music had always been a huge part of 4Kids' approach to the franchise, and they replaced any of the anime score that they found to be ill-fitting, usually leaving in the action scene bits, and produced new pop songs that tied into the show. "We felt like what was really gonna make Pokémon work is if kids incorporated it into their lives," Grossfeld said. "And music is one of those ways. One thing that was important to me and Gail and everybody is respecting our audience. So, when we started thinking about infusing music into kids' lives, we wanted to make sure that we weren't doing music that sounded like kids' albums. So, we decided to do a pop album that sounds like music people would listen to, whether you're an adult or not. Just songs that you might want to hear on the radio."

Tracks like Jason Paige's *Pokémon* theme, the Pokérap, and other millennial classics like "What Kind of Pokémon Are You?" and "Together Forever" found their way onto the *2.B.A. Master* album, a *Pokémon* soundtrack that would sell millions of copies, become Certified Gold in the US, and top the charts for Billboard Kids Albums in 1999. Grossfeld's plan worked, and the songs sound reminiscent of the pop hits of the time—with a slight Pokémon angle, of course. When asked about the first moment that they knew Pokémon was becoming huge in the United States, both Jason Paige and Gail Tilden said that it was when they heard Pokémon music playing, over and over, on the Radio Disney station.

The album's success likely spurred Rave Music, who coordinated the music for the American localization of the anime, to attempt to put together a group that would provide more of it—a Pokémon-themed S Club 7, if you will. Sadly, the group, which was going to be called Johto after the most recent region explored in the games and anime, never kicked off their promotional tour, and then plans for them were quietly shuttered. We'll never know how a pop group dedicated solely to singing about how great Pokémon's themes are would have fared in a world dominated by Destiny's Child and NSYNC, but I guess that's what dreams are for.

Despite the blend of successes and setbacks, optimism reigned. There were more monsters, more music, more movies, and more merchandise in store—Pokémon was something that you were never actually meant to stop collecting. "It's so far from over," 4Kids' senior VP of marketing told Kidscreen near the end of 2000 in reference to the Pokémon craze. The support that 4Kids and Nintendo had shown and would continue to show the franchise would ensure that. At that time, they likely had the greatest proof possible of how much confidence they had in the brand: They brought it to life.

Pokémon Live!

Ash Ketchum and Team Rocket's leader Giovanni used to be roommates. Well, the actors that played them in *Pokémon Live!* did. Studying at the Boston Conservatory, Dominic Nolfi and Darren Dunstan were both subletting in the same apartment and were both part of the group called up to audition for a Pokémon musical. It was exciting, as it would be the first major show for both, even if they didn't exactly know what Pokémon really was.

"I was aware that it existed. I'm not sure I'd ever seen it," Dunstan remembered. "I'm sure I scrambled to try and find something somewhere but that was 2000. The internet was limited and I didn't have a smartphone. I'm not even sure I saw my character in the show until after *Pokémon Live!* existed." Nolfi, on the other hand, would enlist some help from people much more likely to be adept in Pokémon studies than two busy theater students: "I remember I called my cousins who were in middle school and they gave me the whole rundown. I had to ask 'What does Ash do? Who is Pikachu to him? What's their relationship and who are the evil people?' We did a crash course."

Nolfi would end up playing Ash, and Dunstan the evil Giovanni, with two other students from the conservatory playing Misty and Professor Oak.

"Such a great group of people," Dunstan said, remembering the show, a production that was the brainchild of Norman Grossfeld. Grossfeld met with various Broadway producers, but was unable to locate a fit that would work for *Pokémon*'s audience, and his desired time frame, until he partnered with Radio City Music Hall. Concocting a story that would lead Ash and the other characters of the show to take on Giovanni, reunite with Mewtwo, and ultimately face a MechaMew2, he wanted it to have a "true Pokémon experience from a story perspective."

Plus, with it being a musical, some of the work had already been done. "I also felt that we at that point had a really good library of some songs that could work in a musical and that we were maybe twenty-five percent of the way there already," Grossfeld said. To write the rest of the script, veteran playwright Michael Slade was hired. Slade, who passed away in late 2020, was experienced with writing family theater and had also been nominated for a Writers' Guild Award for his soap opera work. One thing he wasn't experienced with was Pokémon, a fact he lied about when contacted by Radio City. "I said 'Oh, I know all about Pokémon! Ya know, Pikachu!'" Slade told the Game Informer Show. "Fact of the matter was, other than that word, [Pikachu] that was the extent of my Pokémon knowledge."

"I don't know what drugs these people are on," Slade recalled thinking when he was sent *The First Movie* to watch for research, but despite his hesitations about the short writing and production schedule and the budget, Slade found it to be a "really cool" gig. His script, one that was approved by 4Kids and Nintendo, and implied that Ash was Giovanni's son, was filled with as many Pokémon as money would allow, ones that would be brought to life with a mixture of puppetry and little people in costume. In the latter category were Pikachu and Team Rocket's Meowth, with his voice actress, Maddie Blaustein, among others from the show, dropping by to offer her feedback. She would also voice the character in *Live!*, as would Pikachu's anime actress Ikue Ōtani, their voices dubbed over loudspeakers.

The entire show was planned to be very akin to *The Lion King*, a massively successful costume- and puppet-heavy show that had recently won copious awards. It wouldn't just be a typical performance, though. From the first previews in Albany, New York, the show was a multimedia event constructed to recall the joy of the anime in a theatrical setting, with screens above the performers and props playing clips of the show that Grossfeld had edited himself. Describing a well-received joke in which the Pokémon Snubbull appears on Ash's underwear as he jumps out of bed to start his adventure, dancing like Tom Cruise in *Risky Business*, Grossfeld said, "It's because the kids knew the character from the TV show. And they were connected to it."

Along with the videos playing edited clips, the puppets, props, and costumes all replicated elements found in the show. Of course, this meant there would be at least a problem or two, though one would end up being quite important: Ash's hair. In the show, Ash Ketchum has the spiky hair of an excitable adolescent anime protagonist, something that's much easier to pull off in a cartoon than in real life. It didn't mean that the creators of *Pokémon Live!* didn't try. The results left Nolfi with one of the most unpleasant experiences of the whole show. "The director was like 'Keep growing your hair,' so it grew and it looked kinda like Ash's hair. But when the Japanese artists came, they pictured the show, like, more cartoon-y, and the director pictured the show more real. And they were like 'Cut his hair and put a wig on him.' And I was like 'Please, no. I don't want to wear a wig. I already have to wear a hat anyway, so what's the point? Just style the back, right?' They insisted, so we tried the wig. Wig didn't work. Everyone hated the wig. So I went to a place in Tribeca and got hair weaves and these women gave me a plastic track of hair. It was the most uncomfortable, itchy, awful thing, and after the Radio City run, I just ripped them out. I said 'I'm done. I'm done. Just put the wig on me until it grows.'"

Having to match the designs of the anime combined with the hectic schedule of a stage performance made for an arduous experience. While performers like Dunstan and Nolfi, who would have his face in the *New York Times* thanks to an ad for the show, were thrilled to be touring at Radio City Music Hall at such an early point in their careers, they soon realized that acting and singing in such a production multiple times a day was no easy task. The show was around two hours and "We'd finish the show, we'd have about forty-five minutes to regroup, and on certain days we did it four times a day," Dunstan recalled. "Dominic had the heaviest lift of all. He's on stage pretty much the whole time and he's crankin' out the high notes."

Live!'s director, Luis Perez, was an experienced dancer and choreographer, and he kept a steady hand on something that could easily have spiraled into chaos. Ensuring that the curtain didn't fall on a pile of costumes and Pokémon puppet corpses was a constant battle. "Jennifer Risser, who played Pikachu, she and I would get into arguments about blocking because I had to hold her hand a lot of the time," Nolfi remembered. "We had to skip around on stage together. And she'd be like 'You're pulling too hard!' and I'd go, 'Just go where I say you go because there's pyro!' One time she got a little too close to the pyro shooting up and that was scary for the both of us."

After being kicked off with a somewhat glib *Playbill* announcement of "Move Over Rockettes!," the show toured from September 2000 to January of the next year, moving from Radio City Music Hall to arenas in Cleveland, Detroit, and Toronto, leaving kids entranced across North America. "They'd be transfixed," Nolfi recalled. "There was a show we did in Chicago, which had steps up to the stage. So kids in the front row would just wander up and their parents were dealing with other kids. At one point, a little kid was just there, looking up at me, and I held his hand and walked him down and gave him back to his mom. And then we kept on going."

Despite the best efforts of its creators, *Pokémon Live!* wasn't meant to last. A little over four months after its debut, the North American run of the tour was shut down. Versions showed up in places including Dubai and Belgium over the next year or so, but overall, it was never as much of a financial hit as intended. Grossfeld attributed the show's lack of success to Pokémon's aging fan base, one that might, by that time, be a little embarrassed to be seen watching it in a theater, away from the privacy of their Game Boy and

TV screen. Regardless, he remains proud of his efforts. "I felt like the show was better than its success."

If *Live!* had seemed like a long shot in 2001, then *Digimon* was preparing to do the exact opposite. Three seasons in, its anime would go back to basics, taking the concept of the "digital monster" and distilling it to what it had been in the first place, a battle-ready beast.

Digimon Tamed

In the final episode of *Digimon Adventure 02*, we see that the Digi-Destined have grown up . . . *way* up. In a flash-forward set twenty-five years after the events in the show, the kids who had once valiantly saved both the Digital and the Real World on multiple occasions were now adults, and some even have their own kids. Their epic story is over as they follow their respective careers and entrust the safety of the Digital World to the next generation of children. It's up to them to "follow their dreams" and "take that first step into adventure."

Where do you go from there? Well, series director Hiroyuki Kakudou had no idea. He and the creative team spent a few days after they finished work on *Adventure 02* mulling it over, but they couldn't find a satisfying next step. "I think we cleaned up so much that we didn't even leave behind the weeds," he said in an interview for a DVD box set of the *Adventure 02* season. To be fair, it was a conclusive ending, one that could even apply to real life, instructing Digi-devotees to pass on their love to new fans to come. If *Digimon* was to end there, it would be a fitting conclusion. But it wouldn't, it couldn't—*Digimon* was still far too popular, and in the wrong hands it would be all too easy to just jump into a lazy *Digimon Adventure 03*.

Enter Chiaki J. Konaka. Konaka had spent the last few years establishing a list of credits that would turn him into one of the most definitive names of the nineties. Anime like *Serial Experiments Lain*, *Devilman Lady*, *Hellsing*, and *The Big O* had become cult classics partly due to his scripting work.

He'd even penned an episode of *Digimon Adventure 02*, using his love of the works of H. P. Lovecraft to deliver a plot that was half Digimon tale and half tribute to stories like "The Shadow over Innsmouth" and "The Call of Cthulhu." With that as a precedent, allowing him to become head writer of the third *Digimon* series would make for a show that was, at the very least, conceptually interesting.

Rather than follow the example set by the previous *Digimon* seasons, Konaka returned to the franchise's blueprints with *Digimon Tamers*, setting his narrative aim on how Digimon were portrayed before the anime and even before the video games. Konaka feared that the "monster-like spirit" of the Digimon would be diminished if he simply continued with another "adventure," so he set out to "rethink what it is to be a Digimon." And this meant going back to the standard set by the virtual pets, creatures that fought first and befriended second.

Battling was a Digimon's true nature. It was how it connected with the world on a base level, and how it communicated with others. In the original *Digimon* virtual pet, there were no niceties between linked-up monsters, no emotional progress granted to their human shepherds through victory. There were simply rage, fireballs, and furious button mashing. If you worked with a Digimon through its fighting spirit, then sure, it *might* eventually trust you enough to consider you its partner. This theme would work to the benefit of Konaka's story, one full of betrayal and techno-angst. The "digital" aspect of Digimon would be explored here in further detail than the two prior series, too, calling into question their innate humanity. *Digimon Tamers*, as it would come to be titled, examined why we have relationships with Digimon at all.

If it sounds out of line with what came before it, that's because it was. A few years into the monster-collecting craze, *Tamers* was the prominent example of an onscreen dissection of the series', and to some extent the genre's, tropes and its methodology. For the most part, *Pokémon* and *Digimon* hadn't really questioned the legitimacy of the connection between man and monster, other than to say that it existed and deserved to be treated with importance. It was there and it was real, even if the monster was from a world of computer networks. *Tamers* asks us to consider the validity of it, and as such the validity of these franchises. Is it a relationship that we feel, or is it the nostalgia of childhood affinities regurgitated in techno form?

Aside from the fact that the protagonists use cards to help increase Digimon powers or help them evolve—cards designed to look like those you could buy in a store, hint *hint*—*Digimon* the series remains fairly dark. The idea of rebirth is all but done away with here as Digimon do not "respawn" as eggs when they pass away. When a supporting monster is killed, he does not return in "Circle of Digital Life" fashion. This take on digital "death" and other grittier aspects are what have transformed *Tamers* into one of the most beloved entries in the entire Digimon franchise. These were also aspects that Fox and Saban would respect and wouldn't tamper with to any extreme degree. In comparison to *Pokémon* or earlier entries of *Digimon: Digital Monsters*, *Tamers* was a dour affair.

Fox Family knew what they had on their hands here, airing promos that repeated the phrase "Game over," as if to say that the past two seasons of *Digimon* had been mere kids' stuff. They also took advantage of the recent popularity of the sci-fi film *The Matrix*, the fifth highest grossing movie of 1999, with a plot that also dealt with the conflict between the real and the digital worlds. Binary code flashed across the screen with the announcer asking ominously, "What if the game became real? What if you were the only one that could see it?" It was an obvious attempt to associate *Digimon* with how cool Neo looked when he was checking out computers, dodging those bullets in slow motion, and doing all that kung fu.

Tamers refrained from delivering the hopeful overtures about growing up that capped off both *Adventure 01* and *02*. Instead, *Tamers'* final episode closes on bittersweet ambiguousness, positing that sometimes the sadness we feel as adolescents isn't to be grown from, but rather to be carried with us. This thoughtful new direction wouldn't be able to stop the monumental change that was coming, though. *Digimon* remained Fox Kids' top show with strong, but slipping, ratings, but it was becoming clear that placing all their eggs in that basket hadn't been the best idea. In the spring of 2001, Fox

Kids' executive VP of programming and development spoke of reducing *Digimon*'s time slots and trying to find shows to complement it.

They never would. *Digimon Tamers* would be Fox Kids' last trip to the digital world, and if certain outlets were to be believed, it was about to be sundown on *Pokémon* as well.

Replacement?

"So Long, Pokémon; *Yu-Gi-Oh!* Is Coming."

A month before Warner Bros.' press release joyfully announced that the hit anime series *Yu-Gi-Oh!* had been licensed by 4Kids Entertainment and would be joining *Pokémon* on Kids' WB in the fall 2001, the *Los Angeles Times* turned it into a harbinger of doom. Its trading card game, one that had moved about 3.5 billion cards in the three years it had been around in Japan, had inspired its own sense of panic: crowds so big and unruly that the authorities were called, robberies, and anxiety among parents who weren't eager to open their wallets again so that their kids could collect an entirely new genus of creatures.

In fact, *Yu-Gi-Oh!*'s *Duel Monsters* cards had become so popular that it wasn't even the first time that the *Los Angeles Times* had opened an article by stating that it was close to bumping *Pokémon* off the throne. A little less than two years earlier, "Forget Pokémon" had kicked off an explanation as to why Yugi was to play Macduff to Pikachu's Macbeth, even at the height of Pokémania. It centered around the aforementioned unruliness—riot police were being forced to quell the extreme dissatisfaction that more than 10,000 *Yu-Gi-Oh!* fans felt about not getting the chance at some new cards at a Tokyo Dome event—and also the merchandise sales. Millions in home video and in manga volumes.

To be fair, it wasn't a totally unfounded feeling. *Yu-Gi-Oh!* would not replace *Pokémon*, but the rise of its anime and trading card game had been huge, with the latter certainly surpassing *Pokémon*'s in sales and eventually becoming the top selling trading card game in the world. The "Just how far will people go to prove they like this monster thing?" brand of news that had once been reserved for *Pokémon* was now allocated for this whole new franchise, too. The manga regularly ranked in the top ten most popular manga in *Weekly Shonen Jump*, sometimes hitting the top five, the top three, and even the number one spot. Not bad for a monster card battling series that wasn't even originally intended to be a monster card battling series.

In the grand scheme of things, *Yu-Gi-Oh!*, like *Digimon*, would serve as equal parts alternative, companion, and stepping stone for *Pokémon* as the years went on. As mentioned before, the themes of the manga and anime, and even the artwork on the cards, with some monsters looking straight out of the *Dungeons & Dragons* or *Magic: The Gathering* pantheon, skewed older. The series is chockful of possession, doomed souls, a "shadow realm," a gothic aesthetic—in fact, Takahashi based Yugi's outfit on Tim Burton's Edward Scissorhands character—and even some body horror from time to time. The body horror is best handled in the manga, as one gets the sense that Takahashi, though settled into a series about escalating duels with collectibles, still really enjoys creeping his readers out with David Cronenberg-esque panels of horror.

All these aspects of this series turned 4Kids' localization into something inherently more serious, even if the US version wasn't necessarily intended to be more mature than *Pokémon* and was subject to many of the same over-hauls that they'd brought to *Pokémon*. "We thought it was just a different audience," Grossfeld said, describing his aims for *Yu-Gi-Oh!*'s demographic. "I think the *Pokémon* card game, from my understanding at the time, was played, but it was mostly collected." Thus, *Yu-Gi-Oh!* would be for fans who were into playing competitive card games instead of just collecting; it was "more strategy driven and less about the attack or what it looked like," Grossfeld thought. "It was more of a thinking kind of game. So I didn't really see it competing with *Pokémon* at all."

In fact, according to Grossfeld, 4Kids licensed *Yu-Gi-Oh!* because they "didn't want *Yu-Gi-Oh!* competing with *Pokémon*." 4Kids' original deal with *Pokémon* and Nintendo had dictated that they couldn't get involved with another property that would have trading cards as a major aspect. However, Grossfeld, Al Khan, and 4Kids knew that *Yu-Gi-Oh!* was hot enough that it would come to the United States, sooner rather than later. Worried that a competitor would slot it at the same time as *Pokémon* on Kids' WB and ignite a rivalry, "we made a decision to go after that show," Grossfeld said, "which involved Nintendo and the *Pokémon* people to allow us to do that." Eventually, 4Kids was able to convince the parties involved that *Yu-Gi-Oh!*, and *Pokémon*, would be best served if it found a home at Kids' WB.

If pulled off correctly, *Yu-Gi-Oh!* could be a merchandising behemoth in the United States just as it had been in Japan. With *Pokémon* or *Digimon*'s card game, you're playing with a cardboard representation of a fictional creature. With *Yu-Gi-Oh!*, you could own the same deck as Yugi or Kaiba, or assemble a monster team never before seen in the show. *Yu-Gi-Oh!* was perhaps the ultimate realization of the aims of its peers, the Pokémon and Digimon toys that would allow you to carry around your favorite monster partner, the virtual pets that hinted at what it was like to take care of them. With the combined power of a *Yu-Gi-Oh!* anime and cards, one could be a player exactly like a character on the show, just without all the "chance of losing your spirit to eternal darkness" malarkey.

While this aspect was great for immersion, it presented a small issue, because the cards used in the Japanese anime of *Yu-Gi-Oh!* looked identical to the actual trading cards, a bit of synergy that's illegal in the United States. Like the hesitancy over creating a Pokémon catchphrase that would be an encouragement and not *technically* tell kids to go buy products, 4Kids would have to create a workaround so that they weren't knee-deep in accusations from the Federal Trade Commission. So one of the most painstaking aspects of the localization was redoing the card art on the show. The summoned monsters would remain intact, but the cards placed on the field or podiums or, eventually, the clunky wrist gauntlets that the duelists wield had to be redrawn so as not to be slapped down for breaching any marketing ethics.

The look of *Yu-Gi-Oh!* was set, and when it came to the sound, there would be a mix of the new and the comfortably familiar. The memorable opening theme started with Yugi shouting, "It's time to d-d-d-d-d-d-d-d-duel!" which was a "darker, cooler, hipper sounding thing that wasn't really a song," said Grossfeld, and a far cry from *Pokémon*'s original aspirational ballad. But among the cast, fans could hear the voices of *Pokémon* performers like Eric Stuart, Darren Dunstan, and Ted Lewis. In a total 180 from the goofy James and Brock, Stuart would portray the über-cocky Seto Kaiba, flexing his ability to sound like a narcissistic jerk with nearly every line of dialogue.

Dunstan had played Giovanni in *Pokémon Live!* and he got the chance to read for the role as mysterious bad guy Maximillion Pegasus because 4Kids figured, hey, if he's good at being a bad guy there, he'd probably be pretty good here. Dunstan remembers it as his first voice acting role and relished every time he said, "Yugi boy," a term full of taunting malice in the Japanese version but that would be turned into a meme thanks to Dunstan's tone in the English version. Meanwhile Lewis, fresh off Tracey Sketchit and *Pokémon Stadium*, voiced characters like Bakura and Bandit Keith. In *Yu-Gi-Oh!*, he would once again find himself shouting attack names. "They can be really exhausting, especially when they'd be like 'Do it again!' That line that you just ripped your spleen out screaming. 'Do that again.'"

As with *Pokémon*, it would be a little while after the anime was released in North America before the *Duel Monster* card game came out as well, but it didn't hurt *Yu-Gi-Oh!*'s chances. On September 29, 2001, the show aired for the first time on Kids' WB at eleven-thirty a.m., the final show in the programming block's lineup. It debuted at number one. Monsters were flying high.

Icons

The moment was important, but the NBC host's delivery was a little off, "Calling all Pokéfans. Are you ready to do what you have to do, to take what it be, take, to do what it takes to be a *Pokémon* master?" he announced as the massive Pikachu float entered the focus at the 2001 Macy's Thanksgiving Parade. Set to an instrumental of the first *Pokémon* anime theme, the NBC commentators rattled off Pikachu's résumé in obligatory fashion. Recalling Brian Williams's disaffected delivery two years earlier on the MSNBC Pokémania segment, the most passion shown is the determination to get through the opening question despite flubbing it three separate times in the span of a sentence.

The importance of Pikachu, a Japanese character, showing up in the classic lineup of American cultural iconography during the Thanksgiving Day parade supersedes any amount of indifference from the hosts. Two and a half months earlier, the events of 9/11 had rocked the country, a tragedy that had ignited a state of über-patriotism. Along with very, very temporarily thrusting President George W. Bush to the highest approval rating of any sitting president in history, it meant that any large public event to occur after would indicate a return to the status quo, a symbol of the fact that the United States and New York City were okay and ready to not just survive but thrive.

The parade is sponsored by Macy's department store chain, itself a product of a particularly American breed of success story. The holiday honors the feel-good representation of an encounter between the incoming British people and the Indigenous people, and the other characters that floated in the parade—Big Bird, Curious George, Jimmy Neutron, and the Kraft Macaroni and Cheese mascot Cheese-a-saurus Rex—were a blend of the currently marketable and the eternally recognizable. That Pikachu had been included meant that Pokémon was no longer an "other," and had gone from being accused of "invading" American culture to becoming a part of it.

Obviously, it had not been a quick evolution. Even though, in the last year, the Vatican had blessed Pokémon, stating that its intentions were good and that it had no "harmful moral side effects," it had been and still would be the bane of certain religious groups for years to come. Along with Harry Potter, it was the poster child in the late nineties and early aughts for the malicious brainwashing of children through secular media, inheriting the mantle that had once been held by Dungeons & Dragons and eighties slasher films. Whether Pokémon was something that taught kids to summon devils or betray their parents or become generally unruly differed depending on which panicked self-published pamphlet you were reading. What really mattered was that kids loved it and adults didn't always understand it, and so it was wrong.

But *Pokémon* was Americana now . . . or at least the closest thing that a little game from a handful of people in a small development studio in Japan can get to being Americana. As Pikachu floated above the streets of New York City, it wasn't an indicator of the height of Pokémon's popularity, but rather of its permeation into culture. It was now as recognizable as any lovable critter from Disney World, as any long-running figure from Western animation, and any big-name video game protagonist that had preceded it. Despite all the criticism of the franchise, some half-baked reactions and some legitimate concerns, it had outlasted any notion that it would just go away and join the globe's collection of has-been entertainment, a box filled with the likes of the Pet Rock, Beanie Babies, the Furby, and POGs.

That meant Pokémon was here to stay. The question, though, lay in exactly what capacity.

Chapter 10

AGE OF MONSTERS

By late 2001, the landscape that Pokémon inhabited had expanded drastically. In the three years since its arrival in North America, things had shifted, some due to the franchise's impact and some due to inevitable mutation in its surrounding ecosystem. Regardless of its causes, the Pokémon world had evolved, and it was becoming a little crowded.

By now, the Game Boy had been replaced by its successor, the Game Boy Advance, which had exploded onto the American market in the summer of 2001 with better graphics, more vivid colors, and the same ethos that had driven the Game Boy. Gunpei Yokoi's doctrine of "Lateral Thinking with Withered Technology" acknowledged that, yes, there would likely be more powerful machines out there, but if you were smart and creative about how you handled your tech, you'd succeed in the end. After twelve years, the rectangular block that had surpassed everyone's expectations by not going gently into that good gaming night was officially on its way out.

What wasn't on its way out were games about collecting monsters, something that had seemed so novel in the United States when *Pokémon* had introduced the concept to millions of children and was now a burgeoning genre in its own right. The latest game, *Pokémon Crystal*, would be the series' Game Boy Color swan song and the most extensive version of the adventure yet released. *Digimon World 2* also made it to North America along with another video game based on Digimon's trading card game. Not to mention that plans were in place for *Yu-Gi-Oh!*'s digital debut in the West, and *Monster Rancher* was continuing to chug along. *Jade Cocoon.* Various installments of *Shin Megami Tensei.* Monsters were everywhere you looked.

Most notable at the time, perhaps, was the resurgence of *Dragon Quest* in the United States. The iconic JRPG series had set the standard for its genre and had also been a major influence on *Pokémon.* Its fantastic fifth installment, released in 1992, introduced to the series the ability to fill your party with monsters that you'd caught and then use them later in battle. However, that game never made it to the United States, and the whole Dragon Warrior series, as it was known in America, seemingly doomed to the lack of interest that many initially thought would cripple *Pokémon.* A new game called *Dragon Warrior Monsters* changed that. Featuring a complex breeding system, an aspect that wouldn't become a part of the Pokémon universe until a year later with the release of *Gold* and *Silver, Monsters* debuted in Japan in 1998 and then in North America in 2000. Its sequel, *Dragon Warrior Monsters 2,* even came with two tradeable versions, which according to Enix developer John Laurence, "was one of the things that made . . . *Pokémon* so popular." Hot on its heels, *Dragon Quest VII,* coming off massive success in Japan, would mark the return of the main series to the US. You could collect monsters in that one, too.

During this time in the world of television, worldwide fans were catching *Pokémon, Digimon,* and *Yu-Gi-Oh!,* while fans in Japan would get to enjoy soon-to-be global exports like the underrated robot collecting and battling anime *Medarot* and *Mon Colle Knights,* a franchise based on a trading card game simply entitled *Monster Collection.* There was also the culinary-based *Fighting Foodons,* the manga *Zatch Bell!,* and *Beyblades,* a series that took the ancient idea of spinning top toys and applied monster summons to them to create a franchising goliath.

In North American theaters, kids would get to see *Pokémon 3: The Movie–Spell of the Unown*, which earned reviews that were pretty much in line with what was said previously about the first two films. However, there would be no vindication of being successful despite the naysayers and critics. The third film, and the last one to be distributed by Warner Bros., earned less than half of what its predecessor did—which, as a reminder, was also a film that had earned far less than its predecessor. In the grand scheme of anime films released in the US, it was still in the top ten, but considering the number of theaters it was screened in—wide release numbers the franchise would never come close to again—the results had to be a bit sobering.

By the year 2000, over half of the United States was actively using the internet, reflecting its rapid growth all over the world and ensuring that the people who'd once argued about Pokémon in the lunchroom could increasingly take those same thoughts online. Sites like Serebii.net, an exhaustive (and extremely useful) collection of Pokémon information, had outlasted its peers, and thanks to the tireless efforts of Joe Merrick, its hardworking webmaster, it had become a go-to site.

Merrick, who began the site as a bored student in the UK, created Serebii before the games had even been officially released there. "I just decided to do it as a hobby project and it just really snowballed from there," Merrick said. Merrick found that many sites at the time "typically ignored the Japanese audience" and put far more stock in rumors that "dominated the online world," so there was room for a site that would aim to be as accurate as possible in its Pokémon coverage. People flocked to it—when the first Game Boy Advance pair, *Ruby* and *Sapphire*, was released, fans were so hungry for information that they crashed Serebii's servers and the site was unavailable for months.

For those who liked cute monsters but could never get into Pokémon, the internet offered another popular option: Neopets. Created in 1999 and earning over 600,000 page views a day within two months of its debut,

Neopets not only provided colorful creatures but games and, eventually, seemingly endless amounts of customization. The virtual pet, which had escaped the confines of the computer with the Tamagotchi and the Digimon, had come back home. Six years later, it would be purchased by massive media conglomerate Viacom for $160 million, a number that would have been unthinkable when its two founders had just begun concocting the site as curious university students.

One of the biggest transformations of all was anime. Since *Pokémon*'s debut it had gained a vast amount of traction and a bit of notoriety in the US. Anime had existed in the US in various forms since the early sixties, and the various monster-collecting series were helping it to break out of its niche. In fact, if you ask people who grew up in the late nineties and early 2000s, a lot will probably tell you that they started watching anime on Kids' WB or Fox Kids. But others may explain that their love of anime grew because of one special programming block, one with a name that's now legendary in the North American anime community: Toonami.

Toonami

A robot figure strolls through the Ghost Planet Spaceship *Absolution*. His stride is confident, and the atmosphere of the ship around him combines futuristic science fiction with nonchalant electronic music vibes. Then he sits in his chair on the main deck and explains that his job is to watch anime with you, introducing them with the casual demeanor of a cool older brother. His name is TOM, and he is the host of the Cartoon Network programming block called Toonami—and he is about to change everything about the way that the United States watches anime.

Toonami was invented in the spring of 1997 by Sean Akins and Jason DeMarco, men who'd been tasked with creating an afternoon action cartoon block on Cartoon Network, which was owned by Warner Bros. at the time. This block was originally meant to manifest as something like Kids'

WB, just aimed at a little older demographic. And, for its first year, that's what it did, showcasing cartoons long past their heyday like *Jonny Quest* and *ThunderCats*. However, change was soon on the horizon.

Though they hadn't been asked by the network for an anime block, DeMarco and Akins had always planned on including it. "We said if you're going to talk about great action cartoons, it must include anime." So, in January 1998, it did. *Robotech* was Toonami's first acquisition, a series about starships and giant robots that was actually, and rather tragically, pieced together from three other Japanese anime. Sorry to all you mecha fans out there, but *Robotech* was mostly a stepping stone in Toonami's quest to catch the big one: DeMarco was after *Dragon Ball*.

Despite the growing interest in anime in the US, *Dragon Ball* was a risky acquisition, with a series of initial pitfalls that belied its quality as a popular franchise in Japan. It had been created by one of the most talented manga artists in history, Akira Toriyama, who also worked on the *Dragon Quest* series as a character designer, thus turning the *Dragon Quest* and *Pokémon* connection into monster-filled ouroboros. "What the heck is a role-playing game?" Toriyama recalled as his initial reaction to the job.

Despite its pedigree, *Dragon Ball* had a history of false starts. In the late eighties, production company Harmony Gold licensed *Dragon Ball* and attempted to localize it and a few of its movies. Test markets gave poor results, and the project was quickly abandoned, with the dub never to be officially released. Then in 1995, *Dragon Ball* was licensed by anime distributor Funimation, but was also swiftly cancelled thirteen episodes in due to poor ratings.

The next year, Funimation licensed the sequel, *Dragon Ball Z,* and began working with Saban Entertainment to localize the story of Goku and his many, many battles. This time they felt like they had a winner because if any anime was going to be a hit among tweens and even teenagers, it would be *Dragon Ball Z*. It was pretty much a superhero story after all: a buff, overly powerful guy saves the earth from all manner of charismatic warlords and looks cool while doing it. Replace his spiky hair with a spit curl and he'd fit right in among the heroes at DC. Once again, though, the show was cut short, this time because Saban had turned their attention elsewhere. They'd cut off the syndicating wing of their operations and devoted more resources to the Fox Kids children's programming block, which would soon be the home to *Digimon: Digital Monsters*. So, *Dragon Ball Z*, which currently sits in the pantheon of anime that have become household names in America, spent a few years stumbling around before finding a long-term home.

That home would be Toonami, airing in the fall 1998 along with another anime that had spent the mid-nineties trying to find its footing, *Sailor Moon*. "It was never packaged up and presented properly," DeMarco said of *Z*, a problem that was very applicable to *Sailor Moon* as well. Toonami aired the episodes just after school was ending, turning *Dragon Ball Z* into something to rush home for. "We also pushed it pretty hard. We advertised it heavily, and we emphasized just how fucking cool we thought it was."

It was a winning formula, giving anime a comfortable bundle "within a context that wasn't totally out of the blue, which is what it was on local cable systems where you would go from *Green Acres* to *Dragon Ball* or whatever," DeMarco said. Ratings spiked, and by the turn of the millennium, Toonami had become synonymous with anime in the United States. DeMarco, who'd grown up as an anime fan and spent his adolescence scouring TV stations, sci-fi conventions, and video rental places on the East Coast for traces of *Gaiking*, *Brave Raideen*, and *Robotech*, knew that getting potential fans to accept anime wasn't a hard task; you just had to illuminate how incredible it was.

During this era of monster-collecting shows and Toonami creating a shelter for anime, an article was published in the *Los Angeles Times* in 2001 called "Anime Hits Critical Mass," a title that's painful to read now. It featured the heads of various programming blocks, and companies discussed their takes on what made anime appealing. Donna Friedman, Kids' WB's executive vice president, who'd just two years earlier told the *New York Times* that *Pokémon* was ready for all challengers, had credited *Pokémon* with anime's burgeoning popularity in the US. Then 4Kids CEO Al Khan explained the immense localization process that went into trying to make series like *Pokémon* and *Yu-Gi-Oh!* approachable for American kids, stating that *Pokémon*'s fans likely didn't even know that it was anime. And Joel Andryc of Fox Kids mentioned the savviness of the young boys who watched it: They knew it was anime and were attracted to its style.

However, it was Dea Connick Perez, the vice president of Cartoon Network's programming, who was the most passionate in her response. "We're desperately trying not to do that," she said of the "Americanization" efforts. "I don't want to change this block to be like a toy block. I want it to be respectable." To be fair, all answers are correct; it just depends on your perspective. The huge success of heavily localized series like *Pokémon* and *Digimon* in the West was indisputable, but only Cartoon Network and Toonami's approach would stand the test of time in the minds of hard-core fans. Toonami embraced its anime-ness for all it was worth and set the standard for many of the localization efforts of today.

The creators of Toonami and others like them could tell that anime posed no threat and would only become more prominent with time. Anime conventions like Anime Expo, Katsucon, and Otakon, all founded in the early to mid-nineties, had seen an increase in attendance on a year by year basis. Companies like Right Stuf, US Renditions, and Manga Entertainment were bringing anime on home video to the US in increasing fashion. *Weekly Shonen Jump*, the manga anthology that was the source material for many Toonami series like *Dragon Ball*, *Yu Yu Hakusho*, and *Naruto*, expanded publication efforts to countries in North America and Europe during the early aughts. Magazines like *Animerica* and *Anime Insider* were on shelves, and in 1998, Justin Sevakis created Anime News Network, which over twenty years later remains the go-to site for anime news coverage in the US.

In short, anime was still something you often had to seek out, but if you wanted to, you could find it. Toonami was an integral part in introducing and fostering the love of anime for a generation of kids, just as *Pokémon* had done for many role-playing gamers and for anime. In hindsight, they wouldn't be competitors, but rather partners in taking a medium and readying it for international success in a way that few could have dreamed of.

Toonami didn't have a monster-collecting show for the first few years of its run, though they would eventually air the Nelvana dub of *Cardcaptors*, something that DeMarco regards as kind of a mistake—and that helped set it apart from places like Kids' WB and Fox Kids, which seemed all too eager to snap up anything full of friendly critters. That said, it was less of a creative stance and more of a practical, financial decision. "Back then those shows were actually considered younger-skewing than what we showed, even though in Japan it was all pitched to the same age group," DeMarco explained. "It was twofold. Those shows were considered too young for our programming department to want to go after. And because *Pokémon* blew up so big, any show that was even remotely *Pokémon*-like was getting looked at and fought over and there were bidding wars . . . and we didn't have enough money for that."

Regardless, it helped set Toonami apart, never having to worry about finding the "next *Pokémon*." Instead, DeMarco and his partners, who scoured video stores in Atlanta for untranslated *Dragon Ball* movies and other anime to see what was available or cool, often were "literally just trying to identify the shows we thought were really quality before they got snatched up by other people." Of course, Toonami would face its own highs and lows over the years—it was cancelled in 2009 due to low ratings, then revived and merged with Adult Swim in 2012—yet it would push anime's recognition in the US in a big way. In fact, one could trace its roots to the explosion of streaming services like Crunchyroll, Funimation, and Pokémon TV, the latter built solely around the fact that people around the world love it when there's easy online access to Ash Ketchum. "I'm taking you guys to the new millennium," TOM told viewers on the night he debuted as the block's host. And he couldn't have been closer to the truth.

Toonami was a revolution, but *Pokémon* would be slowly making its own changes as well, developing into the *Crystal* version. It was the final installment to grace the Game Boy and, to date, the greatest game in the series.

Crystal Clear

If you look at the first two generations of Pokémon games, each new set represents something—a new stage of development, a new position in pop culture, a new boundary being broken. *Red* and *Green* are promising but a little messy, much like their own development. *Blue*—and by extension the *Red* and *Blue* versions released outside of Japan—established a new franchise-friendly approach, with cleaned-up looks that signify a readiness for the global stage. *Yellow*, with its inclusion of virtual pet aspects, emphasis on Pikachu, and references to the anime, symbolizes *Pokémon* as not just a game but as a collection of media and ideas working as a tandem package. And then *Gold* and *Silver*, the "ultimate" games that would add so many little intricacies along with a hundred more monsters, reflects *Pokémon*'s relationship with progress. Not a complete overhaul, but like the eggs and baby Pokémon revealed as new stages in the games, a hint that there will always be more to offer, and that potential is around every corner (or inside every egg).

So, what about *Crystal*? The third version of Generation 2 was released in Japan in December of 2000 and then in North America in July the year after—as usual, Europe would have to wait a little while longer—and featured the legendary Pokémon Suicune on its box art. It was designed by Muneo Saito, the Game Freak artist and manga creator who would also draw the other two Johto legendary Pokémon, Entei and Raikou. Suicune is a majestic, doglike Water-type, seen running through the opening animation of *Crystal* and, eventually, spotted by the player throughout the region. These appearances tease the player, driving them forward and hinting at bonds between Pokémon and mankind only just being realized in the series.

Of course, the major plot points from *Gold* and *Silver* are still there: defeating the reformed Team Rocket, taking down your rival figure, who mostly exists to trash talk your training methods, defeating all the gym leaders, the Elite Four, and the mysterious Red, aka you. But it changes certain requirements, too. Now, in order to meet the legendary Pokémon from *Gold*, Ho-Oh, the player has to have captured Suicune, Entei, and Raikou, the latter two moving around the map and forcing the player to either hunt them carefully or hope for random encounters. Piggybacking off *Gold* and *Silver*'s focus on fostering the Pokémon world, *Crystal* presents something even more reverent to their unknowable magic. It is fully aware of their power as fictional beings and even as symbols.

Crystal's Johto is filled with ancient temples, some based on real ones in the city of Kyoto, Japan. This isn't a new feature; plenty of locations in *Red* and *Blue*'s Kanto region were based on actual places as well. Here, though, we find Pokémon becoming a source of spiritual strength for the characters involved, a pseudo-religion formed around these emissaries from the forests, oceans, and grasslands. Suicune is the crux of this idea, existing as an irresistibly tangible part of the world and also as myth. *Crystal* is Pokémon as the grand realization of Satoshi Tajiri's ideals, that something as simple as bug-catching can come to be an examination of how we form relationships with one another, with the natural, and with the fantastical.

By this point, though, Tajiri's role with Game Freak had changed. *Gold* and *Silver* had been his last in the series as a director and game designer. With *Crystal*, he passed over the reins to Junichi Masuda, who directed the main series games for over a decade after, while Tajiri served as executive director and then executive producer, a title that he continues to hold.

While *Crystal* remains intensely nostalgic for the perfect, childlike vision that Tajiri created, it also pushed the franchise forward. Some of these methods were necessary and would become lasting features. It was the first game to feature moving monster sprites, adding kinetic life to the *Pokémon* art as they entered battle. It was a seemingly small change, one that wouldn't be implemented again for a few more years, but it lent energy and character to the simple designs and only enhanced *Crystal*'s strong atmosphere of a place indebted to the vibrancy of the earth.

Even more important was the addition of a playable female character, available from the start, as Professor Oak asks, "Are you a boy or a girl?" As with the Game Boy editions, females had always made up a notable chunk of the *Pokémon* fan base, and now, if they wished, they could play as Kris, a trainer who also wanted to catch 'em all. It made no impact on the game aside from the fact that, now, the player's sprite had long hair, but it was a step in the right direction as an acknowledgment that the idea that video games existed to be dominated by male players and characters was an illusion. Rebecca Stone, staff writer for the video game site Twinfinite and a *Pokémon* fan since elementary school, was more than delighted. "For the first time ever, it finally felt like it was *my* journey when I named my character 'Rebecca' and it wasn't a boy's sprite," Rebecca remembered. "This type of inclusion is such a simple concept, but it meant so much to be playing as a character that better represented me, especially since this was a less common occurrence at the time."

HOT NEW RATTATA NEWS

The release of *Crystal* coincided with *Pokémon*'s first flirtation with real-world cell phones, decades before one could use them to play *Pokemon GO*. The cell phone had been introduced as an in-game feature in *Gold* and *Silver*, and the player could use it to contact certain characters, usually in order to find special items. It also allowed characters to call the player, imbuing the games with a broader sense of inner community, as well as giving Youngster Joey the chance to show off all the dope moves his Rattata has learned since you crushed his dreams about two hours earlier. Being a kid with a cell phone in a video game may have seemed like a novelty to Western kids, since in 1999, only 32 percent of Americans used one, but that was swiftly changing. In fact, the number would grow by 29 percent in 2001, and Japan's population had latched onto the technology even faster. So, in 2000, Nintendo joined forces with Konami to create Mobile21, a company dedicated to taking the Game Boy and *Pokémon* online.

Konami, the entertainment company responsible at the time for *Yu-Gi-Oh!*, aided in inventing the Mobile Adapter GB. The Game Boy line had a long history with linking attachments, and the Mobile Adapter GB was another addition, running from the side of the Game Boy Color to a real-life cell phone. While certainly paying for the data spent during play time, users could now download cool new items, get news updates, battle others, and even access otherwise restricted parts of *Crystal*. Oh, by the way, it only worked with *Crystal* at first.

It expanded to other games and to the Game Boy Advance, but still, its lifespan turned it into a Game Boy footnote, and by the end of 2002, the whole deal was shuttered. North American fans would never even know that it existed, and the only cell phone–related feature in the game was the fake one that could only hold ten numbers and was often busy with Joey's Rattata newsbreaks.

The sales of *Pokémon Crystal* painted a different picture than its outstanding quality. *Pokémon Red, Green,* and *Blue* had sold over 31 million copies, while *Yellow* had nearly hit 15 million. *Gold* and *Silver* would come close to 24 million; however, *Crystal* only hit 6.36 million units sold worldwide, and sold far better in America than it did in Japan by around 250 percent. Nintendo of America's executive vice president of sales and marketing praised its debut numbers, as *Crystal* had sold over 600,000 copies within the first two weeks of its release. Reviews were favorable across the board, but many carried a dual blend of "This again?" and "What's next?" *Pokémon Crystal* was a great game, but mostly for people who hadn't yet bought the other games. Plus, with the Game Boy Advance on the horizon, *Crystal* was unfortunately lumped into the same role that many had assigned to *Yellow,* a simple stopgap, something to bide time until the next leap in hardware.

When the game came to the original Game Boy set, it was only designed to work on the Color, which meant that Game Boy and Game Boy Pocket owners would find little use in it. And while it would be packaged in Japan and North America with a Game Boy Advance system, whether it was a good deal to buy a current generation's system with the last generation's game is anyone's guess. Hitting store shelves at the same time as the Game Boy Advance in North America sadly rendered it a relic.

In the Sprout Tower, an ancient building designed to resemble the root-like Grass Pokémon Bellsprout, one of the tower's "sages" prefaces their battle with you by saying, "Here we express our gratitude to honor all Pokémon." It's a line that captures the tone of *Crystal* perfectly. Building upon the foundation of the earlier games, it takes the Pokémon world past the realm of the regular interacting with the fantastical and makes it truly whole, tying the series so far together. If it was out of time, it was beautifully so.

Despite its sales being a far cry from the combined sales of the other sets of previous Pokémon games, *Crystal* was still an overachiever in the grand scheme of Game Boy games. It became the seventh best-selling of all time and the most successful Game Boy Color–exclusive game ever released in

North America. That last part is key, though: In Japan, it had to settle for the silver medal, with the top spot occupied by a *Yu-Gi-Oh!* game, one that used *Pokémon*-esque tactics to propel its record breaking to boot.

Nightmare versus Nurture

While the *Yu-Gi-Oh!* video games, much like *Digimon*, wouldn't hit the United States until at least a few months after the debut of the anime, they could be found in Japan back in 1998. And the number one game there for the Game Boy Color, selling 2.5 million copies, was the fourth in the Duel Monsters series. Each game was bundled with physical copies of promotional cards as an added bonus, but with the fourth game, *Battle of Great Duelist*, there were three different versions of the games that were sold, allowing players to buy a Yugi Deck, a Jonouchi Deck, or a Kaiba Deck. Like the different Pokémon games, each set offered a unique catalog of monsters to trade, and each of these games allowed players to play different main characters with different cards.

It was a popular marketing tactic for handhelds, especially in the Game Boy days. Obviously *Pokémon* did it, and so did *Yu-Gi-Oh!*, as well as *Medarot* and the *Digimon* games for the Game Boy and WonderSwan. It was such a popular method that when a pair of *The Legend of Zelda* games popped up for the Game Boy Color, some likely didn't know that *Oracle of Ages* and *Oracle of Seasons* were actually entirely different games. Action fans could relish *Season*'s polished gameplay and, if they were like me, be deeply frustrated by the puzzle-centric *Ages*.

However, *Duel Monsters IV* went a step further than *Pokémon*. Rather than just having different sets of monsters to trade between games, some cards could *only* be obtained in a certain game but be unusable unless traded to another. For instance, you can acquire the Winged Dragon of Ra card in the Yugi Deck, but unless you're packing the Jonouchi Deck to trade it into, its wings are clipped.

These "god cards," much like the legendary Pokémon that would play such a big role in the movies, games, and on the game box art, are tied to the greater lore of *Yu-Gi-Oh!* It's a series with plenty of backstory about Egyptian gods, pharaohs, and the "shadow games" they played, and likely a complex narrative for anyone who mostly just wanted a nice array of cards. For instance, that Millennium Puzzle that I mentioned that turns Yugi into Dark Yugi holds the spirit of the Pharoah Atem, who happens to look just like him.

Bits like this are fully fleshed out in the manga narrative, one that would be adapted in the anime. This is a fairly typical production timeline—a successful manga is pretty much a shoo-in for an anime, but it's something that *Yu-Gi-Oh!* has that neither *Pokémon* nor *Digimon* had when they launched. *Pokémon*'s main anime was loosely based on the world of the game, while the creators of *Digimon* were often free to take bits and piece from the virtual pets, games, and manga to craft the anime story. As such, the *Yu-Gi-Oh!* anime bears a sense of completeness that *Pokémon* or *Digimon* seemed to lack. You can watch it knowing that, even during its adjustments, it's at least based on *the* version, whereas *Pokémon* and *Digimon* offer totally different experiences based on whether you're playing the games, toying with the cards, watching the shows, or reading any one of the manga.

Yu-Gi-Oh! offers a different breed of participation from its monster-collecting peers, one that shuns the nurturing qualities in favor of something more self-gratifying. As mentioned in the last chapter, a strength of *Yu-Gi-Oh!*'s combined media was that players could replicate one to the next, allowing them to own and use close to the exact decks of their fictional heroes, and it was something that the series' various licensors knew as well. Two months after the anime's debut, but before the games launched in America, a Warner Bros. press release asked, "Are you ready to play like Yu-Gi?" before offering a sweepstakes for Yu-Gi-Oh! merchandise.

Aside from the fact that that's very much not how you spell Yugi's name, it does nail home the fact that any sort of wish fulfillment in *Yu-Gi-Oh!* was twofold. In *Pokémon*, no matter how cool or well designed a character is, they mostly serve as a human avatar for their team of monsters. They're an outlet so that we're not listening to monster grunts all day. In *Digimon*, the humans are a little more closely tied to their monsters, with the emotional growth of the former binding with the growth of strength of the latter. However, the humans are still, for the most part, regular kids and teens with all the foibles that come with it.

Yu-Gi-Oh!, on the other hand, was based on a *Weekly Shonen Jump* manga, an anthology full of stories of power fantasies. Everything from Goku and his Z Fighter pals in *Dragon Ball Z* to Luffy and the Straw Hat Crew in *One Piece* are based around a main guy and his pals getting stronger, wiser, and potentially able to shoot way more laser beams and do way more cool punches. *Yu-Gi-Oh!* is no different, with Yugi and his friends gaining better cards and becoming more skilled at their game of choice. By the end of the original run of *Yu-Gi-Oh!*, they are some of the best in the world, performing card combos and wielding a deck full of ridiculously ominous monsters with ease.

Yu-Gi-Oh!'s localization strategy seemed to be built on that, hoping that kids would want to become the "King of Games" like Yugi. "So, when you watch the show, the first thing you want to do is go out and buy the cards and play the games for yourself," 4Kids' Al Khan told the Bismarck *Tribune*, confident that *Yu-Gi-Oh!* was poised to conquer. 4Kids had a new franchise and Kids' WB had a hit new show. Things were looking pretty good for them.

Expanding Their Collection

Fox Kids was in its final stretch.

In early July 2001, Fox Family Worldwide was bought by Disney for $3 billion, taking it out of the hands of News Corp. and Saban. Disney's then CEO Michael Eisner was excited to have made the acquisition because it gave Disney unlimited access to Saban Entertainment's vast library, but it would also broaden their reach. The Fox Family channel would be renamed ABC Family, and there were big plans to overhaul its content over the next few years.

This move had not come out of nowhere. Even as they'd scored scattered wins, Fox Family and, more specifically, the Fox Kids block had faced consistently declining ratings as they struggled to stand up to fierce competition like Warner Bros. and Nickelodeon. A quick look at the Saturday morning block's schedule in 2001 revealed that any plans to find a show to directly complement *Digimon* or assist in carrying the block in the same way would not come to fruition in the first half of the year. The amount of *Digimon* aired had not been reduced, either, and chunks of it were now placed alongside a stream of ever-present favorites like Saban's original heavy hitter *Power Rangers*, the soon-to-be-forgotten like *Los Luchadores* and *Kong: The Animated Series*, and even one that had been shoved aside during *Digimon*'s early days on the block, *Big Guy and Rusty the Boy Robot*.

Feeling burned by its attempts at marketing shows at girls, Fox Kids settled into something specifically aimed at boys. "We like to say, 'if Bart Simpson were real,'" general manager Maureen Smith said, "'he would be our target audience.'" However, it did all feel trivial, a biding of time until something, anything, could fit in with the *Digimon* and *Power Rangers* puzzle. And while they wouldn't stop the inevitable, two series would pop up in quick succession that would at the very least click into place with *Digital Monsters*.

Mon Colle Knights and *Medabots*, the former showing up in July 2001 and the latter in September, occupy an odd, desperate spot when it comes to their presence in the United States. In terms of the monster-collecting genre, their presence is dwarfed by Pokémon, Yu-Gi-Oh!, and the rest, as these are franchises that got tremendous reach across Western media and merchandise. The *Mon Colle Knights* and *Medabots* anime are just the tip of the iceberg, and in America, it's pretty much the only part of that iceberg we got.

Mon Colle Knights was based off the *Monster Collection Trading Card Game*, a game that rivaled *Pokémon* and *Yu-Gi-Oh!* in late-nineties Japan. Originating in 1997 and amassing strong popularity with their anime-esque art—they were designed by Ryuusuke Mita, creator of the classic *Dragon Half* fantasy manga—the game was eventually spun off into a manga itself titled *Six Gates Far Away Mon Colle Knight*, named after the gates connected to the world, gates that are also connected to each monster's element. The writers of *Mon Colle Knight* were appropriate: Satoru Akahori is best known for his work writing on *Sakura Wars,* a franchise that has also never really been given a fair chance outside of Japan, and Katsumi Hasegawa would later work on the *Pokémon* adjacent monster series *Bakugan Battle Brawlers* and *Beyblade*.

The plot of *Mon Colle Knight* is simple: Two heroes are trying to find magical items and by using a spell are able to wield giant monsters for battle. Their adversary is Count Collection, who'd like the same items except, ya know, for bad guy reasons, and, like *Pokémon*'s Team Rocket, employs two goofy lackeys to (attempt to) get the job done. Each new installment usually provides a cool new monster, many of which are based on legends like dragons, Pegasus, orcs, or centaurs, while some are simply cartoon whimsy like my personal favorite, the giant who just wants to play baseball, or the nightmarish Terror Dragon with the giant eye in the middle of its mutated torso. I'm a man of varied tastes.

The show was licensed by Saban for North America in October 2000 but didn't show up on Fox Kids until almost a year later where its release schedule was mangled. Episodes were shown out of order for nearly its entire run, and while *Knights* wasn't as heavily serialized as *Digimon*, it did give the show an uneven quality that likely harmed its ability to amass a fan base, one that was necessary as Fox Kids continued to look for shows it could hang its hat on.

Faring a little better was *Medabots*, known as *Medarot* in Japan, a series that followed the monster-collecting format but with a variety of robots. Operating with different kinds of medals that complement or increase different attributes in a Medabot, the owner sends their robot into battle. It debuted in 1997 with a Game Boy game simply titled *Medarot*, and players could choose between two versions: Kabuto and Kuwagata, each named after a kind of beetle, one whose horn corresponded to the armored decorations/weapons on the cover robots' heads.

Quickly also spun into a manga series by Rin Horuma, the first *Medarot* game looks a lot like *Pokémon Red* and *Green* when the players are just walking around the world, though American audiences wouldn't know that, at least for a while. A *Medabot* game didn't hit the United States until near the end of the second season's Western broadcast in the summer of 2002. And even then, it wasn't the role-playing experience that the series was known for, but rather a platform fighting game, of which the best thing that can be said is that it's extremely colorful.

Much more memorable is the anime that was based off the video games and manga, one whose first two seasons were produced by the studio Bee Train. Established just two years before *Medarot* originally aired, Bee Train's approach stands out in the genre of anime based on monster video and card games, mainly because, at times, it looks really, really good. Crackling with intricate animation and energetic action sequences, *Medarot* had a fantastic staff to bring it to life. For example, Tensai Okamura, who had been a contributing director to the *Cowboy Bebop* movie and played numerous creative roles on *Neon Genesis Evangelion*, was head director here. He'd later go on to be head director of *Blue Exorcist*, *Wolf's Rain,* and *Darker Than Black*, all of which could attribute a chunk of their success to the visual prowess on display.

The best clashes in *Medarot* all tend to relish a dynamism that's typically absent from the early years of *Pokémon, Digimon,* and *Yu-Gi-Oh!*, most of which at the time were powered by relatively static shots of creatures shooting their attacks at one another. Though *Medarot* followed the template of young heroes standing on the sidelines and shouting orders at their monster friends in the arena, its battles are thrilling in a way that many of its peers aren't. The physical combat feels a bit more visceral, even when it's just little robot parts flying everywhere.

And though it was licensed by Nelvana, the same company that had attempted to Frankenstein together a *Pokémon* clone out of *Cardcaptor Sakura*, they did a solid job here. This is perhaps owed to the fact that it's a show that features robots fighting rather than an elementary school girl collecting cards and cooking. One of the reasons that the giant android Sentinels are such a common favorite among *X-Men* cartoons isn't just because they're famous in the comics, but because they give Wolverine and his pals something to carve up without the censors fainting. Eviscerate the earth's supply of robots and no one bats an eye, unlike in *Pokémon* and *Digimon,* which were often edited to ensure that the animalistic title monsters weren't getting pummeled *too* badly.

However, like *Mon Colle Knights, Medarot*—now *Medabots* in North America—was tossed around the Fox Kids lineup, its episodes shown out of order even after it had established a fairly firm time slot. Not that it would have mattered in the long run. Two months after *Medabots* premiered in September 2001, it was announced that the Fox Kids weekday afternoon lineup would be cancelled, with the time handed to Fox affiliates to program on their own. And that was just the first half of it.

By the start of the new year, it became clear that the Saturday morning Fox Kids block had been looking for potential buyers as well. They'd need it, as soon their mine of Saban offerings would be stripped. If Fox Kids hoped to continue, it would require an owner with a history of licensing shows and turning them into hits. And on January 18, 2002, that buyer made a deal to pay $25.3 million a year over four years and turn around the bleeding block.

4Kids bought Fox Kids.

Chapter 11

EVOLUTION

The business of Pokémon had changed.

A few months before 4Kids acquired Fox Kids with the intentions of turning around the programming block's fortunes, they entered into a five-year agreement with the Pokémon Company, gaining a 3 percent stake. This meant that they would continue to be licensors for merchandise, television, and home video outside of Asia, while also gaining a cut of the Pokémon Company's sales and turning in some of their own profits to the business as well.

It was likely a necessary move if 4Kids wished to remain a part of the franchise—the establishment of the Pokémon Company, and later Pokémon Company USA and UK, had meant that efforts were being made to bring Pokémon under one roof after Ishihara's huge, *Gold* and *Silver*-hyping licensing binge. In one instance, Wizards of the Coast, who'd served as the trading card game's publisher under Hasbro in North America, handed over the rights in the summer of 2003. The Pokémon Company eventually came to represent Pokémon around the world, swallowing up all the pieces that had been scattered during its earlier years.

Confident that Pokémon could still move merchandise with the best of them, a Pokémon Center store was opened in Rockefeller Plaza in New York City. Seated in the same building as NBC's *Today* show, this 13,000-square-foot space was devoted solely to Pokémon products, including some pieces of merch and monster giveaways that were exclusive to the location. It was a lavish operation, filled to the brim with Pokémon models and themed animatronics, while handles shaped like halves of a Poké Ball adorned its double doors. Very rarely has any franchise that originated in Japan received such a singular treatment in the US. In 2001, it was still very much acknowledged among fans that while America would get a few video games and anime products, the truly *good stuff* still remained in Japan. Considering that, a Pokémon Center in Manhattan was a miracle, albeit one with a shelf life of just a few years.

In April 2002, Warner Bros., who had distributed the first three Pokémon movies, lost their bid on the film series. Though they retained the anime on Kids' WB, Miramax Films, then still owned by the Walt Disney Company and run by the Weinstein brothers, was said to have made a $1 million deal for the fourth and fifth films with a pledge of 75 percent of the profits to the Pokémon Company. The localization of the films was still to be done by 4Kids, but Miramax would now be responsible for putting them in theaters with what they said would be a "bolder, smarter marketing concept." They would be released under the Miramax Family division, which with very few exceptions mostly served as a dumping ground for imported children's fare. Whatever better concept that Miramax was working with had not yet been hinted at.

Unfortunately, 4Kids had seen massive revenue drops at the end of 2001—apparently as large as 74 percent—thanks in part to Pokémon just not bringing in the amount of money that it used to. However, it and Yu-Gi-Oh! were still among the most popular brands in children's entertainment, and buying into the Pokémon Company would, hopefully, bring strong returns. This would mean, though, that with the acquisition of the Block Formerly Known as Fox Kids, 4Kids would have to play two fronts: Kids' WB had the rights to the *Pokémon* anime for, according to *Variety*, an indefinite amount of time, so it wasn't going anywhere. Which meant that 4Kids would effectively be producing its own competition.

Though 4Kids producing content for Kids' WB and Fox Kids, and Disney being the parent company of both Miramax and the newly purchased Fox Family Worldwide with all of Saban's output, made the world seem a little bit smaller, new ground was still being made. The Digimon brand kicked off the new year by expanding into territory that had yet to become an all-encompassing video game genre but was certainly gaining steam. And it would produce the most memorable results that this branch of the franchise had seen in years.

Digimmo

Massively Multiplayer Online Role-Playing Games (usually referred to as MMOs) would come to be one of the defining game genres of the aughts. *World of Warcraft* was a hit of unimaginable proportions, earning billions of dollars, and, by its tenth anniversary in 2014, netting over 100 million player accounts. Based on the popular *Warcraft* strategy games and with a design that was simultaneously sprawling and yet utterly approachable, its influence across pop culture rivals that of *Mario* and *Grand Theft Auto*. Memes about it would show up in *Jeopardy!* questions. The main character on the CBS sitcom *How I Met Your Mother* plays it, and characters in shows including *The Big Bang Theory*, *My Name Is Earl*, and *How to Get Away with Murder* were open fans. Though it would come to define the genre, it wasn't the first MMO.

Even before *WoW* was announced, *Digimon* would make its MMO debut. Now, admittedly, *Digimon Battle Online* didn't make the splash that *WoW* did, but it's notable for a few reasons. First, it didn't come from Japan, since Japan's development of MMOs, while existent, had always been a bit more cautious than other countries'. Eventually, they'd build a roster that included *Lifestorm*, *Phantasy Star Online*, and *Final Fantasy XI*, but for a few years, these efforts seemed minuscule in comparison to the overwhelming success of Western-produced MMOs like *Everquest*.

Instead, *Digimon Battle Online* was created by South Korean developer Move Games. MMOs had always found a home in South Korea, with many like *Nexus: The Kingdom of the Winds*, *Ragnarok Online*, and *Lineage* becoming huge hits. Unlike in North America, the social stigma around gaming as a ravenous devourer of time was never as harsh in South Korea, a country that launched its own professional e-sports association as early as 2000. Combined with the fact that the country made playing in public and around others extremely easy with internet cafes and "PC bangs," locations mostly devoted to providing you a cheap place to hang out and game, it was the perfect place to launch a Digimon MMO.

Digimon Battle Online itself isn't much to look at, though a lot of its aesthetics and even its choices in starter monsters were based around the Digimon Tamers series, and the graphics were clunky and plain. The fact that you choose four characters designed after the four leads from Tamers typically meant that every space is littered with a smattering of the same faces and outfits, which makes everything a little eerie. However, amid the chaotic application of what is effectively another variation of the "bugs on a wire" idea, there's a sense of haphazard togetherness.

Plus, the idea of role-playing as characters who were destined to meet their digital monster partners is a great match for an MMO. It supersedes any clumsiness of this first attempt to a degree. It feels cool to finally be able to live out the gratifying high points of the anime series in a way that you can't find with virtual pets or solo adventures or card games or multiplayer fighting games. You're not just among other players, but other special chosen ones with Digimon pals that reflect them. It's why on chat rooms and forums, *Digimon* has always had a vibrant online role-playing community. You're becoming immersed in something that's only limited by your own creativity, the extent of your passion for *Digimon,* and your willingness to be involved.

Even as the kinks were being worked out in presentation, it's clear that there's a match between the themes of *Digimon* and the mechanics of the MMO. And it's likely due to the rising popularity of the latter that *Digimon World 3* would base its narrative around the idea that, even in the fictional *Digimon* universe, there was a *Digimon* MMO. In a way that resembles Digimon Tamers introducing us to a reality where the *Digimon Trading Card Game* is a popular craze among kids, *Digimon World 3* exists in a place where people love to play "*Digimon Online.*" If it was in any way an attempt at cross-promotion, it was a shortsighted one (*Digimon Battle Online* would stay in South Korea alone for about another half decade), but with its story about kids getting trapped in a *Digimon* MMO and having to fight back against evil hackers, it would lead to a stable RPG experience. After the dull dungeons of *World 2*, it was a welcome cohesion.

Digimon, a franchise whose emotional core is built around the relationships we form with the unreal and how they can become so important as to rival any flesh-and-blood ties, obviously had its eyes on the future. By using MMOs as a cultural touchstone, it signifies an understanding of trends, even if there's some hesitancy to fully latch onto them. Released in North America in June 2002, a full month before Japan, *World 3* was the final *Digimon* effort on the original PlayStation. But, rather than burst onto the next era of game consoles, a few years would go by until anywhere but Japan received another *Digimon* RPG.

This wasn't the only part of the franchise to slow down. The 2002 Toei Summer Anime Fair had been a disaster, making less than half of what the Spring Fair had. Used to promote its offering of animated series and typically showcasing various anime films based on its properties, the Toei fair had been highlighted for over a decade by series like *Dragon Ball*, *Dr. Slump, Sailor Moon,* and in the last few years, *Digimon*. The fairs were held on breaks from the Japanese school year, meaning that they were a great way to gauge which series were running particularly hot with kids. And in the Spring Fair, they'd shown the Tamers film *Runaway Locomon*, which had been fairly successful.

The same could not be said for *Island of Lost Digimon*, the first and only film based on the fourth *Digimon* anime series, *Digimon Frontier*. *Tamers* had been a more solemn, introspective take on the Digimon material, but *Frontier* turned the franchise on its head. In it, the main group of children use "Spirit Evolution" in order to merge and become Digimon themselves. As such, the immediate evolutions are very humanlike, resembling people in elaborate Digimon armor cosplay more than the reptiles, robots, and beasts that made up the previous groups of monsters. It was an interesting approach, one overseen by returning *Tamers* director Yukio Kaizawa. Chiaki J. Konaka, *Tamers*' head writer, did not return for *Frontier*, instead being replaced by longtime anime journeyman Sukehiro Tomita, whose approach to this revamp was perfunctory.

Frontier had only been running for two months when the fair was held. Much like people's tepid responses to the last part of *Digimon: The Movie*, which had featured new anime characters that were unfamiliar to audiences, perhaps they simply had not been given enough time to care. Or perhaps there simply wasn't enough of an audience to care in the first place, as the proportion of *Frontier*'s episodes that would crack the top ten charts in Japan would only be 14 percent, a disappointing number considering the original *Adventure* had nearly 80 percent and even *Tamers* had a modest 58.8 percent. *Frontier* remains a fairly underrated series, though even director Kaizawa admitted in an interview that in the fourth year of *Digimon*'s anime run, "they didn't do well."

Regardless, the fair where *Digimon Frontier* would make its cinematic debut was the final Toei Anime Fair. *Frontier* would also be the first series to make its Western debut outside of Fox Kids, but we'll get to that in a bit. While *Digimon* was still on the block, they would continue a two-year tradition that mixed Fox's love of sports broadcasting with Fox Kids' love of constant Digimon programming. Hosted by an NFL legend and pitting groups of cartoon children against one another in a way that can best be described as "terrifically arbitrary," it was the Digi-Bowl.

The Big Game

Terry Bradshaw was a quarterback for the Pittsburgh Steelers for fourteen seasons and won four Super Bowl titles. He's a member of the Pro Football Hall of Fame and, post-retirement, quickly moved on to becoming a commentator on CBS. As Fox acquired the rights for NFL broadcasts, Bradshaw moved to their pregame show *Fox NFL Sunday,* where he remains a fixture to this day, blending his massive grin and football knowledge with a kind of "aw shucks" charisma. His greatest achievement, though, is unanimously agreed to be his role as the host of Fox Kids' Digi-Bowl in 2001 and 2002.

Kicked off with the blaring brass of the *NFL on Fox* theme, the Digi-Bowl ran for just two years, though it was a strange delight each time. It's uncertain who it was for. Nine-year-olds watching *Digimon* probably didn't have any strong ties to Bradshaw's status or sports legacy, and football fans likely weren't too inclined to tune in to short, competition-themed segments based around a series that pop culture usually considered *Pokémon*'s second cousin. It wasn't cross-promotion as much as it was Fox's ludicrous attempt at a branding Venn diagram.

Bradshaw, alone in the Fox studio, interacted with various members of the animated cast, who, through looped lip flap movements and voice-over, did most of the *Digimon* info heavy lifting. Credit goes to Bradshaw, though: While many *Pokémon* segments involving media personalities often included at least a hint of puzzled timidity, Bradshaw went all in. "Super Bowls? They come and go! But the Digi-Bowl? Now *that's* exciting stuff!" he shouted to kick off the 2001 edition.

The duels were between the cast of the current season of *Digital Monsters* and the one previous, with points administered due to attacks landed in the episodes shown. Between every episode, Bradshaw names his Most

Valuable Digimon ("Ah-Goo-Mon. Love that pepper breath, baby!") and offers analysis like "That Mega-Myotismon is meaner than John Randle!" "Mega-Myotismon," by the way, isn't the name of the actual Digimon on the show, nor is it the name of any Digimon at all, but it doesn't really matter at this point.

When we discuss why *Digimon* didn't succeed in the same way as *Pokémon* in North America, we often blame it on kids, the target audience for both. While it's true that too much of one thing can saturate a market, children are not blind in the things they gravitate to. *Digimon* wasn't drowned out by *Pokémon*, nor were kids likely confused by the pair. Ask a kid to tell you the names of all the DC and Marvel superheroes or what Nintendo series each character from *Super Smash Bros.* comes from, and you'll discover that it was entirely possible to keep up with both *Digimon* and *Pokémon*.

Instead, what *Digimon* lacked was a coherent branding ethos, the "Gotta catch 'em all!" that would lead consumers from one bit to another. The marketing for the games was entirely different from how the cards or the anime or the virtual pets were presented. And though things like the Digi-Bowl are fun in that they seem like nostalgic hallucinations, they do not drive to introduce anything outside of themselves. So, when fans recall *Digimon* and its impact in the West, they typically have memories of the anime, not just because it's actually a solid show that provided a good gateway to serialized anime storytelling, but because it existed alone for many.

The final months of Fox Kids would be unassuming. The third season of *Digimon: Digital Monsters*—this was the "Tamers" season—concluded in June 2002, and its message of growing up and moving on without very much handholding about future promise was a pretty apt metaphor for the block itself. On September 7, Fox Kids aired for the last time, coming just a day short of a twelve-year lifespan. The final show broadcast was a rerun of *Mon Colle Knights*.

The next weekend, over the 4Kids logo, viewers who tuned in heard, "And now, from the producers of *Yu-Gi-Oh!* and *Pokémon*, it's FoxBox! Get set for an all new way to watch TV!" Neither of those shows would be airing, but hopefully they provided name value and a reason to stick around with an entirely new schedule. Meanwhile, the Digital Monsters would need rehoming.

Card Tricks

"Psssh, it's bigger than *Pokémon*."

In a segment for CBC Edmonton news, a hobby shop employee offers his opinion on *Yu-Gi-Oh!*'s success. The card game, introduced in North America in March 2002, had already become top dog by the summer, and reports about it seem incredibly familiar—parents relaying gentle confusion and children passionately explaining their new obsession. In front of the employee are full boxes of *Pokémon* cards, labeled "25 cents or 10 for $1." Their positioning is suspect, but the way *Pokémon* is framed—just as baseball and other sports cards were handled in 1999 when kids flocked past them for the chance at unwrapping a holographic Charizard—tells a story, one about an upheaval in the world of trading cards and the monster economy.

It was hard not to see it that way. The year 2002 was the first without a new *Pokémon* game hitting shelves in North America in four years. There would be three new sets of the trading cards released, with one of them, a "Legendary Collection," simply offering reprints of older cards and adorned with packaging and a name that seemed to imply that perhaps the Golden Age of Pokémon was long behind us. For the first time since its debut in the United States, the anime stood alone as the figurehead of the operation. Luckily, it was still the shining star of the Kids' WB lineup.

Yu-Gi-Oh!'s presence was extremely sizable, though. 4Kids and Mattel had wrapped up 2001 by signing a deal to produce toys and other products based on the series. It wasn't the only license that the toy giant Mattel acquired around the time—in July 2002, they also joined with Warner Bros. and gained the rights to sell toys based on characters like Batman, Superman, and the Looney Tunes. But no doubt Mattel saw promise in

Yu-Gi-Oh! similar to what Hasbro had seen with Pokémon merchandise a few years prior. As for the trading card game, distribution for that would be handled in North America by Upper Deck, a company that, at that point, had primarily been concerned with the production of sports cards. In little time, *Yu-Gi-Oh!* would outdo all of them.

Between April and June of 2002, sales reached $17 million, with two starter decks themed after Yugi and Kaiba's decks, of course, and an expansion pack named after the Blue Eyes White Dragon. This behemoth was one of the closest things that Yu-Gi-Oh! had to a Pikachu figure when it came to a character that symbolized the franchise's preferred aesthetics and could be printed on everything from a t-shirt to school supplies. Unlike Pikachu, though, the Blue Eyes was a gigantic, laser-spitting monster owned by a gloating industrialist. Though, depending on how you feel about Pokémon's franchising, Pikachu might be that to you, too.

While *Yu-Gi-Oh!* didn't have a *Pokémon Red* and *Blue*, it did release two games in the United States launching almost simultaneously on different platforms. Those with a Game Boy Color could enjoy *Yu-Gi-Oh! Dark Duel Stories* on March 18, 2002, the third in the Duel Monsters line and a blockbuster success in Japan. Meanwhile on March 20, PlayStation owners could pop in *Yu-Gi-Oh! Forbidden Memories*, which took place, for the most part, in ancient Egypt with you playing as Atem, the Yugi-looking pharaoh.

Sadly, neither was very good, though *Dark Duel Stories* is the better way to enjoy what makes *Yu-Gi-Oh!* so popular if you don't feel like rummaging around in the hobby aisle of a Target for cards. They come off as ungainly alternatives to the physical thing. *Pokémon Red* and *Blue*, despite their flaws, had an instantly addictive quality, one that drew you in and left you, as Elizabeth M. Hollinger, author of the *Red* and *Blue* strategy guide for Prima, wrote, "playing this game everywhere and anywhere, from my bedroom in the wee hours of the morning to the checkout line at my local grocery store."

Through it all, news of *Yu-Gi-Oh!* cards being banned at schools thanks to the actions of bedeviled children was relatively uncommon. Whether publishers had exhausted their will to turn every confiscated deck into a headline or they just realized that maybe it wasn't that big of a deal in the first place is unknown. Whatever anxieties that *Pokémon* had awakened, the old-rooted nightmares of eighties economic competition with Japan, religious qualms, and simple annoyances that your kid wouldn't be quiet about Charmander, Bulbasaur, and Squirtle, had been at least partly tempered for *Yu-Gi-Oh! 60 Minutes Australia* had run a nearly fifteen-minute segment pondering *Pokémon's* grip on the childhood psyche with lines like "Look in almost any Australian backyard and you'll see our kids have been captured . . . *by monsters.*"

Yu-Gi-Oh! was not granted the same trading card trumpet of the apocalypse. But it did herald something new for Kids' WB. *Yu-Gi-Oh!* had a formula, one that kept kids coming back episode to episode, week to week: multi-installment fights. It's a staple of battle anime, a constant series of power-ups, cliffhangers, and moments of near defeat until the good guy finally reaches a point where he can vanquish the bad guy. Fans of Toonami were already acquainted with this: Goku's climactic battle with the intergalactic conqueror Frieza in *Dragon Ball Z*, an animated battle with scale and intensity so grand that the likes of it had never been seen on American television, lasts around a dozen episodes. Sure, you get recaps aplenty, but missing an episode means missing the cool move that all your friends will talk about the next day.

Pokémon didn't really have a ton of multi-episode battles in this period. Aside from two-parters during important matches, cliffhangers were fairly rare, meaning that the episode where Ash started his contest with a gym leader was usually the episode where Ash finished the contest. Though 4Kids would combine certain episodes, it was the norm for *Yu-Gi-Oh!* duels to last two episodes or more. In fact, Yugi's duel against Pegasus, the first season's arch-villain, lasts five. It's the kind of serialization that was usually considered poor planning in the creation of many Western cartoons, with executives fearing that forcing kids to keep up with a show to that extent would just drive them from it. A strictly episodic approach was also used to safeguard against production hiccups, meaning that if one episode was delayed, another could be slotted in its place without hesitancy.

Though 4Kids' localization process was indeed heavier than what was typically featured on places like Toonami, and can seem extravagant by today's standards, it's in things like this that its role in introducing kids to anime, particularly battle anime, and turning them into supporters of the medium was solidified. They weren't turned away by these long competitions but rather they relished them—that Yugi versus Pegasus duel started on September 21 on Kids' WB, and viewers would have to remain tuned in until October 5 to see the final results. It was something different, like a soap opera, but instead of betrayals, affairs, and models, it was monster combos, trap cards, and a card game expert with very tall, very spiky hair. And in a way, it was the exact opposite of what *Pokémon* seemed to be offering at the time.

The Long Road

Ash Ketchum's journey through the Johto region is a double-edged sword.

The first portion of the anime, the "Indigo League" section that takes place in Kanto, had ended with an embarrassing defeat for the trainer. It hadn't come out of nowhere, as many of Ash's major victories in Kanto weren't really victories in the traditional sense. Out of the eight gym leader battles, Ash technically only earned half of the badges through winning matches. He'd receive the others through some act of kindness or valor that the gym leader appreciated, usually after the gym leader's team had utterly dominated Ash's. This feeds into Pokémon's themes of battling only being a worthwhile pursuit if you're kind to your monsters and others. It also makes sense that, in a climactic tournament filled with top ranked competitors where Ash is unable to win any awards for simply being a good dude, he would find himself in over his head. This would give him room to grow.

And grow he does in Johto. All of Ash's gym badges in Johto are earned the proper way, with Ash showing a recognition for battle strategy that he barely possessed in the show's first arc. It leads to the Silver Conference and his tournament round with Gary Oak. The eternally taunting Gary had bested him at the end of the Orange Islands and had, to this point, played the part of both bully and rival, teasing Ash while also bragging about his own copious accomplishments. Ash is able to beat him here, though, serving as his final major win in the Johto region. It's a nice story, seeing as Ash and Gary had started their Pokémon journeys on the same day, grew up in the same town, and received their starter monster from the same person (Gary's grandfather, which adds a hint of nepotism to Gary's bristling character). It also turns the Kanto/Johto portions of the anime into something akin to the *Red/Blue* and *Gold/Silver* pairing: a two-part story (only this one had an actual main character instead of *you* at the center of everything).

The problem is the structure of the adventure that the character arc takes place in. Ash's journey through Kanto was relatively abbreviated, reflecting the year and a half that its production team was given to work with. As such, he really flies through some of the early game checkpoints. For instance, he got his third gym badge by the fourteenth episode, and in that span of time, only two episodes either a) Didn't take place in a recognizable video game location, or b) Didn't feature Ash Ketchum filling out his roster of Pokémon. In comparison, it took Ash forty-three episodes to do the same in Johto, with many of those episodes simply serving to showcase a "Pokémon of the week."

In anime, this is what's known as "filler," episodes that don't move the plot forward and, if excised, would not be noticed in their deletion. Filler is not automatically bad—there are plenty of episodes later on in the Indigo League that have no real impact on the overall plot but are delightful in how lively their translation of the Pokémon world is. Johto, sadly, becomes a bit of a slog to get through, a near constant cycle of meeting inconsequential new characters.

With *Gold* and *Silver* originally planned to be the final games, and their delayed release date, followed by a full three years before the next games, the anime might have had to twiddle its thumbs a bit more openly than usual. Dampening it even more is the fact that there's really no B-plot for Ash's companions. Later seasons would give the group members their own goals that ran alongside Ash's quest to be the best. Here, Misty and Brock often feel more like sidekicks than friends, there mostly to react to whatever Ash is doing or feeling at the time.

It was a weird period for the anime, and this feeling carried over into the movies. Miramax and the Weinsteins' promise to give Pokémon films a "bold, smarter marketing concept" didn't carry over into action. Instead, the wide release seen for the first three films was whittled down for the fourth (the third movie was shown on nearly 2,700 screens; *Pokémon 4Ever: Celebi—Voice of the Forest* wouldn't even get 250), with its box office reflecting this downgrade: *4Ever* earned less than $2 million theatrically in the United States, with the film's aims being mostly set for home video.

It's a shame, because for fans of the series, *4Ever* offers quite a bit to chew on. It inserts Ash's goofy mentor Professor Samuel Oak into the mix, with a main character revealed to be Sam from the past, thrown into the present thanks to some well-meaning time travel courtesy of the titular Celebi. The villain is the Iron Masked Marauder, a character with little depth who simply wants to overthrow Team Rocket and make himself boss, but the environmental themes of the story resemble something a little more akin to the work of famed anime director Hayao Miyazaki.

Miyazaki is the founder of Studio Ghibli and the man behind classics including *Princess Mononoke* (a film that was distributed by Miramax, the localization of which found Miyazaki butting heads with the Weinsteins, to no one's surprise) and *My Neighbor Totoro*. Ghibli was and still is perhaps the most famous anime film company in the world, and Miyazaki infuses his work with themes of the troubled connection between man and nature. These ideas are fitting for a Pokémon film, and *4Ever* concerns itself with man's ruinous impact on the earth in a way that's more direct than ever before.

In the climax, little green Celebi, regarded as a mythical spirit of the outdoors, dies in the arms of Ash and Sam. Dipping it in a lake won't work as it had before, as it's been tainted by the devastation. Even when the water is purified by the presence of Suicune (an apt fit for the film, considering its own ethereal relationship with the wild), it still won't work, and Ash even

182

tries feeding it berries, which simply dribble away from Celebi's inert form. Celebi is eventually revived thanks to other Celebi "spirits of the future and the past" coming in to save it, but just as you saw in the games these monsters are from, *Gold/Silver/Crystal*, the whole thing's emotional core lies in the depth of your connection not just with nature, but with Pokémon nature.

Like Studio Ghibli's output, *4Ever* presents the natural world as profound, outside of our understanding, but never free from our choices. It was a similarity that did not go unnoticed by critics at the time, as Ghibli's latest effort, *Spirited Away*, had just gotten an overseas release, too. And the comparisons were often far less than kind. "Thank god there's a Miyazaki film opening simultaneously," wrote the *Austin Chronicle*. "Why not just treat the little yard apes to the real deal and take them to *Spirited Away*?" asked the *Boston Globe*. *4Ever* and *Spirited Away* represented the "enormous artistic chasm" between the production of the former and the latter, according to *Variety*. And, as always, most of the publications wondered why *4Ever* existed at all. Wasn't *Pokémon* dead? Hadn't anyone gotten the memo?

Spirited Away's theatrical run in the US was initially even more limited than *Pokémon*'s (though it would gain a major increase after the film took home the Academy Award for Best Animated Film). And it's certainly a gorgeous feature, lavishly animated with a story based around certain aspects of Japanese mythology and yet delivering a poignant tale about adolescence and how we handle the responsibility that growing up thrusts at us. This isn't too remarkably different from *Pokémon*, the story of a preteen faced with leaving home and finding their destiny among monsters. But one was the latest project from the powerhouse imagination of a freshly lauded anime studio and the other was the fourth annual feature length project done by a company that was also tasked with completing fifty-two other weekly half-hour installments about the same subject.

So while not opposites thematically, they were received totally antithetically. *Pokémon 4Ever* was tired franchising, a vestige of pre-millennium toy sales. *Spirited Away* was boundary pushing, an example of where not just anime but animation as creative expression could be heading if we were lucky. The subsequent Oscar win only sealed this. "It really transformed the image of anime in the States," said historian of Japanese culture Matt Alt. "It was already a booming subculture, but that represented a real coming out for the medium and its fans."

Though the advertising was muted (it's odd to watch the preview and not hear the "Pokémon Dance Mix," a Eurobeat-sounding track that punctuated the trailers for the first three Pokémon films) and the reception condemning, *Pokémon 4Ever* did contain an interesting Pokémon first: footage specifically created for 4Kids' localization and the United States release. Previously, bits that seemed understated or perplexing could be changed through rewriting. In this way, Mewtwo in the *First Movie* was altered from a genetic experiment lashing out and questioning its own birth to an outright villain that has to be placated with a lesson about friendship.

In the fourth film, called *Celebi: A Timeless Encounter* in Japan, the realization that Sam, transported from the past, is Professor Oak is hazy and only hinted at. With the newly produced scenes, Oak basically confirms it: "True friendships can withstand the test of time. And I have a feeling that this one will. I'm sure that you and Sammy will be friends forever," Oak reminds Ash, having never actually been told Sam's name. Misty calls this fact out, providing the "Aha!" moment that puts the nudges together while essentially winking at the camera.

Overall, it was a monumental moment for anime filmmaking: an auteur and his production company garnering one of the most notable prizes in animation and being exposed to a massive global audience. The fourth in a yearly series of films about a worldwide hit franchise finding new depths to explore despite a lackluster reaction. A Western licensor editing in not just adjustments but additions to a Japanese work in order to make its storyline more palatable, providing another stepping stone toward North American companies like Netflix getting in the game of producing their own anime today. Pokémania was over, but Pokémon was *4Ever*.

Chapter 12

CATCH AND RELEASE

In the beginning, Pokémon's Hoenn region doesn't look too dissimilar from Kanto and Johto. It's got the same blend of small towns, forests, and roads, populated by people who either want to fight your team of monsters or just stop and have a chat about them. Later, the region will expand into a blend of tropical landscape and surf-ready oceans, but for the first hour or so, it's simple and perfectly manageable. Whatever promise that the late 2002 games that house this new land, *Ruby* and *Sapphire*, hold for you seems to be a familiar one, just with a visual upgrade courtesy of the Game Boy Advance hardware.

Then, as you cross a bridge, two young girls stop you, with the one standing on the right stating, "We are twins, so we battle Pokémon together." You're immediately thrown into your first double battle, a two-on-two match that not only fills up the screen with more monsters but forces you to consider twice as many potential strategies as you fight. It's one of a few new features that *Ruby* and *Sapphire* implemented, along with over a hundred new Pokémon to find and collect. It didn't flip the series on its head, but instead would install the basis for every new Pokémon game to come along with Nintendo's new pieces of hardware. There were some minor adjustments and additions here and there, but you can count on it to still be definitively and utterly *Pokémon*.

This was Junichi Masuda's first time as a solo director, a role that was well earned but did not come without its fair share of work. *Ruby* and *Sapphire* were made under different circumstances than the previous two sets, namely in that they were going to kick off *Pokémon*'s next era. *Red* and *Green* had been devised under the impression that they might be Game Freak's only shot, while *Gold* and *Silver* were created to be the grand finale, only to see that plan reversed when they were huge hits, too. Now Masuda was tasked with steering a franchise with bigger plans than just hoping that whatever they were working on at the time would pan out. He had the future to think about.

"It was a very stressful project for sure," Masuda told *Game Informer* magazine while listing the sequels that they'd already had planned at the time, like the *Diamond* and *Pearl* game, and remakes of the original games. They required more manpower, too, all efforts being taken under a specter that had loomed around the world for a few years: that *Pokémon* was dead. Masuda and Game Freak not only had to present a good game, but also "there was a huge pressure to prove people wrong." *Ruby* and *Sapphire* had to stand out as sequels, a reinvention, a comeback tour, and a loose reboot all at the same time. It was pressure that would send Masuda to the hospital for a checkup—luckily, nothing major was wrong aside from having to deliver a follow-up to a renowned game franchise—and when Computerandvideogames.com asked Masuda about his nightmares, he claimed that he and Game Freak staff tend to have nightmares that systems will break down. No doubt partly a holdover from the crash that nearly deleted everything during *Red* and *Green*'s production, a fire that Masuda had also put out.

In the end, Masuda had no reason to fear. *Ruby* and *Sapphire* were quick and massive successes, eventually leading the pack when it came to Game

Boy Advance games in general. Their sales, 16.22 million, wouldn't match *Gold/Silver*'s or *Red* and *Green* and *Blue*'s, but no other game in the series ever would. Nor did they need to. Explosive success followed by cultural irrelevance had been the fate of things like the Beanie Baby, stuff Pokémon was compared to and stuff with a trajectory many expected Pokémon to follow. This wouldn't be the case here. *Ruby* and *Sapphire* had not ushered in the next great *Pokémon* craze, but they had solidified its livelihood. Many pieces of the franchise had seen an immense rise and a dramatic fall over the last few years, but Pokémon itself was safe. And the company responsible for much of its notoriety around the world was trying to assure the same for itself.

FoxBoxing

"We're always reliant on some gatekeeper, so what can we do to mitigate that?" was what Norman Grossfeld said about 4Kids' decision to purchase the Fox Kids block. Kids' programming had changed, and what once had been extremely profitable wasn't as viable. Advertisers were fleeing local markets, the markets that had once been home to programming blocks like Kids' WB and Fox Kids. They saw bigger potential on cable and channels like Nickelodeon, which were increasingly becoming a part of kids' common entertainment diet. "It was always going to be a short-term thing. We knew that going in. Unfortunately, the deal was very expensive for us. I think we clearly overbid," Grossfeld admitted.

On the positive side, it meant that aside from having to comply with the FCC's rule that at least three hours per week had to be devoted to "informative and educational" programming, 4Kids was able to manage a full lineup of shows they felt had potential. "The shows we selected had to have one predicate, and that was success somewhere else," CEO Al Khan told Kidscreen. This meant two different things: Many of the shows had been licensed by 4Kids from Japanese studios and publishers, and they had already been a hit over there. It also implied that, like *Pokémon*, they'd had success in other mediums, meaning they were ripe for franchising. For example, *Ultraman Tiga* was the latest in the long-running Ultraman series, one that was no stranger to toys and figurines. *Ultimate Muscle* was based on a manga series and merchandise heavy. *Fighting Foodons* had video games. *Kirby* was a Nintendo mainstay and needs no real introduction.

4Kids had also begun co-producing an animated reboot of *Teenage Mutant Ninja Turtles*, one of the most recognizable kids' action brands in the world at the time. It wouldn't debut until early 2003, but its grittier take stood out among their comedy-heavy localized anime fare, and it was a ratings and critical triumph. It also fit the 4Kids trend of acquiring properties that some thought promoted violence. "Some parents believe *Teenage Mutant Ninja Turtles* encourage aggression. Others say the turtles are just harmless fun," read one *Los Angeles Times* headline from 1990, back when the turtles' animated adventures mostly consisted of clunky karate sequences and obsessive pizza eating.

Thanks to FoxBox's focus on a more coherent lineup and weeks of advertising, their debut outdid Fox Kids' final week. They also remained dedicated to counterprogramming *Pokémon* and *Yu-Gi-Oh!,* ensuring that whatever they were airing wouldn't step on their shows at Kids' WB—for example, not placing *Kirby: Right Back at Ya!* in *Pokémon*'s timeslot so as not to annoy Nintendo. But this tricky balance wouldn't be a concern for much longer. FoxBox outlived 4Kids' association with *Pokémon,* and in 2005, they sold their stake in the Pokémon Company. A few months later, most of the voice actors associated with 4Kids since the beginning had their characters recast, a controversial decision that raised the ire of fans and the actors themselves, who mused whether it was truly a creative decision or simply blind cost-cutting.

"It was a sad day for us in the studio—like saying goodbye to a dear old friend," Grossfeld said of the final wrap on their production. 4Kids had been associated with *Pokémon* for almost eight years at that point, meaning that their involvement had defined it for an entire generation of fans. The benefits and downsides of 4Kids' handlings of it remain debated to this day. On one hand, it's hard to imagine *Pokémon*'s wildfire global popularity in the late nineties without 4Kids' eagerness. The first *Pokémon* anime theme in the English dub remains a battle cry of millennial nostalgia, the voice acting seared into our brains. The commercialization presented by 4Kids and Nintendo of America rendered *Pokémon* ubiquitous, setting the standard for the Pokémon Company International's current and borderline impenetrable branding.

On the other hand, anime fandom was changing rapidly. Online discussion propagated, with access to foreign media and merchandise going from a slow trickle to a stream. 4Kids' approach to *Pokémon* had been built around the idea that it could take place anywhere, its adventures applying to any child who watched it. However, as with many anime franchises at the time, ranging from *Pokémon*'s monster-collecting peers to even things like *Dragon Ball Z*, *Gundam Wing*, and *Yu Yu Hakusho*, the growing available information about the shows' formats in Japan led to a perceptive chasm: the shows weren't simply alternate versions, but represented a true dichotomy. On one side lay the "pure" originals, on the other, the censored "Americanized" treatments. This, too, is a debate that rages on today, advancing and often mutating based on its participants.

Thanks to their ties to such an enormous franchise, 4Kids will remain the poster child of this argument for as long as it exists. They began as a licensing company and took a financial risk that could have spelled their doom. Over the next few years, they oversaw ridiculous growth, and then grappled with the nagging attitude that they were stewards of a dying brand—"Surely a form of child abuse," *the New York Post* said of *Pokémon Heroes*, the fifth film of a series that, at that point, had become an arms race for the escalating jabs of critics. Now 4Kids has entered the annals of an eternal discussion about anime, localization, and how we consume Japanese pop culture. While their role in *Pokémon* is long over, their role in how we discuss *Pokémon* sees no real end.

Final Frontier

Nowadays, Disney's purchase of things like 20th Century Fox, as well as the Star Wars and Marvel Entertainment brands, is immensely newsworthy. It delights fans who enjoy the "more of the stuff you loved as a kid, all the time" approach of the company, but raises the concerns that having a monopoly on the largest film franchises in history is the antithesis of what makes good business and good creative storytelling. Twenty years ago, though, the acquisition of something like *Digimon* raised far fewer eyebrows, partly because, even though Disney now owned both Fox Family Worldwide and Saban Entertainment, not much seemed to have changed.

The part dedicated to localizing *Digimon* was renamed Sensation Animation, and the change occurred midway through the third season. Saban Entertainment itself would be renamed BVS Entertainment, Inc. *Digimon* had begun to air on ABC Family in late 2001, Disney's renamed Fox Family Channel. In late 2002, it would also move to UPN, which aired a Disney programming block. However, that's all fairly trivial stuff, the monotonous checklist of name changes that typically accompany any large company sale.

The final season of *Digimon: Digital Monsters*, known as *Digimon Frontier* in Japan, received no big overhaul now that it was owned by the most well-known purveyor of kids entertainment in the world—excess violence, hints of sexuality, all the things that had been altered when it was a part of the Fox Kids lineup, were consistently excised here, too.

In fact, the biggest change came with *Digimon* finally getting a new theme song. *Tamers* had *technically* received a new one, this one laced with more prominent guitar to accentuate its new, edgier nature. But these, like the *Yu-Gi-Oh!* theme, had been more chants than anything, copious reminders of the name and the fact that *Digimon* "are the champions." Seeing that "Champion" is a stage that *Digimon* can evolve into, it was something that could be used as both a theme song and a sales jingle.

Frontier, on the other hand, had a ballad arranged for it, one that kind of sounds like it was modeled after the work of the band Toto, famous for their 1982 mega hit "Africa." "Look to the past, as we head for the future" and "with faith in ourselves, and trust in each other" are just two of the lines dropped into the closest thing that *Digimon*'s American releases would get to the original *Pokémon* theme song. It was applicable to any brave adventure among friends, even when taken outside of the context of Digital Monsters, and it remains a high point of an extremely weird show.

As mentioned, the Digi-Destined in this case fuse with spirits to "Spirit Evolve" and become Digimon themselves. For the most part, this renders all the evolutions to look at least vaguely humanoid, but it also means that the impact of the emotional growth is lessened. *Digimon*, until this point, had been centered around the threads of humanity that tie the real and unreal together. As such, moments of personal triumph are shared by the person and their monster companions alike. One helps the other embrace their hidden, innate strengths, fortifying a theme of union.

It's something that any kid that grew up making their first friends online around that time could identify with. The people you chatted and hung out with over the internet might have just seemed like glorified pen pals to older generations, parents, and clueless bullies, but to you, they were as authentic as flesh and blood. By not having these kinds of affiliations, visually represented by a young kid and their monster, but instead merging the two, you wind up with something that rings a little hollower within the scope of the series. The final episode ends with the kids returning to the Real World at the same point in time when they'd left, and though they do affirm their friendships and the traits that they've improved thanks to taking down villains, it loses the wistfulness that made the first three seasons so effective.

There is no accompanying goodbye, no worry that going back to normal life will mean losing out on something held dear—that conclusion of summer vacation moment as the clock ticks toward the first day of school. *Digimon Adventure* ends with this, the kids waving goodbye to their monster pals, unsure if they'll meet again, but sure of the nurturing effect they have all had on one another. *Frontier*, on the other hand, opts for simply recognizing that everyone got better and became friends while in the Digital World, and will probably do pretty well going forward. It lacks the sentimental nuance of the first three series, which allowed you to parse your own ties to *Digimon*. Are they affectionately viable fictional characters, well-made toys meant to be shipped out at the first sign of a child's interest, symbols for the way we bond in a world increasingly driven by technology and the "unnatural," or a mix of all three?

Frontier would be Digimon's final bow before an extended hiatus. Enthusiasm for the franchise had waned, meaning that the brand, as a whole, would see breaks of various lengths. It wouldn't be until 2006 that another anime series was released, while the main world series of video games didn't return until 2005, with the titles released until then being a mix of fighting games and, bizarrely enough, a racing game for the Game Boy Advance. *Digimon Racing* (2004) isn't very good, but if you played *Mario Kart: Super Circuit* and thought to yourself, "Needs more arbitrary fireball-shooting dragons," then I imagine you'll find a few minutes of deeply singular bliss.

Despite its distinct voice and narrative, *Digimon* never really proved the people that accused it of being a *Pokémon* clone wrong. Then again, they likely wouldn't have cared to see the evidence anyway. For its fans, though, it provided something different to latch onto, an anime that seemed to understand that growing up was intrinsically hard and that others might not understand the importance of the friendships you make, but you do. It was inspiring in that way.

Maddie C., who would later become a popular internet artist and move to Japan to teach English, found some of the seeds of her interest with anime and Japanese culture in *Digimon*. "It's hard to put into words how much this series means to me when it's been a part of my life for this long and continues to be my favorite anime to this day," Maddie said. "But *Digimon* to me will always be this charming, shockingly deep experience. It's also the home to Kari Kamiya, the character in media I relate to the most, a character who shows that sensitivity and thoughtfulness can be an incredible strength."

The games were quirky and channeled a kind of niche enchantment that made them easy to obsess over. The digital pets, the ones sprung from their older Tamagotchi sibling, built their own storylines and networks out of something that was, on the surface, fairly elementary. *Digimon* wasn't perfect, but its intricacies helped it feel tailor-made for whoever was interacting with it. You were a Digi-Destined.

Pokémon in Court

Despite the trading cards not being as prominent as they had been just three years ago, a new set of *Pokémon* video games could mean another chance to appeal. Newly added monsters attracted older fans looking to keep their collections up to date and fresh fans who wanted to find an entry point into the game, so Wizards of the Coast was eager to produce and distribute them. They'd been at the front of the operation since the cards first hit North America in early 1999 and along with things like *Magic: The Gathering*, they had become a vital part of the company. This time, though, the Pokémon Company USA said no.

The 2003 card releases to coincide with *Ruby* and *Sapphire* would not be handled by WotC. Chuck Huebner, WotC CEO at the time, released the news on the Wizards website, directing the announcement to "Loyal Pokémon Players," and adding a seeming tinge of resentment. "We felt our proposal was fair and appropriate based on what we knew the property to be worth through first-hand experience," Huebner explained, later mentioning the "nearly ten billion cards sold globally" to affirm the company's expertise in these matters.

WotC's handling of *Pokémon* had proven lucrative, especially in the early years, which saw *Pokémon* card sales skyrocketing past anyone's expectations. However, it seemed like it wasn't just sales, but the relationship between Wizards and the Pokémon Company that had declined. The year prior had seen numerous employees head over to the Pokémon Company USA, or at least that's what WotC's lawsuit argued. Among them were a vice president of marketing, a senior vice president who was involved in card games that weren't *Magic: The Gathering*, a designer, and an art director, adding steam to their claims that not only had there been "patent infringement," but a "misappropriation of trade secrets" that had allegedly undermined a non-disclosure agreement.

Nintendo of America had stated months earlier that it would be moving forward to oversee distribution of the trading cards, and cards were already being distributed shortly before the suit was filed. Meanwhile, WotC felt that there had been a major breach of contract, one that was framed as a sort of artistic robbery. Making matters murkier, in the late nineties, WotC had received the patent for "Trading card game method of play." Its broad description sounds like a way to keep a hold on *Magic: The Gathering* and to protect them from anyone trying to duplicate that game's specifics. Considering that the *Pokémon TCG* has some very *Magic*-esque aspects, one could see where a patent like this could be used for some leverage. Online discussions flourished: Did Wizards somehow own the rights to trading card games in general? How had *that* happened?

This was no grand breakdown of what had seemed like a well-oiled machine, though. Despite the hints that there was a *Pokémon* versus *Pokémon* brawl in the works, the companies would settle out of court before the end of the year. Like 4Kids, though, WotC's effect on *Pokémon* is far from over. In early 2021, a combination of social media influencer interest and auction attention gave the trading card game a massive second wind in North America. The Charizard that had been the most requested Christmas gift in 1999 was once again making headlines, with one being sold for $800,000. Videos emerged of men rushing into department stores and cramming into tiny aisles, mosh pit style, to fill up their arms, baskets, and carts with *Pokémon* cards. Target had to stop selling them for a bit to cut down on the chaos. News reports broke of scalping, phony card fraud, and emotions running high. *Pokémon* cards were back, all right.

All Caught Up

In *Pokémon*'s English dub, Ash, Misty, and Brock had been companions since September 1998. If you had begun first grade that fall, then you would have found yourself entering sixth grade by the time they split apart in October 2003. You would have potentially gone to middle school, leaving behind some of the friends that you'd known for five years. Your interests would likely have changed or at least evolved; you may have moved, you might have become an older sibling, and you might have even experienced the loss of a family member. Then, that autumn, when Ash, Misty, and Brock hit a crossroads and each went off to meet some new challenge or adventure alone, you may have been sitting in a new, unfamiliar school, surrounded by new, unfamiliar people, wondering how exactly you were going to be able to handle the changes that life had dealt you.

Luckily Ash Ketchum had your back.

"Gotta Catch Ya Later" is the penultimate episode of the original series, the one that spans from the beginning of Kanto to, well, the beginning of Kanto again. After traveling through there, surfing the Orange Islands, and roaming through Johto, the trio of friends and Pikachu find themselves back in Viridian City. It's the first new city that Ash Ketchum visited in the second episode of the show, the one where Misty joined him, the one where he initially faced Team Rocket, and the one where he'd made a call back to his mom, telling her how unexpectedly rough his journey had been so far.

Now, he was there again after so many years—or maybe a single year by the anime's timeline. Keeping Ash Ketchum around ten years old means that any attempt to figure out how time passes in the *Pokémon* anime universe is painfully futile—each is compelled to head their own way. Misty jumps back into the role of gym leader due to her flighty sisters, while Brock is asked to come home by his father. And Ash, of course, is drawn to new lands, new Pokémon, and new video game–adjacent stories.

There are sad little touches about the group splitting up, mostly because Misty and Brock both view Ash as someone who is still growing up. "Just keep on doing your best," Misty tells him, a simple remark that Ash asks the meaning of. "Well, you know, without me there?" Misty answers. It's in this simple bit of dialogue that Ash's character arc in the opening anime seasons becomes clearer. This is the story of a kid who learns to be okay on his own. His first arrival in Viridian City was marked by chaos, a gravely hurt Pikachu, an annoyed supporting cast, and a call home to worry if the adventure was a good idea in the first place. His final exit is serene and contemplative.

Ash Ketchum is no hero. He is not meant to rise above others, but rather to rise because of them. Brock and Misty gave him a fighting chance to be able to go out and tackle this next step in his journey on his own. Of course, he isn't alone for long. Ash meets new people to travel with, and Brock would return only a few episodes later, but, in this moment, *Pokémon* is able to tell a complete story before launching off into the next part of the franchise.

And that part would come . . . after the commercial break.

Funnily enough, the episode doesn't end with Ash running away in tears, declaring that he'll miss his pals. Halfway through, the episode cuts back to Ash waking up in his childhood home, just like he did in the first episode. He then visits Professor Oak, like he did in the first episode, and leaves all the Pokémon in his team behind, except for Pikachu, of course, so that he can have a "fresh start." He sees Ho-Oh in the sky, as he did in the first episode, an omen of a new adventure, and he receives a new Pokédex from the professor like he did in the first episode. He's given a new outfit by his mom and a cool new hat. He even runs into Gary Oak, only this time the rival is a much more humble, friendly person, a sharp contrast to the one who would write, "Gary was here! Ash is a loser!" on public signs just to piss Ketchum off.

In short, after a story that has been building since *Pokémon*'s first episode ends, the anime performs a soft reboot in less than eight minutes. It's not shocking that it happened this way, and there had even been preview episodes on Kids' WB back in March 2003, showing Ash in the new Hoenn region with the new supporting cast in order to promote the release of the

Ruby and *Sapphire* games. So, really, fans had likely known for a while that Misty and Brock were on their way out. Instead, it was just indicative of the franchise, as a whole, one that was deeply nostalgic yet kept moving constantly forward with more monsters, more characters, and more worlds to explore.

Even the title of the episode served as a sort of farewell. "Gotta Catch Ya Later" referenced "Gotta catch 'em all!," the slogan that had driven Pokémon's expansion through North America and the rest of the world since 1998. It had appeared not just commonly in the *Pokémon* anime openings—like when Ash arrived in Johto, the theme reminded us "But ya still gotta catch 'em all" as if we'd be quizzed on it later—but had been on the cover of nearly every main series game: "Gotta catch 'em all!" is slapped under the title. Early box art for *Ruby* and *Sapphire* had even featured it. But when the games finally released, they were devoid of it. It had been on the packaging of Pokémon merchandise and on the sides of trading card sets to the extent that it was almost as common to see as the name of the franchise itself. "Nintendo's ad agency did a lot of research measuring popularity of characters and franchises and offering insights," Gail Tilden remembered. "There were efforts towards bringing new players into the franchise." Younger players may find the concept of "catching them all" to be daunting and impossible if they hadn't played *Red/Blue/Yellow* and *Gold/Silver*. So, from both a marketing perspective and, really, a legal perspective, it would not be to the company's advantage to keep pushing that slogan.

The phrase was referenced and used sparingly from time to time in the coming years, but never again was it at the forefront of *Pokémon*'s marketing. That didn't stop players from trying to catch them all, though. That was too grand of an idea to give up on, a feat that required patience, obsession, and a ton of game cartridges, but resulted in a point of immense pride like few role-playing game achievements have ever granted. "Gotta catch 'em all!" is no longer on the box, but to *Pokémon* fans around the world, the millions that buy the games despite claims that at one point it was all heading to extinction, it's a call that still rings clear.

EPILOGUE

I t looks like something out of a blockbuster movie: hundreds, maybe thou- sands of teens and adults rushing forward, temporarily blind to any pos- sible danger. Some dodge cars on their way across a busy street and others abandon their vehicles entirely to join in, leaving other drivers frustratedly honking their horns behind them. The tone of the group is nothing less than thrilled, an excited mass heading to one single location for one single purpose: *Pokémon*.

But this isn't a movie, it's real life. Shortly after the July 6, 2016, launch of *Pokémon GO*, an app that in just a few years would become one of the most successful mobile games in history, all these folks have just discovered, staring down at the screens that illuminate their faces among the horde, that there is a Vaporeon in Central Park, New York City. So they hustle together, united by a franchise that many predicted would leave our cultural consciousness before the twenty-first century even kicked off. Amid the chatter, you can even hear shouts of "I GOT 'EM!"

We're not in ToPikachu, Kansas, anymore.

Now *Pokémon* thrives all around the world, with *GO* being just one of the latest outlets. It ticks off all the familiar boxes, highly addictive in nature and often the subject of controversy. A nineteen-year-old girl found a dead body while playing it; then there were the two men who fell from a cliff while immersed in it. Robbers used its geolocation features to find potential victims and the US Holocaust Museum had to make a statement telling players to refrain from playing it when visiting. When acclaimed German film director Werner Herzog was asked about it by The Verge, even the indomitable auteur is curious: "When two persons in search of Pokémon clash at the corner of Sunset and San Vicente, is there violence? Is there murder? . . . Do they bite each other's hands? Do they punch each other?"

All this happened within the *first two months* of *GO*'s release, and while the initial rush has been tamed, interest remains sprawling—in fact in 2020, it would have its most profitable year ever. *Pokémon*, as a whole, is lucrative: One of latest sets of new games, *Sword* and *Shield*, have sold more units than any other since *Red* and *Blue*; the anime can currently be found on Netflix in dozens of countries; and the trading card game saw a massive resurgence, one that has managed to both titillate and frustrate collectors. *Pokémon* celebrated its twenty-fifth anniversary on February 27, 2021, a day headlined by a virtual concert with popular rapper Post Malone. A CGI avatar of the musician sang among various 3D Pokémon animations, something that might seem weird if, years earlier, *Pokémon* hadn't launched various commercials showing real people interacting with the cartoonish monsters as if they occupied the same physical space. "We all live in a Pokémon world," of course.

The people behind its global efforts have changed, too. They're now old enough to have grown up as fans, which means they bring a sense of familiarity and nostalgia to their efforts, even as they break new ground. Dan Hernandez and Benji Samit, who worked on the screenplay for 2019's *Detective Pikachu*, the first live action Pokémon movie, were in high school when the series debuted in North America. "It was not something that we were like 'Oh no, this is for nerds.' We *were* the nerds," they said. And both were deeply invested in bringing the "fun, imaginative" world of *Pokémon* to life: "There were times when we were writing with a Pokédex, a book in one hand, going 'I wish there was some kind of bioluminescent mushroom . . . Oh, Morelull! Perfect!' We really tried to utilize the classics that we had been familiar with from the beginning, and then sort of synthesize that with stuff that came a little bit later."

Henry Thurlow, who at the time of this writing works for Toei, the animation studio behind *Digimon*, was inspired by *Pokémon* and eventually got to work as an animator on the show itself. "I imported the *Pokémon Silver* game when it first came out in Japan, and even though I didn't know a word of Japanese at the time, fought my way through it," Thurlow recalls. Years later, *Pokémon* would become his very first animation credit, credits he's been able to multiply with time. "I think all artists get into this profession to 'be a part of something they enjoy,' though a lot never end up actually working on the franchises they specifically love. I consider myself very fortunate to be able to have the chance to actually work on series I enjoy."

Geoff Thew, who goes by the online moniker Mother's Basement, built his career on analyzing anime series, and holds a deep love for the monster-collecting genre. "The first three seasons of *Digimon* were some of the best storytelling I'd experienced at that point in my life," Thew said of his formative anime-watching years. Growing up during *Pokémon*'s rise to prominence, he watched it change the way the West approaches anime as a whole as well. "I don't know if we'd have theatrical anime releases at this scale right now if it wasn't for the groundwork laid by *Pokémon: The First Movie*." However, Thew's true monster-collecting love lies with *Medabots*, a series he called "low-key one of the best anime of its era." Having produced a video about its amazing production staff entitled *The Most Slept-On Anime Ever*, Thew's adoration is unabashed. "Almost every show in this book is going to be better in your memories than it is to actually go back and rewatch it. *Medabots* is the exception. It's better now than it was twenty years ago."

Recently, the web series *Pokémon: Twilight Wings* amassed enormous critical success thanks to its combination of gorgeous animation and stories meant to evoke pure Pokémon bliss. "I really wanted to channel those pure, childlike feelings," director Shingo Yamashita told Pokemon.com about one of the series' battle scenes. The monsters had felt so immense to him as a child, titanic in their wonder in a way that belied the little Game Boy screens that they were seen on.

Series writer Sou Kinoshita could "never forget the thrill of going on an adventure through unfamiliar towns, forests, and mountains with Charmander and Pikachu." Like Satoshi Tajiri, he'd also searched for insects as a youth, and was elated whenever he found one like those he'd seen in his encyclopedias. "Being that type of kid, how could I not fall head over heels for *Pokémon*, where you go on an adventure filling up your Pokédex?"

Even when working outside of *Pokémon*, artists still found inspiration in it. Kevin Zuhn, creator of the surprise hit *Bugsnax*, was influenced by *Pokémon Snap* when crafting his game about catching bugs that are shaped like various foods. "It's still something we loved," Zuhn said about *Snap*, even after the development of his game moved the finished project further and further from its *Snap* roots and became a delightfully original experience. "In *Pokémon*, the idea that the monsters are unique in some way, that there's something special about each of them. It's not just collecting," Zuhn said of the genre. "Like you're not particularly compelled to collect ten rat skulls in an MMO outside of the fact that it's what you must do to continue. The uniqueness of Pokémon as individual creatures, and also Bugsnax, is what drives you to want to get them. Variety itself is extremely compelling."

Though its influence and impact is undeniable, *Pokémon* is not the only one that continues to be celebrated and loved by fans. The eight original Digi-Destined from the anime received a send-off with the film *Digimon Adventure: Last Evolution Kizuna* in 2020, a tear-jerker for all those that grew up alongside the protectors of the Digital World. In the same year, *Digimon Adventure* received the reboot treatment and was now a series that was both a nostalgic tribute and an action-packed journey that often eschewed the adolescent sentimentality of the original for borderline superhero antics. More games, cards, and virtual pets would see releases in the West, and despite its struggles with growing its audience, the excitement over these affirmed the evergreen nature of *Digimon*'s fan base's passion.

And let's not forget *Yu-Gi-Oh!*, which has a steady stream of spinoff manga and anime, card releases and games. The original series was eventually capped off with 2016's lavishly animated *The Dark Side of Dimensions* film, featuring the return of franchise creator Kazuki Takahashi as writer and was a fine send-off for characters who had also grown a little bit since the early aughts. Most impressive, perhaps, is the *Yu-Gi-Oh! Duel Links* game, which features playable characters from the series' twenty-plus-year run and, as of the end of 2020, had hosted 5 billion online duels.

None of these franchises show any signs of stopping, either. Their focus might shift, sometimes toward homage and sometimes toward reinvention, but for the time being, they remain comfortable with their place in the world and in pop culture. They are no longer indicative of fads, no longer looked at as the byproducts of fleeting trends; instead they've developed their own legacies. Their fans range from children to adults, some new and eager, and some carrying a lifetime's worth of memories.

For its twenty-fifth anniversary, the Pokémon Company released a well-edited video that took fans through eight generations of Pokémon, generations that amassed a myriad of games, TV series, toys, and nearly a thousand monsters. The hardware that *Pokémon* was played on shifted from the blocky glory of the original Game Boy to the Color, the Advance, the Nintendo DS and 3DS, and finally to the Switch, the latest Nintendo console, which can be docked and played as a home system or taken on the go. The graphics of each game improved, going from the tiny black, white, and gray monsters of 1996 to full-blown 3D models of 2021 that seem to bounce along and breathe as they wait for your order in combat. Tie-in products came and went: the voice recognition unit for the Nintendo 64's *Hey You, Pikachu!*, the card e-reader for the Game Boy Advance, the Pokéwalker that paired with *HeartGold* and *SoulSilver*, just to name a few. Ash Ketchum's wardrobe and sometimes his design changed, as did his team of Pokémon, as he traveled to new regions in search of new adventures.

There was a sense of evolution, but only on the surface. All the inner workings, all the things that made *Pokémon* appealing and defined the series, remained intact. *Pokémon* as we know it in 2022 is very much *Pokémon* as we knew it in 1996. The way we see it has changed and so has the world around it, but that feeling, the one that begins when you find yourself in the childhood bedroom of your virtual hometown at the beginning of the game, on the cusp of starting your journey, that seems immovable.

Nintendo of America's role has only gotten larger, with its Treehouse, their name for the localization team, becoming bigger and more high-profile. Game Freak now has hundreds of employees instead of a handful and has developed dozens of games. The Pokémon Company is massive, overseeing or at least helping to oversee every aspect of the series.

For the most part, the major players have all moved on to new endeavors, but they all remain grateful for the fact that they got to work on *Pokémon*, a franchise they described in roller coaster fashion. Many of them, like Sara Bush and Norman Grossfeld, are delighted in the knowledge that they made so many children happy over the years. And some are constantly reminded of *Pokémon* through their own children. "We went to an island in the San Juan Islands for a wedding," Gail Tilden recalled. "And we're walking down the street, we're going to lunch, and my son's like 'WAIT. There's a Pokémon on this corner. We have to stop until I catch it.' Stuff like that makes you think that it's so fun that you were there from the beginning."

And the future? Well, I think it's safe to say that whatever lies ahead for *Pokémon* will likely be successful. Earlier in 2022, we saw the release of *Pokémon Legends: Arceus*, an open-world game set in the universe's distant past. With an adventure no longer restrained by the routes and strictly defined paths that had been a staple of nearly every previous *Pokémon* title, its announcement was greeted with almost unanimous enthusiasm. Finally, the *Pokémon* game of tomorrow was here, the one that would push it forward and defy the expectations we'd built over the last two decades. Still, it looked pretty Pokémon to me. You're a kid traveling around and meeting monsters, monsters that you catch, battle, and take with you as your travel companions. The land is lush and filled with opportunity, the odyssey is brisk and curious, the tone is grand. You are a child leaving to go into the woods, to flip over rocks, and wade through streams. The things you encounter are larger than life, not just because they're fantastical beasts, but because of the way they're presented renders them as far more dignified than the TV screen or handheld device they're trapped in. In *Pokémon*, nature and exploration are more than just an alternative to the stuffy living that comes when real everyday life is dominated by small apartment walls, economic uncertainty, and the stringent process others often enforce on growing up.

Instead, it's how we come to love the species of the world and how we relate to them. It's how we meet others and form relationships that can last a minute or a lifetime. *Pokémon, Digimon, Yu-Gi-Oh!, Medabots, Monster Rancher,* at their best, they embody the spirit of union through the excitement of play. When the game starts and someone welcomes you to the world of *Pokémon,* they mean more than just an area where these creatures exist but a community that's bonded over shared experience. We trade not just monsters with each other, but knowledge, admiration, and joy.

It is communication and competition and connection. Back and forth, like bugs on a wire.

Acknowledgments

I first had the idea for *Monster Kids* while I played *Pokémon Sun* in a laundromat in Brooklyn. The game, released on the year of *Pokémon*'s twentieth anniversary, was not only really fun, but lit a spark in me to tell *Pokémon*'s story, or at least the part that I grew up with. Books about the era had been written before, but I didn't want to view my subjects from a distance. I'd been there and I'd spent my late childhood and preteen years in the weeds. The literal weeds. Ya know, the ones in Viridian Forest as I toured the labyrinth in order to push my Charmander to be strong enough to beat Brock's Onix with my incredible strategy of "Do nothing but attack and pray."

That idea became the book that you're holding, and while it was a ton of work, I never would have gotten it over the finish line without the help of all of those who lent their knowledge and their memories in interviews. So I absolutely have to thank Nob Ogasawara, Michael Haigney, Jason DeMarco, RJ Palmer, Kevin Zuhn, Dan Hernandez, Benji Samit, Bill Giese, Mike Toole, Matt Alt, Henry Thurlow, Rebecca Stone, Lynzee Loveridge, Geoff Thew, Norman Grossfeld, Sara Bush, Ted Lewis, Jeff Kalles, Dominic Nolfi, Darren Dunstan, Gail Tilden, Jason Paige, Jeff Nimoy, Tommy Priest, Nate Ming, Joshua Seth, Laura Summer, Joe Merrick, Maddie C., and Alexander "Touya" Fisher.

Along with interviews, certain sources became indispensable over time. Most prominent of these were sites like Bulbapedia and Joe Merrick's Serebii, especially in the early days of research when I had to create a timeline lest I be crushed by an avalanche of release dates and names. There's also Dr. Lava's Lost Pokémon Content, a fantastic resource for translated interviews, and Dogasu's Backpack, which is an absolute treasure. The DigiLab is a gold mine of interviews relating to the *Digimon* anime over the years. And I'm honestly surprised that more sites don't reference Kidscreen.com, which has decades of information and press releases about children's programming just sitting there. Finally, I need to thank Crunchyroll Japanese correspondent Daryl Harding for the translation work he did. You're the best, dude.

Over the past two years, there are others that have put up with near constant Pikachu chatter with me as I worked through the book. Some of them even read the book when it was in its earliest stages, and for that, I am sorry. Thank you, Joe Luster, Mark Hill, and Jonathan Dantzler. Another big thanks to the members of the Crunchyroll Audience Development Team: Cayla, Kyle, David, Carolyn, Miles, Cameron, and Jesse. Y'all were so accommodating to my schedule, as writing a book essentially filled it with rocks and then threw it into a river. Your support and encouragement were invaluable.

I don't know what I did to earn the partnership of my agent, Cassie Mannes Murray, and the entirety of Howland Literary. I also don't know of anyone better at her job in this entire industry and the expertise and advice she gave helped turned *Monster Kids* into an actual story when, in the beginning, it was just a collection of *Pokémon* ravings. I am too lucky to know you, Cassie.

If you're a writer working on a book, I can only hope that you find an editor like Brit Brooks-Perilli—intelligent, empathetic, and always down to discuss the fine art of tiny monsters that you collect and battle with. Brit not only made my work better but made me more confident about it. The entire team at Running Press has been nothing but kind, talented, and resourceful, and this book would not have been possible without the help of production editor Melanie Gold, designer Rachel Peckman, copy editor Becky Maines, proofreaders Kimberly Broderick and Stephanie Finnegan, the marketing and publicity team, and illustrator José Elgueta, whose artwork brings the spirit of this book to life in a way that I'm in awe of.

A big thanks to my parents for never telling me to "grow up," and for always reminding me to dig deeper into the subjects that I love. My siblings, Rob and Sal, have listened to me talk about *Pokémon* since we were all children playing Game Boys on the floor of my bedroom, and I'm so grateful for them. Finally, I don't know where I'd be without my wife, Audra, my son, and my dog Elmer, all of whom remain the greatest things to ever happen to my whole dumb existence. I love you dearly.